arabian
wildlife
encyclopedia

arabian
wildlife
encyclopedia

Published by Trident Press Ltd,
175 Piccadilly, London W1J 9 TB;
www.tridentpress.com

Editor: Peter Vine
Text Editor: Daniel Gilpin
Consultants: Simon Aspinall, Peter Hellyer
Research, compilation, design, typesetting and illustration: Jane Stark

© Photographs remain copyright of the photographers or alternate copyright owners
(listed alphabetically): A.N.T. Photo Library /NHPA, Rob Baldwin, Mark Beech/ADIAS,
BP Archive, Pete Atkinson/NHPA, Gary Brown, Tina Carvallo, Phil Coates, Ronald Codrai,
Stephen Dalton/NHPA, Nigel J. Dennis/NHPA, Reinhard Dirscherl/FLPA, Lorraine Egan,
Birgit Eichseneher, Hanne and Jens Eriksen, David Fleetham/Oxford Scientific,
Xavier Eichaker, Gary Feulner, Drew Gardner, David George, Graham Giles, Michael Gillett,
Christian Gross, Daniel Heuclin/NHPA, Richard Hornby, David Hosking/FLPA, David John,
Marijcke Jongbloed, Jumeirah?, T Kitchin and V Hurst/NHPA, Jürgen Kuchinke, Yves
Lanceau/NHPA, Linda Lewis/FLPA, Lucy Monro, NASA, Natural History Museum, London,
Mark Newman/FLPA, Philip Perry/FLPA, Linda Pitkin/NHPA, Dan Potts, Jany
Sauvanet/NHPA, Kevin Schafer/NHPA, Hagen Schmid, Malcolm Schuyl/FLPA, Seapics,
Hans Sjoeholm, Alex Smailes, Dieter Stark, Chris and Tilde Stuart, Barbara Tigar/Patrick
Osborne, M. Turkay, Peter Vine, Tony Waltham, Mark Webster/Oxford Scientific, Peter
Whybrow & The Natural History Museum, Tony Wharton/FLPA, D P Wilson/FLPA,
Winfried Wisniewski/FLPA, Adam Woolfitt

© Additional illustrations:
Judy Roberts; Steve Roberts

British Library Cataloguing in Publication Data: A CIP catalogue record for this book is
available from the British Library.

Front cover photographs: Lorraine Egan, Hanne and Jens Eriksen, Hagen Schmid,
Back cover photographs: Hanne and Jens Eriksen

ISBN:978-1-905486-66-3

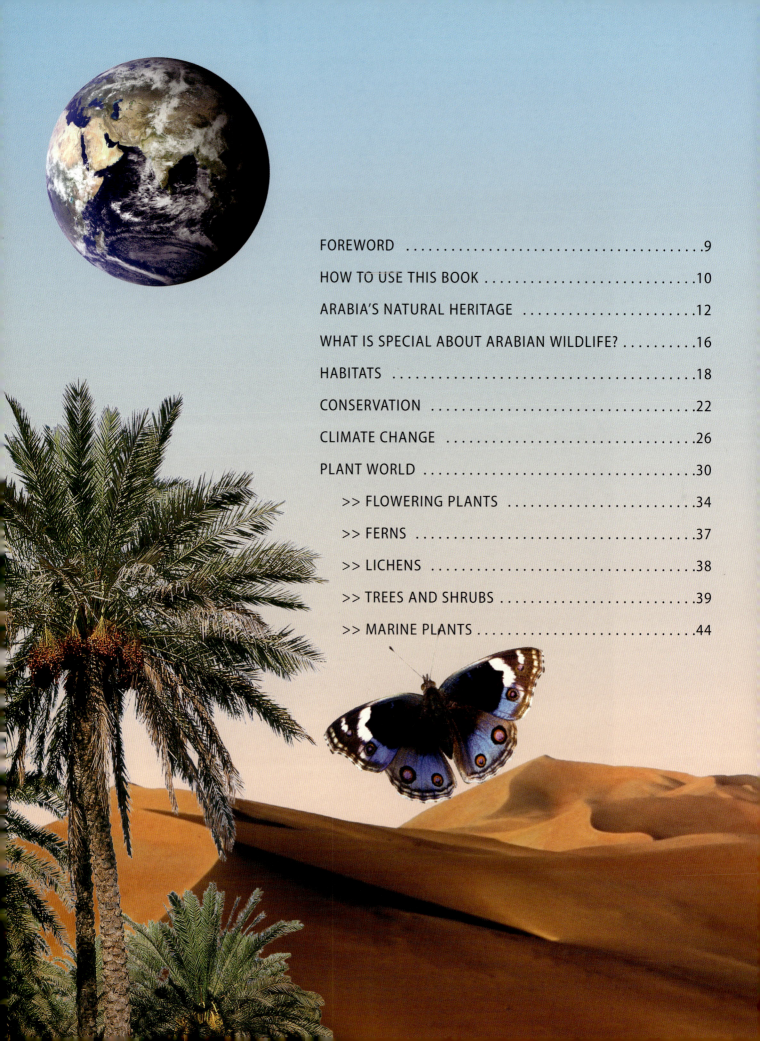

contents

FOREWORD

This broad-ranging and beautifully illustrated encyclopedia once and for all explodes the myth that Arabia's natural world is nothing but desert!

Our purpose in producing the encyclopedia was not only to celebrate the diverse wildlife of Arabia, we also wanted to provide in-depth knowledge on Arabia's natural world; thereby empowering young people with the understanding required to defend and preserve key environments.

As our societies become increasingly focused on city living, we are growing apart from nature and there is a danger that we will lose the 'balance' that is necessary, both for our own existence and for a healthy planet.

Knowledge is the first step to put things right: knowledge about Arabia's wildlife, once ingrained in Bedouin society, and respected as a pre-requisite for survival in the region's deserts, mountains and seas, has sadly diminished among the general population.

But acquiring knowledge about Arabia's animals, plants and environments does not have to be an onerous task restricted to the classroom or lecture theatre. It can and should be engaging, fun, stimulating and rewarding. It should inspire students to delve deeper and use their knowledge. It should become a hobby that lasts a lifetime, enriching every stage of one's growth, from childhood to 'grandparenthood'.

That is what this book is all about. It is ostensibly aimed at 13 to 19 year-olds but could be read and enjoyed by 7 to 70 year olds and beyond.

It illustrates, describes and reveals some of the most interesting facts about Arabia's animals and plants and guides the reader on how to find out more.

It will be of huge benefit to schools throughout Arabia, where such a book is simply not available, and should be part of every home library in every Arabian country.

As publishers, we really want this book to make a difference to the future of Arabia's natural world. With your help, we think it can.

Good reading! Good nature watching!

Peter and Paula Vine
Trident Press Ltd.

HOW TO USE THIS BOOK

The *Arabian Wildlife Encyclopedia* is designed to be used in combination with additional information posted on the Internet, and contains many links to specific web pages. However, the book can also be used alone as a useful reference work for both students and teachers, or anyone with an interest in natural history. It contains extensive information on the plant and animal life of the Arabian Peninsula, and endeavours to show many of the unique features that enable Arabian species to survive the often harsh environmental conditions of the region.

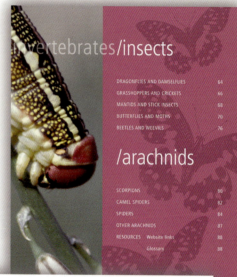

invertebrates/insects

/arachnids

>> This volume begins with an overview of the natural history of the Arabian Peninsula, along with general information on plants and animals. More detailed information about Arabian species is arranged according to taxonomic order, beginning with plants and ending with mammals. Section pages list the contents of each major division within the book (e.g. Insects and Arachnids).

In addition to detailed information about Arabian species, the book also contains numerous 'fascinating facts' boxes containing a variety of interesting and often surprising data about wildlife, both in Arabia and worldwide.

<< A navigation bar at the bottom of each page provides a URL for the relevant section of the website.

Numerous Arabian species are described in a series of identification boxes.

Each section of the encyclopedia ends with a resource page, featuring a list of selected websites containing further relevant information, along with a glossary of terms that are used and highlighted in the text.

Throughout the book, a number of Arabian 'key species' are featured in colourful two page spreads. In addition to the date palm spread (pictured left), other spreads feature the Arabian leopard, oryx, gazelle, tahr, houbara bustard, flamingo, spiny-tailed lizard and camel spider.

Red boxes containing warnings and basic first aid advice are found on pages featuring venomous species.

Environmental and conservation notes pertaining to specific Arabian species are located throughout the text. The introductory pages also contain information on global warming and related issues.

ARABIA'S NATURAL HERITAGE

For perhaps 200,000 years, humans have occupied the Arabian Peninsula. Archaeological evidence shows that by at least 7,500 years ago, in the Late Stone Age, or Neolithic period, some people were living in settled communities, while others lived nomadic lives. It was essential for these early inhabitants to know what natural resources were available to provide them with food, shelter and other items for survival. As a result, they learned when and where to find various plants and animals, as well as how to make use of them in a sustainable way. This knowledge was passed from one generation to another and became part of a rich heritage that can help today's inhabitants of the peninsula face the challenges and opportunities of the modern world.

ARCHAEOLOGICAL EVIDENCE

Archaeologists play an important role in finding evidence of how humans interacted with nature in the past. Excavations have unearthed a wide variety of artefacts, including stone tools, arrowheads and spearheads (below right), which were used to hunt and prepare animals for food. In coastal regions, fish hooks and net sinkers, along with **shell middens** and bones, indicate that the inhabitants included fish and other marine life in their diet. In addition to practical implements, there is considerable decorative evidence of how humans used the natural resources around them. Pictures on coins (top right), seals (centre right) and in rock drawings (below left), illustrate aspects of early human habitation in the region.

DOMESTICATED ANIMALS

Over the last few thousand years, three animals have become domesticated in the Arabian Peninsula: the camel, the Arabian horse and the saluki dog. All of these share the same characteristics of endurance and adaptability that are needed for living in the desert climate.

CAMELS

Superbly suited to the desert environment, domesticated camels made it possible for humans to continue to live in the Arabian Peninsula as rainfall declined and the region became more arid. Camels have been a source of meat, milk, transport, clothes and household items for over 3,000 years.

THE SALUKI

For thousands of years, Arabia's nomadic tribes have bred the graceful, silky-coated saluki. It is mainly used for hunting gazelles and hares, but sometimes also used in conjunction with falcons. Highly prized for its stamina, speed and intelligence, the saluki is thought to be one of the oldest canine breeds in the world.

THE ARABIAN HORSE

The Arabian horse is renowned for its beauty, speed, intelligence and endurance – qualities that have been nurtured by the Bedu over many centuries. Purebred Arabian mares have always been highly valued, and as their reputation spread, their bloodlines were used to establish other famous breeds.

FALCONRY

The use of falcons by inhabitants of the Arabian desert to hunt houbara (pictured right), stone curlews and hares probably dates back to pre-Islamic times, and was an important means of obtaining food.

Traditionally, desert nomads captured and trained the wild saker *Falco cherrug* and the peregrine *F. peregrinus*, but modern falconers use mainly captive-bred birds in order to preserve wild falcon populations.

Falconry was not only a way of varying the diet; it was also an important part of the traditional way of life, making use of skills for life in the desert that had been developed over generations. It was also a means of bringing people together as a community.

PEARLING AND OTHER MARITIME TRADITIONS

Archaeological sites along the coastline of the Arabian Peninsula indicate that early inhabitants made good use of the resources available to them from the sea. In addition to catching a large variety of fish species, they also included shellfish and crabs in their diet. The shells of smaller molluscs were often pierced and used as jewellery.

PEARLING

The harvesting of pearls in the Arabian Gulf appears to date back to the Late Stone Age. In later times, it became an important industry. Gulf pearls were exported to the markets of Imperial Rome and later, to the courts of India and medieval Europe. The main harvest took place in the summer, between June and September. During the rest of the year, many pearl divers either engaged in fishing or tended date palm plantations. The industry finally came to an end in the early 20th century.

EGG COLLECTING

In the past, birds' eggs and turtle eggs were collected for food. Of particular importance were the Socotra cormorant *Phalacrocorax nigrogularis* and various species of tern. Their close-packed breeding colonies provided easy access to eggs, which were generally collected early in the season, before incubation had begun. The birds would then lay again. This pattern of exploitation was ecologically sustainable, with fishermen never taking more eggs than the breeding population could stand.

DUGONG

Dugong (pictured below) have been found on Late Stone Age archaeological sites, and continued to be harvested until relatively recent times. Meat from the dugong was eaten both fresh and dried, while the hides were used to make sandals. The oil produced from fat was used on both the insides and the outsides of boats, to prevent the wood from drying out, and also to keep it waterproof. The short tusks were carved to make sticks for the application of kohl as make-up for women's eyes.

THE DATE PALM

For over 8,000 years the people of the Arabian Peninsula relied on the date palm to help them survive in the harsh desert climate. Although it is best known for its highly nutritious fruit, nearly every part of the date palm can be put to good use.

POLLINATION

Pollination of the date palm is a very labour-intensive process because each tree supports only male or female flowers. Since male trees cannot bear fruit, most of them are destroyed in date palm gardens. This means that the female palm must be pollinated manually, using a variety of techniques.

TRADITIONAL USES OF THE DATE PALM

These are just a few of the many and varied uses of the date palm:

• The strong leaf fronds of the date palm were dried, and used to construct *'arish* (palm-frond) shelters (pictured above), wind-breaks and fencing.

• The dried fronds were also split into strips, known as *khooss*, that were then woven into matting for floors, or used to make simple containers for household use.

• In some areas, the long, tough stalks of the leaves were used to make *shashas*, small boats capable of carrying one or two fishermen.

WHAT IS SPECIAL ABOUT ARABIAN WILDLIFE?

The Arabian Peninsula contains one of the Earth's largest continuous areas of sandy desert, an arid region with little to offer in the way of shelter and where the extremely high daytime temperatures plummet dramatically at night. In such a challenging environment, plant and animal life forms have developed a variety of special adaptations in order to survive. Other ecosystems in the region include mountains and wadis, gravel plains and shrubland, coastal mangroves and mudflats, as well as a variety of marine habitats in the waters surrounding the peninsula. Each ecosystem supports its own array of life forms, resulting in a surprisingly wide diversity of animals and plants.

See page 18 for more information about habitats

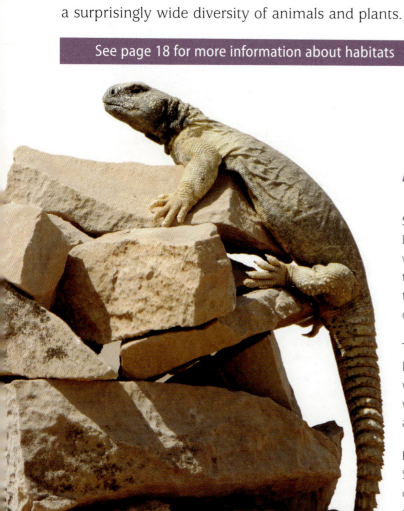

ADAPTING TO LIFE IN THE DESERT

STAYING COOL

Desert animals have developed a number of ways in which to deal with the heat and intensity of the sun's rays. Larger mammals, such as the Arabian oryx (above), usually have light-coloured coats that reflect the heat. The oryx has evolved a number of remarkable adaptations to desert life, which are discussed in more detail on page 212.

THICK-SKINNED

Like many other reptiles, the distinctive spiny-tailed lizard (*dhub*) is well-suited to life in the desert, with a thick, tough skin that minimises water loss. Many invertebrates, such as scorpions and various beetles, also have tough outer coverings that prevent dehydration.

FAT STORAGE

Since body fat keeps heat in, some desert mammals, such as the camel, carry their fat in a hump, rather than having it distributed all over the body.

FLOWERING DESERT

Just as animals have developed ways of adapting to the extreme conditions of the desert, so plants have also evolved specialised means of survival.

Plants such as buck's horn groundsel (right) have shallow root systems, along with a short growing season, which allows them to take advantage of infrequent periods of rain. Seed from these plants may remain dormant in the ground for long periods, until rain allows germination. Plants that do this are known as 'ephemerals'.

Some **perennial** plants have especially small leaves, or leaves that drop off after long periods without rain. Others have stems and leaves covered with fine, light-coloured hairs that help to reflect the sun's rays. All of these are adaptations to prevent water loss.

Succulents have fleshy, waxy leaves and stems that can store water, allowing them to survive long periods of drought.

See page 30 for more information about plants.

A young Rüppell's sand fox cub (left) ventures out of the underground den in which it lives with parents and siblings. The pads on the feet of this desert species are covered with hair to protect them when walking on hot sand. Blanford's fox (below), however, has bare foot pads, more suited to walking over the rocky terrain where it is found.

SMALL MAMMAL ADAPTATIONS

Small mammals, reptiles and insects commonly deal with high temperatures by staying in the shade, either under bushes or rocks above ground or by burrowing. Many desert animals remain inactive during the heat of the day, hunting at night instead, when it is cooler. Some desert mammals manage to survive without drinking, obtaining all of the water they need from their food.

SLOWING DOWN TO CHILL OUT

Desert Cape hares have a much slower metabolism than their European counterparts, which helps to keep thire body temperature lower. They can also tolerate more salt in their drinking water than European hares. Cape hares have large ears that help to radiate body heat, but when it gets too hot they may restrict blood flow to the ears and flatten them against the body to provide shade.

HABITATS

Although the landscape of the Arabian Peninsula is dominated mainly by sandy desert, other important habitats provide shelter for a broad range of species. In addition to a variety of desert landscapes, mountains, plains, wadis, date palm plantations, urban and agricultural areas, the waters surrounding the region hold another diverse group of ecosystems.

SABKHA

Sabkha is an Arabic name for flat, salt-encrusted desert that occurs in areas where the water table remains close to the surface due to hard, underlying rock. As the water evaporates, it leaves behind a crust of salt. Very little life can survive in such a salty environment, but a number of salt-tolerant plants may be found around the edges of *sabkha*. Salt-tolerant plants like this are known as **halophytes**.

DEW-FORESTS

In a few regions of the Arabian Peninsula (such as inland south and west of Abu Dhabi) the moisture from seasonal fog allows the growth of an interesting plant community that is dominated by saxaul trees *Haloxylon persicum*. These shrubby trees obtain water from the dew that forms on their branches and then drips onto the ground around the trunk. Animals that are found in this habitat include the Cape hare *Lepus capensis*, gerbil *Gerbillus* spp., red fox *Vulpes vulpes* and over-wintering eagles *Aquila* spp., as well as the stone curlew *Burhinus oedicnemus*, desert wheatear *Oenanthe deserti* and desert warbler *Sylvia nana*.

SAND SHEETS AND DUNES

By far the largest area of the Arabian Peninsula is covered with sand. Arabia's sand deserts range from vast, flat expanses to impressive mega-dunes. Stable sand sheets can provide a favourable environment for vegetation, due to the water that is held just beneath the surface, within reach of plant roots. Mobile sand dunes, however, support few plants. This is partly because of the coarse-grained sand that allows water to rapidly drain away, leaving it inaccessible to most plants' roots. The shifting nature of the sands is also an important factor: many seeds become too deeply buried to germinate, while those that do germinate have to be capable of withstanding the harsh conditions associated with the dunes. There are few perennials that exist in areas of mobile sand dunes, and even the annuals that make their appearance after rains are few in number and variety.

PIEDMONT ALLUVIAL AND INTERDUNAL PLAINS

Alluvial plains are made up of rocks, gravels and pebbles washed from surrounding mountain regions. They are characterised by a type of vegetation consisting of small trees, shrubs and succulents.

Interdunal plains, consisting of sand and gravel, form a connection between dune systems. The high salt content of the soil on some of these plains results in vegetation dominated by salt-tolerant **halophytes**, such as *Zygophyllum* spp..

MOUNTAINS AND WADIS

At first glance, Arabia's mountainous areas may appear barren, but in fact, the mountain regions contain a higher diversity of plant life than other habitats. Mountain wadis and high plateaux can support relatively lush vegetation. The increased rainfall and lower temperatures found at higher altitudes create a more favourable climate for plants. The wadis themselves often support a rich variety of plants.

COASTAL WHITE SANDS

Coastal white sands originate from recent marine deposits. They are fairly stable and often have a high coverage of vegetation, dominated by the **perennial** tussock grass *Panicum turgidum*. Other grasses and dwarf shrubs are also a feature of coastal sands, along with a number of annuals, such as *Eremobium aegyptiacum*, *Lotus halophilus*, *Neurada procumbens*, *Plantago boissieri* and *Silene villosa* (pictured above).

CAVES

There are a number of cave systems in the Arabian Peninsula. One example is the multi-chambered system of Magharah Qasr Hafit at Jebel Hafit, south of Al Ain. A **stalagmite** sample from this cave has been dated at 337,000 years old, but the connecting passages are much older, dating back to a time when the climate was much wetter. Arabia's caves support some invertebrates, such as bristletails (primitive insects). Like most cave-dwelling creatures, these are almost invariably colourless, having no need of body pigment in the darkness underground. Caves also provide roosting places for several species of bat.

SHORELINE HABITATS

Natural habitats of the coastal zone include mangroves, saltmarsh, tidal flats with **cyanobacterial mats**, sandy and rocky beaches, coastal flats and low sand dunes, *sabkha*, cliffs and rocky headlands. With the exception of mangroves, coastal vegetation is dominated by salt-tolerant, succulent dwarf shrubs. Two **parasitic** plants, the desert hyacinth *Cistanche tubulosa* (pictured below left) and red thumb *Cynomorium coccineum*, are commonly found with their **host plant** *Zygophyllum qatarense*.

MANGROVES

Dense stands of mangroves commonly occur along sheltered stretches of shoreline and often border lagoons. Mangroves provide an essential habitat for numerous birds and marine species.

DATE PALM PLANTATIONS AND AGRICULTURAL LAND

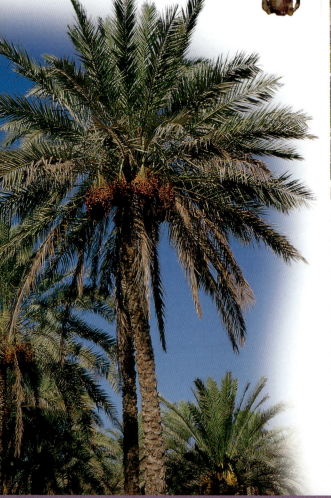

The moisture, shade and food sources provided by date palm plantations and desert oases, as well as agricultural fields in the mountains, attract numerous species of birds, mammals and invertebrates. Two types of traditional irrigation systems supply water to these areas. In the falaj system, underground water is diverted to fields and plantations by means of open channels. In the mountains, water is extracted from the wadi bed, and directed along open watercourses built into the sides of the wadi, then channelled to terraced fields.

Fruit bats are frequent night-time visitors to date palm plantations.

MARINE HABITATS

INTERTIDAL

The intertidal zone is the area of the shoreline that is usually under water at high tide, but is exposed at low tide.

On rocky shores the range of intertidal habitats is generally greater than on **sediment shores**, but sheltered tidal sand and mudflats may contain many microscopic surface-dwelling organisms (particularly microscopic algae known as diatoms) as well as large numbers of small invertebrates that provide food for shorebirds.

Stands of mangrove trees (see opposite page) in intertidal areas help to stabilise the sand by reducing current and wave action, thereby providing a habitat for a greater number of invertebrate species. Mangrove trunks and breathing roots (pneumatophores) also provide a hard surface on which rock-dwelling species can become established.

CORAL REEFS

Although coral reefs occupy only about one quarter of one per cent of the total marine environment worldwide, they are important ecosystems that provide shelter and food for a quarter of all sea life.

The entire Arabian Peninsula is fringed by some of the world's most beautiful coral reefs. Compared with the harsh and often seemingly barren habitats on land, they support a vast number of animal species, ranging from prawns, crabs and other crustaceans to multitudes of fish.

Sadly, although they may look robust, corals are highly sensitive to disturbance caused by humans through dredging, toxic waste, overfishing and careless diving practices.

SUBTIDAL

Sandy shores: The subtidal zone just below the low tide line is always covered with water, and in the sheltered shallow waters and lagoons of the Arabian Gulf, often features extensive seagrass beds (see photo above). These provide a vital habitat for large endangered vertebrates, such as turtles and dugongs, which depend on them for their food supply. Smaller organisms such as fish, crustaceans, sea cucumbers and molluscs also find shelter in seagrass beds.

Rocky shores: Rocky areas below the water-line provides a habitat for species unable to withstand exposure to air at low tide. Invertebrates and small fish find shelter here in natural crevices, while seasonal growth of fleshy seaweeds also provides temporary refuge for other marine life.

Man-made habitats: Harbours, marinas, breakwaters, artificial islands, jetties and piers are not always harmful to marine life. Some of these have created new habitats for intertidal and subtidal species that favour hard rather than soft **substrates**.

CONSERVATION

Before the discovery of oil in the Arabian Peninsula, the harsh climatic conditions of the region posed enormous challenges to the survival of human inhabitants. An adequate supply of food, water and shelter required a wide knowledge of the natural resources available and how to use them in a sustainable manner. This knowledge has become part of the traditions and culture of the region. As the world faces major climate changes and depletion of resources in the 21st century, this rich heritage, combined with modern scientific and technological knowledge, may once more play an essential part in surviving extreme conditions.

HEMA RESERVES

The hema system is an ancient traditional method of land management based on the core Islamic principle that man is the custodian and guardian of the natural environment. Commonly practiced in the Arabian Peninsula until the mid-20th century, the system is still used in some places, but is no longer widespread. In the managed areas, restrictions were placed on animal grazing, the cutting down of certain species of trees, such as *Acacia* and *Haloxylon persicum*, and, in some instances, on the harvesting of hay. Designed to preserve valuable rangelands from over-use, the restrictions varied according to local conditions.

Protected areas such as the Al Wathba Wetland Reserve in Abu Dhabi and Dubai's Ras al-Khor Wildlife Sanctuary provide food, shelter and breeding areas for a wide variety of birds, including the greater flamingo (pictured left).

PROTECTED AREAS

The International Union for the Conservation of Nature (IUCN) defines a protected area as "an area of land or sea especially dedicated to the protection and maintenance of biological diversity, and its associated natural and cultural resources, managed through legal or other effective means." Protected areas are essential tools in the protection of biodiversity against increasing development and habitat destruction. In addition to protecting a wide variety of plant and animal species, these areas provide valuable educational and recreational opportunities.

PROTECTING MARINE LIFE

Marine protected areas play a vital role in preserving the diversity and quality of coastal and underwater environments. In 2007, the Marawah Marine Protected Area west of Abu Dhabi was designated as a Biosphere Reserve by UNESCO. A large population of dugongs, bottlenose and hump-backed dolphins, hawksbill (pictured right) and green turtles are among the species protected, along with coral reefs, mangroves, seagrass beds and potential turtle nesting beaches.

RESCUING ENDANGERED SPECIES

In common with the rest of the world, the Arabian Peninsula has a number of species that are on the brink of extinction in their native habitat. Others may already be extinct. Major efforts are being made to save these species from extinction through captive breeding programmes and eventual reintroduction into the wild.

REINTRODUCED

Some species have been successfully reintroduced, such as the endangered Arabian oryx, sand gazelle and the Arabian gazelle, and are protected within a number of reserves. Overgrazing by livestock, off-road driving, and human destruction of habitat are the main threats to this desert ecoregion.

SOME ARABIAN SPECIES AND THEIR CONSERVATION STATUS

	Common name	Species name	Status
1	Arabian leopard	*Panthera pardus nimr*	Critically endangered
2	Arabian tahr	*Hemitragus jayakari*	Endangered
3	Arabian oryx	*Oryx leucoryx*	Endangered
4	Arabian gazelle	*Gazella gazella cora*	Vulnerable
5	Sand cat	*Felis margarita*	Near threatened
6	Sand gazelle	*Gazella subgutturosa marica*	Vulnerable
7	Lesser kestrel	*Falco naumanni*	Vulnerable
8	Sooty falcon	*Falco concolor*	Near threatened
9	Houbara bustard	*Chlamydotis undulata*	Vulnerable
10	Sand boa	*Eryx jayakari*	Appendix II CITES
11	Hawksbill turtle	*Eretmochelys imbricata*	Critically endangered
12	Green turtle	*Chelonia mydas*	Endangered

POTENTIAL THREATS

TO PLANT AND ANIMAL SPECIES AND THEIR HABITATS

- residential and commercial development
- energy production and mining
- agriculture and aquaculture
- transportation infrastructure
- pollution
- introduction of alien invasive species
- human disturbance and interference
- climate change and extreme weather
- geological events

INTERNATIONAL CONSERVATION ORGANISATIONS & CONVENTIONS

As current environmental challenges become increasingly urgent, the need for global action becomes ever more vital. In order to coordinate support, funding and knowledge to address these challenges, a number of organisations and conventions have been established. The organisations assist local initiatives aimed at specific regional problems, while maintaining a global view and providing many online resources that can be used by governments, scientists, universities, schools, community groups and other organisations and individuals. Most have material designed particularly for young people. Conventions are international agreements signed by governments that have agreed to abide by the terms within them.

WHAT IS THE IUCN AND WHAT DOES IT DO?

As the world's oldest and largest environmental network, the International Union for Conservation of Nature (IUCN) provides a neutral forum for governments, non-government organisations, United Nations agencies, companies and local communities from more than 160 countries, assisting them to develop and enact laws and policies concerning development and environmental protection. In addition, the IUCN also supports scientific research and manages field projects around the world.

This unique organisation describes its mission as follows:

". . . to influence, encourage and assist societies throughout the world to conserve the integrity and diversity of nature and to ensure that any use of natural resources is equitable and ecologically sustainable."

More information: http://www.iucn.org

THE 'RED LIST'

The IUCN is perhaps best known for the IUCN Red List of Threatened Species™ – an evaluation of the conservation status of animal and plant species around the world. The number of species currently covered stands at around 47,960. This vast project is by no means complete and gathering information about species already on the Red List, as well as expanding the number covered.

An important part of future work will be in assessing which species are most susceptible to global climate change.

CONVENTION ON BIOLOGICAL DIVERSITY

The Convention on Biological Diversity was established in 1992 at the Earth Summit in Rio de Janeiro, Brazil. It is a pact between 190 of the world's governments to make sure that world development continues in a manner that uses Earth's natural resources in a sustainable way, so that we leave the planet in a healthy state for future generations.

The Convention on Biological Diversity has three goals:

1. The preservation of **biological diversity**
2. The sustainable use of its components
3. The fair and equitable sharing of the benefits derived from the use of genetic resources

The CBD website has an excellent online youth section. It includes a 16 page newsletter *Gincaniño* in PDF format, a children's web portal 'Biodiversity, Food and Farming for a Healthy Planet', as well as resources for teachers.

More information: http://www.cbd.int/youth/

CITES

The **Convention on International Trade in Endangered Species of Wild Fauna and Flora (CITES)** aims to ensure that international trade does not endanger the survival of any wild animal or plant species. Estimated to be worth billions of dollars annually, the international wildlife trade involves many millions of animals and plants. In addition to live specimens, trade includes a wide variety of wildlife products, such as furs from exotic animals, food items, tourist souvenirs, tropical timber and medicines.

Many animals and plants are not endangered, but still benefit from the CITES regulations, which protect against over-exploitation. More than 30,000 species are listed under three CITES appendices, which categorise them according to the degree of protection required.

Appendix I: Species threatened with extinction. Trade in these species is permitted only in exceptional circumstances.

Arabian species listed in Appendix I include the Arabian oryx, caracal, Arabian leopard, blue whale, Bryde's whale, Indo-Pacific hump-backed dolphin, dugong, peregrine falcon, houbara bustard, desert monitor lizard, marine turtles, sawfish and whale shark.

Appendix II: Species listed here are not necessarily under immediate threat of extinction but may become so unless trade is closely controlled. International trade in Appendix II species may be authorised by the granting of an export permit or re-export certificate if the relevant authorities are satisfied that certain conditions are met, particularly that trade will not be harmful to the survival of the species in the wild. No import permit is required for Appendix II species under CITES regulations; however, a permit may be needed in some countries that have enacted stricter measures than CITES requires.

Arabian species in Appendix II include the spiny-tailed lizard *Uromastyx* spp., black corals and stony corals.

Appendix III: Species are included in Appendix III at the request of a country that already regulates trade in a particular species and that needs the cooperation of other countries to prevent unsustainable or illegal exploitation.

More information: http://www.cites.org

WORLD WIDE FUND FOR NATURE (WWF)

WWF is one of the world's largest independent global conservation organisations, acting in over 40 countries to:

- conserve the world's **biological diversity**
- ensure sustainable use of renewable natural resources
- promote the reduction of pollution and wasteful consumption.

WWF's Protected Areas for a Living Planet programme is working to assist governments to meet bold targets for creating a global network of terrestrial and marine protected areas.

Global Ecoregions

WWF scientists have worked with regional experts around the world to develop Global Ecoregions – a global analysis of the planet's **biodiversity**, covering every major habitat type and spanning five continents and all the world's oceans. With this initiative, WWF aims to ensure that regional conservation efforts around the world contribute to a global **biodiversity** strategy. By conserving the Earth's most outstanding places and the most important species that inhabit them, other species that share those habitats will also be conserved.

More information: http://www.wwf.org

CLIMATE CHANGE

Climate change is not a new phenomenon. Throughout the Earth's history, fluctuations in temperature have occurred, with large portions of the planet being covered with ice during cooler periods. As temperatures increased again the glacial ice sheets retreated. These variations were the natural result of changes in the amount of solar energy reaching the Earth's surface, due to small shifts in its orbit. Scientists believe, however, that since the beginning of the industrial revolution in the late 19th century, the Earth's climate has undergone changes that have been influenced by human activity.

EVIDENCE OF CLIMATE CHANGE

Earth-orbiting satellites allow scientists to closely monitor and collect data about changes in the Earth's atmosphere, and its land and water temperatures. Core samples taken in areas with permanent ice cover provide information about the Earth's climate in the past. By looking at both sources of information scientists can build a picture of how the planet's climate has altered.

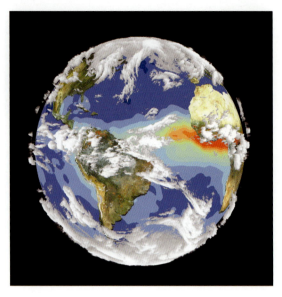

Images of Earth such as the one above give scientists a better view of the Earth's interrelated systems and climate today. Data from a number of satellites contributed to the making of this image. One satellite gave a true colour composite of land vegetation. Another detected fires, which appear as small red areas over South America and Africa. A third collected data about the oceanic aerosol layer caused by biomass burning and windblown dust over Africa. The cloud layer is a composite of infrared images from four geostationary weather satellites.

THE OZONE LAYER

Ozone is a gas that is produced naturally in the **stratosphere**. It forms a protective layer around the Earth, absorbing harmful **ultraviolet** (UV) rays. In 1979, scientists discovered that a hole in the ozone layer had begun to develop over Antarctica. Since then, evidence suggests that the entire ozone layer has been getting thinner, and another, smaller hole now develops over the Arctic each year. A NASA image (below left), with the ozone hole in blue indicates its considerable size.

This thinning of the ozone layer has been caused by human activities, particularly the production and use of **chloro-fluoro-carbon**s (CFCs) in **aerosol** spray cans, refrigerators and air conditioners.

Excessive exposure to UV rays can be harmful to human health, causing sunburn, skin cancer, and eye damage that may lead to blindness. UV rays also kill plankton, which is a vital part of the marine food chain. Plants also may be damaged by excessive amounts of UV radiation, affecting the supply of food on land.

Most countries have now stopped producing CFCs, but there are many still in use. For this reason, it is important to correctly and safely dispose of items that contain CFCs.

Ozone is beneficial when it is in the **stratosphere**, but when it occurs in the air that we breathe, it poses a danger to health. At ground level ozone is produced by a reaction between sunlight and air pollution from vehicles and factories. The resulting smog may cause breathing difficulties and other health problems

THE GREENHOUSE EFFECT

Life on Earth depends on the greenhouse effect to provide warmth and energy. Certain gases, such as water vapour, carbon dioxide (CO_2), methane, nitrous oxide, ozone and **chloro-fluoro-carbons** (CFCs) act like the glass in a greenhouse, allowing the sun's radiation to pass through, but preventing most of the heat radiated upwards from the Earth to escape back into space. Without the greenhouse effect the Earth would be much colder.

Human activities, such as the burning of **fossil fuels** have increased the amount of greenhouse gases, resulting in global warming (see below).

Most solar radiation passes through the Earth's atmosphere and warms the planet's surface.
About half of this evaporates water that condenses in the atmosphere, releasing energy that powers storms and produces rain and snow.

Roughly one-third of the sun's radiation is reflected by the Earth's surface and the atmosphere.

Heat radiates upwards as the Earth's surface cools. Some radiation passes through the atmosphere but most of it is trapped by molecules of greenhouse gases and reflected back towards the Earth.

GLOBAL WARMING

BURNING FOSSIL FUELS

Since the beginning of the Industrial Revolution, large amounts of greenhouse gases have been added to the Earth's atmosphere through the burning of **fossil fuels**. Increased levels of gases such as carbon dioxide (see chart) absorb more energy, causing temperatures in the Earth's atmosphere to rise. Higher temperatures cause changes to the Earth's weather patterns.

CUTTING DOWN TREES

In addition to burning **fossil fuels**, humans have cut down large areas of forest. Trees remove carbon dioxide from the atmosphere during the process of **photosynthesis**. Cutting down forests results in less carbon dioxide being taken out of the atmosphere, thereby adding to the problems of global warming.

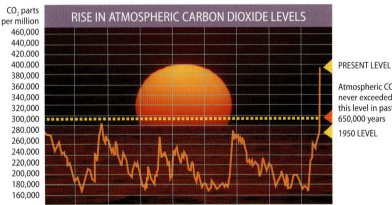

CO$_2$ parts per million

RISE IN ATMOSPHERIC CARBON DIOXIDE LEVELS

460,000
440,000
420.000
400.000
380.000
360.000
340.000
320.000
300.000
280.000
260.000
240.000
220.000
200.000
180.000
160.000

PRESENT LEVEL

Atmospheric CO$_2$ never exceeded this level in past 650,000 years

1950 LEVEL

400.000 350,000 300,000 250,000 200,000 150,000 100,000 50,000 YEARS BEFORE PRESENT

CORAL BLEACHING

In response to rises in seawater temperature, coral colonies expel the single-celled green algae (**zooxanthellae**) that supply them with oxygen, causing the coral to become white and brittle in a process known as bleaching. When coral dies, the survival of many other species of marine life is also threatened.

CONSEQUENCES OF GLOBAL WARMING

Predicting all the consequences of global warming is difficult, but scientists believe that we can expect an increase in sea levels, due to melting glaciers and polar ice caps. As this happens some low-lying areas of land will disappear under water. Some areas of the world are likely to become warmer and drier, while other regions may become cooler and wetter. These changes in global weather patterns may affect the growth and distribution of plants, including food crops, which in turn will affect wildlife. In some cases the results may be positive, leading to higher food production, while in others **biological diversity** may decrease.

WHAT CAN WE DO ABOUT GLOBAL WARMING?

WHAT IS A CARBON FOOTPRINT?

A carbon footprint is a measure of the impact that human activities have on the Earth's environment, expressed in terms of the amount of greenhouse gases generated by those activities. This can be divided into two parts:

- the primary footprint, which measures direct emissions of carbon dioxide as a result of our home energy use and transportation choices
- the secondary footprint, which is the total carbon emissions produced in the entire lifecycle of items that people use.

Carbon footprints vary from person to person and from country to country, depending on lifestyles. In the Arabian Peninsula, the extremely hot and dry climate means that a great deal of energy is used to power air conditioners, refrigerators and desalination plants. Because much of the region is unsuitable for agriculture, many food items must be imported, resulting in further energy consumption and relatively large carbon footprints.

HOW WILL GLOBAL WARMING AFFECT THE ARABIAN PENINSULA?

Temperatures may increase, bringing more drought, as well as more violent storms. Sandstorms may occur with greater frequency and severity. A rise in sea levels will affect coastal regions, including coral reefs and mangrove communities. Sources of freshwater will decrease or dry up. Plant and animal species that are unable to adapt to these changes in the environment may disappear. This, in turn, will affect the rest of the food chain, leading to further decreases in **biodiversity**.

A sandstorm blowing from the UAE over the Arabian Gulf can clearly be seen from space.

BECOMING PART OF THE SOLUTION

Just as humans have been a big part of the global warming problem, so everyone can also be an important part of the solution. While governments, businesses and environmental organisations must work together to find alternative, non-polluting forms of energy, there are many practical ways in which people of all ages can help.

- find out the size of own your carbon footprint
- use energy-saving lightbulbs
- turn off lights when you leave the room
- take showers instead of baths
- use public transport whenever possible
- wash clothes at 30°C
- only run the dishwasher when it is full
- turn off water heaters except when needed
- use rechargeable batteries
- don't leave TVs and other electronic equipment on standby
- choose appliances with a high energy efficiency rating

Long hours of sunshine mean that solar energy is an excellent alternative source of energy for the Arabian Peninsula.

>> LEARN MORE : USEFUL WEBSITES

ARABIA'S NATURAL HERITAGE

http://www.uaeinteract.com/history/trad/index.asp – information on all aspects of Arabia's natural heritage

http://www.mefrg.org/ – the Middle East Falcon Research Group

http://www.arkive.org/houbara-bustard/chlamydotis-undulata/info.html – useful information page about the houbara bustard with links to other relevant sites

http://www.arabianhorses.org/education/education_history_origin.asp – article on the origins of the Arabian horse from the Arabian Horse Association

http://www.alreem.com/protected/nsub6b.asp – very useful list of protected areas in the Arab world

ARABIAN ENDANGERED SPECIES

http://www.ead.ae/en/?T=4&ID=3935 – news articles about release of Arabian oryx into Wadi Rum Protected Area. More information can be found at http://www.ead.ae/en/?T=4&ID=3687

http://www.arkive.org/arabian-leopard/panthera-pardus-nimr/threats-and-conservation.html – good summary of the status of the Arabian leopard, as well as conservation measures being employed

REGIONAL CONSERVATION BODIES

http://www.ead.ae/en/ – Environment Agency Abu Dhabi

http://www.awpr.ae – Al Ain Wildlife Park

http://www.breedingcentresharjah.com – Breeding Centre for Endangered Arabian Wildlife

http://www.ead.ae/en/en-us/national.avian.research.center.aspx – National Avian Research Centre (NARC)

http://www.ddcr.org – Dubai Desert Conservation Reserve

http://www.panda.org/who_we_are/wwf_offices/united_arab_emirates/wwf_uae – WWF in UAE

http://www.ncwcd.gov.sa/English/default.aspx – National Commission for Wildlife Conservation and Development (NCWCD), Saudi Arabia

http://www.environment.org.om/ – Environment Society of Oman

http://www.rscn.org.jo/ – Royal Society for the Conservation of Nature, Jordan

CONSERVATION ORGANISATIONS

http://www.panda.org/about_our_earth/ – the WWF website is an excellent source of information on conservation and the environment

http://www.iucnredlist.org/static/programme – overview page for the IUCN Red List with search facility

http://www.iucnredlist.org/static/publications_links – extensive list of IUCN publications and links to other websites containing information on IUCN Red List species

http://www.unep-wcmc.org/ – UN Conservation Monitoring Centre

GLOBAL WARMING AND CARBON FOOTPRINTS

http://www.heroesoftheuae.ae/en/article/overview.html – a project to reduce the per capita ecological footprint of the UAE

http://www.footprintnetwork.org/en/index.php/GFN/page/calculator/ – calculate carbon footprints for the planet, specific countries and individuals

http://www.zerofootprintkids.com/kids_home.aspx – a footprint calculator specially designed for schoolchildren

INTRODUCTION GLOSSARY

aerosol: minute liquid or solid particles suspended in the atmosphere

biological diversity (biodiversity): the number and variety of life forms in an ecosystem, used as a measure of the ecosystem's health

biomass: renewable organic material, such as wood, leaves and grasses, that can be converted to fuel

chloro-fluoro-carbons (CFCs): organic compounds consisting of carbon, fluorine and chlorine atoms used as propellant in aerosol cans

cyanobacterial mats: mat-forming microscopic 'plants' that contain blue-green pigment and are more closely related to bacteria than other plants

fossil fuels: fuels formed in the ground over millions of years from dead plants and animals

geostationary satellite: a satellite in a position that is always fixed to a relative point on the Earth

halophyte: a plant that has adapted to a salty environment

host plant: a plant on which a parasitic plant depends for nourishment

parasitic (plant): a plant that obtains its nourishment from another species

perennial: a plant that lives longer than two years

photosynthesis: the process by which plants obtain energy from the sun (see page 33)

sediment shore: a shore composed of particles that have been deposited by the flow of water, with few, if any, outcrops of bedrock

shell midden: a mound of shells accumulated by human consumption of shellfish

stalagmite: icicle-shaped column of calcium carbonate that grows upwards from a cave floor (stalactites grow downwards from the cave ceiling)

stratosphere: upper part of the Earth's atmosphere from about 14–22 km above the earth's surface

substrate: underlying surface, such as rock or soil, on which an organism lives

ultraviolet (UV) rays: invisible radiation from the sun that can be useful (UV-A – beneficial to plants and used in some medical and dental procedures) or potentially harmful (UV-B – may cause sunburn, premature aging of the skin or skin cancer)

zooxanthellae: microscopic, single-celled algae that live in a symbiotic relationship with many corals and other marine life, such as jellyfish and sea anemones

plant world

PLANT WORLD

The plant kingdom consists of an amazing diversity of forms, which include flowering plants, ferns, conifers, mosses, and lichens. Although plants have been around for a very long time, they did not begin to look like modern plants do until the Late Silurian, around 420 million years ago. By about 360 million years ago, a wide variety of plants of many different shapes and sizes had developed. Through the millenia, plants have evolved adaptations in order to survive in a wide range of habitats. Many plants that are native to the Arabian Peninsula have acquired protective features that enable them to survive the rigours of an **arid** environment.

THE PLANT KINGDOM

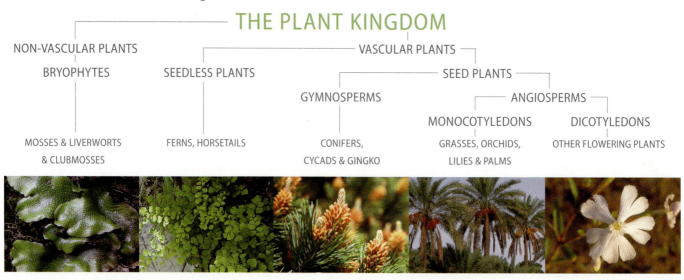

NON-VASCULAR PLANTS		VASCULAR PLANTS		
BRYOPHYTES	SEEDLESS PLANTS	SEED PLANTS		
		GYMNOSPERMS	ANGIOSPERMS	
			MONOCOTYLEDONS	DICOTYLEDONS
MOSSES & LIVERWORTS & CLUBMOSSES	FERNS, HORSETAILS	CONIFERS, CYCADS & GINGKO	GRASSES, ORCHIDS, LILIES & PALMS	OTHER FLOWERING PLANTS

– simple plants with no transport system for food and water; usually found in moist habitats

– earliest and most primitive plants that have a system for transporting food and water

– most primitive plants to have naked seeds: unable to make flowers, so seeds are not encased in fruit

– flowering plants with a single seed leaf (cotyledon), parallel leaf veins and flower parts arranged in threes

– flowering plants with two seed leaves (cotyledons) and usually with net-like veins in leaves

ADAPTING TO THE DESERT

Plants in many parts of the Arabian Peninsula have evolved strategies for living in an **arid** environment, exposed to lack of water, high temperatures, high light intensities and high **salinity**. Most desert **annuals** spend the hottest periods as seeds, a percentage of which then germinate early in the rainfall season. In the event of a drought, this strategy allows the remaining seeds an opportunity to germinate later, after the next suitable rainfall.

Many **perennials** survive below ground as **rhizomes**, **corms** and bulbs during harsh weather conditions, having died back after producing seed. Other species such as *Rhanterium epapposum* (left) shed their leaves in the summer heat and become dormant.

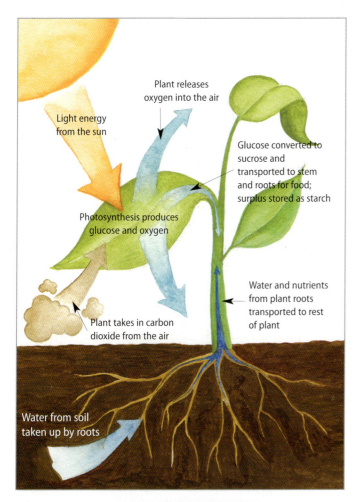

Light energy from the sun

Plant releases oxygen into the air

Glucose converted to sucrose and transported to stem and roots for food; surplus stored as starch

Photosynthesis produces glucose and oxygen

Water and nutrients from plant roots transported to rest of plant

Plant takes in carbon dioxide from the air

Water from soil taken up by roots

THE IMPORTANCE OF PLANTS

PHOTOSYNTHESIS

Plants are the foundation of life on Earth because of their ability to use the sun's energy to make carbohydrates, which provide food for both plants and other life forms, including other plants. This process is called **photosynthesis** (see diagram on left).

The green colour seen in most plants is a pigment known as **chlorophyll**, which absorbs light energy from the sun and uses it to turn carbon dioxide and water from the plant's surroundings into glucose and oxygen. The glucose can be converted to sucrose, which feeds the plant, or it can be stored as starch for later use. The oxygen that is produced is released into the atmosphere.

Most of the food eaten by humans and other animals ultimately comes from plants, and without the complex process of **photosynthesis**, life as we know it would not exist.

As well as releasing oxygen into the atmosphere, plants also absorb much of the carbon dioxide from our surroundings, thereby making the atmosphere suitable for us to breathe. Plants also play a vital part in the fight against global warming. Human activities such as the burning of fossil fuels release carbon dioxide into the air, leading to an increase in the 'greenhouse effect' causing the Earth's atmosphere to become warmer. Without plants to absorb carbon dioxide, global warming would be much worse.

See more about global warming on page 27

A desert bush provides shade and security for a baby oryx. Plants supply vital food, shelter and protection from predators for a wide range of animals.

PLANTS AS MEDICINE

Traditionally, many Arabian plants have been used in the treatment of various illnesses and to improve general health and well-being. The pioneering Zayed Complex for Herbal Research and Traditional Medicine in the UAE works with about 4,000 species of plants in the treatment of 50 illnesses and chronic pain. The Complex has been named by the World Health Organisation as a regional centre for alternative medicine in the Middle East.

FLOWERING PLANTS

Although flowering plants were the most recent to evolve, there is estimated to be about 422,000 species worldwide, many of which are still undescribed by science. In addition to being able to produce seed like the **gymnosperms** (see page 32), plants with flowers (angiosperms) can also attract other organisms, such as insects and birds, to assist in pollination and the distribution of seeds. Flowering plants are found in nearly every habitat on the planet and exhibit a huge diversity of form and size. Whilst **arid** regions such as the Arabian Peninsula have fewer plant species than areas with higher rainfall, native plants nonetheless exist, and have developed unique and interesting ways of adapting to their challenging environment.

FLOWER ANATOMY

STIGMA

STYLE

ANTHER

STAMEN

FILAMENT

PISTIL

PETAL

OVARY

OVULE

RECEPTACLE

SEPAL

PEDUNCLE STEM

POLLINATION IN FLOWERING PLANTS

In order for fertilisation to occur in a flowering plant, pollination must first take place. The petals of a flower indicate the presence of nectar to passing insects. The nectar is located at the inside base of the petals and as the insect crawls into the flower to reach the nectar, it gets a dusting of pollen. When the insect visits another flower, the pollen travels with it and is then deposited onto the stigma of another flower. Fertilisation takes place when the **nucleus** from the pollen fuses with the nucleus in the ovule, allowing a seed to develop.

WHAT IS A FLOWER?

Flowers are the reproductive part of a flowering plant. Species that have both male and female parts present in one flower are known as 'perfect' flowers, while those that contain either male or female reproductive organs, but not both, in the same flower are called 'imperfect'.

MALE PARTS
Stamen: male, pollen-producing part of the plant, consisting of the filament and anther. The number of stamens is usually the same as the number of petals.
Anther: top part of the stamen containing pollen
Filament: fine stalk that supports the anther

FEMALE PARTS
Pistil: female part of the flower, consisting of the stigma, style, and ovary
Stigma: sticky upper portion of the pistil that receives pollen grains and on which they germinate
Style: long stalk through which a slender tube grows down from the pollen grain to the unfertilised seed
Ovary: section of the pistil usually located at the bottom of the flower, containing the ovules, and which turns into fruit
Ovule: unfertilised seed

OTHER PARTS OF A FLOWER
Petal: usually colourful, often fragrant part of the flower that attracts pollinators such as bees, butterflies and other insects
Sepal: The parts that look like little green leaves that cover the outside of a flower bud to protect the flower before it opens

SUCCULENTS

Succulents are plants that have developed the capacity to store water in one or more of their organs (roots, leaves or stem) in order to survive long periods of drought. Many of these plants lack true leaves, but have swollen, fleshy stems with a waxy outer covering. Others have a swollen base called a **caudex**, which may be either the lower part of the stem or the exposed upper parts of the roots. In some **arid** regions of the world many plants fall into this category, but in Arabia, few plants are true succulents, and those that do occur are found in mountainous regions. Among these is *Caralluma arabica* (left), a species that thrives at relatively high altitudes on mountain slopes. It has dark red-brown, unpleasant smelling flowers that attract flies as pollinators. A related species, *Caralluma flava* (right) is rarer. The poisonous succulent spurge *Euphorbia larica* is dominant in some areas in the mountains, even at lower altitudes.

PARASITIC PLANTS

A parasitic plant is one that connects itself to another plant by means of a root-like attachment called a **haustorium** in order to obtain food and water. The plant that supplies the nutrients is known as the **host**. Two families of parasitic plants are represented on the Arabian Peninsula: one is Orobanchaceae (broomrapes) and the other is Cynomoriaceae.

Several species of the broomrape family occur in Arabia, the most common being the desert hyacinth *Cistanche* spp. (pictured below), which can be seen flowering in winter in coastal areas of the Arabian Gulf as well as on inland salt plains. Desert hyacinths attach themselves to **host plants** – usually salt-loving species such as glaucous glasswort *Arthrocnemum macrostachyum* (see photo page 36), jointed glasswort *Halocnemum strobilaceum* and bean caper *Zygophyllum qatarense* – by means of a **haustorium** that can be up to several metres in length. In some regions, gazelles are known to graze on this parasite.

Cynomorium coccineum, also known as red thumb, or **tarthuth** in Arabic, attaches itself to *Zygophyllum* spp.. With its faint, but characteristic smell of rotting flesh, red thumb attracts flies and ants. For centuries, the Bedu boiled and ate the flesh of young stems and used the plant for medicinal purposes.

GRASSES AND SEDGES

Grasses and sedges are a characteristic feature of many habitats of the Arabian Peninsula. Widespread **perennial** grasses include turgid panic grass *Panicum turgidum*, bristle grass *Pennisetum divisum* and plumose triple-awned grass *Stipagrostis plumosa*, all of which are important sources of natural food for many mammals. Many desert grasses have large, tough **lateral** root systems that help to anchor the plants during sand movement.

The common sedge, *Cyperus conglomeratus* (left) is one of few plants that frequently colonise sand dunes. It was traditionally used to make baskets and mats, as well as being used for fuel.

SALT-TOLERANT PLANTS

Plants that have developed characteristics which allow them to grow in highly salty environments are known as **halophytes**. Many salt-tolerant plants have very fleshy, bead-like leaves that are globular, or at least very fleshy in appearance, and allow large quantities of water to be stored for long periods. The stems may have deep grooves that reduce the amount of moisture loss.

Glaucous glasswort (above left) is commonly found along the shoreline in coastal areas and, in some regions, grows in association with mangroves. Jointed glasswort (above right) may also occur near mangroves as well as in saltmarshes. These two species, together with *Salsola drummondii* (right) and string of beads *Halopeplis perfoliata* (left) are members of the widespread goosefoot or **chenopod** family.

FERNS

Ferns were the first plants, along with horsetails, to evolve a **vascular** system that would allow them to grow larger than the mosses and liverworts that existed on earth before them. The **arid** environment of the Arabian Peninsula is not an ideal habitat for ferns, which usually prefer moist, shady surroundings; however, there are a number species that grow mainly in mountain regions, as well as the adder's tongue fern, which is common in some coastal areas around Dubai and is also known to occur after rain in other parts of Arabia.

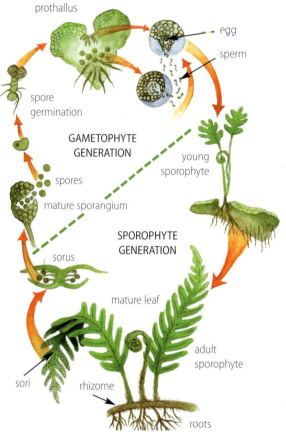

prothallus
egg
sperm
spore germination
GAMETOPHYTE GENERATION
young sporophyte
spores
mature sporangium
SPOROPHYTE GENERATION
sorus
mature leaf
adult sporophyte
sori
rhizome
roots

THE LIFE CYCLE OF FERNS

The life cycle of ferns differs from that of flowering plants. Instead of producing seeds, ferns reproduce from spores over two generations.

GAMETOPHYTE GENERATION

The most easily observed part of the cycle is the development of the green fronds, on the undersides of which are scaly bumps called **sori**. The sori are clusters of small sacs called sporangia that contain the powdery **spores**. These are released when the sori ripen and turn brown. The spores fall to the ground and develop into small, heart-shaped plants known as **prothallia** (singular **prothallus**). This part of the cycle is called the **gametophyte** generation because male and female reproductive organs produce **gametes**, the equivalent of pollen and ovules in seed-bearing plants.

SPOROPHYTE GENERATION

In the presence of moisture, the male and female **gametes** combine to form spores. This process is easily missed because **prothallia** are very small and lie close to the ground. When released, these spores grow into the familiar frond-bearing plant.

The maidenhair fern Adiantum capillus-veneris (below left) grows in moist, shady areas of cliffs, on the banks of wadis and along irrigation channels. It has been used in traditional medicine in the treatment of chest ailments and other complaints. The adder's tongue fern Ophioglossum polyphyllum (below right) is not immediately recognisable as a fern. The fertile organs that are grouped together at the top of a spike gives the plant its common name. The adder's tongue fern grows in sand and silt in both coastal and mountain areas.

LICHENS

Lichens are the result of a unique relationship between a **fungus** and either green algae (see page 44) or **cyanobacteria**, in which the fungus provides shelter and nutrients for the algae or bacteria, and in return receives energy produced by its partner through **photosynthesis**. A number of studies undertaken by scientists in recent years have recorded some 230 species of lichens across the Arabian Peninsula.

Gloeoheppia turgida

Gloeoheppia turgida is common in rocky habitats. Due to its variable appearance and small size, it can easily be confused with other lichens. The **squamules** (scale-like lobes) are slightly inflated and measure up to 3 mm across. In older individuals, they are often 'frosted', as shown here.

Buellia subalbula

Buellia subalbula is a widespread species of lichen found on rocks. It is especially common in coastal locations. The black disc-shaped objects are the reproductive fruiting bodies, which produce spores. These develop on the white, cracked body of the lichen.

The bright yellow lichen Fulgensia fulgida (above), with red fruiting bodies, usually occurs at elevations of over 900 m.

TYPES OF LICHEN

Lichens usually grow in one of four different forms:

Crustose lichens form flat, crusty plates that are tightly attached to the surface on which they grow. Some are brightly coloured and may look like a splash of paint.

Foliose lichens form lobes that are leaf-like in appearance. They are more loosely attached to the substrate than crustose lichens, and may have a holdfast or similar structure that connects to the substrate.

Fruticose lichens are usually branched and either grow upward, like a small bush as in *Ramalina maciformis*, pictured bottom left, or hang down in strands like a beard. Whilst they are usually attached to the substrate at a single point, some are unattached.

Squamulose lichens have small, overlapping lobes that resemble scales.

FASCINATING FACTS

Due to their ability to absorb almost everything from the surrounding air, including pollutants, lichens play a very important role in monitoring air quality. By measuring the amount of heavy metals, carbon dioxide and sulphur present in lichens, scientists are able to determine pollution levels in the atmosphere. The specific properties of individual species can provide scientists with a wide range of useful information.

TREES AND SHRUBS

In addition to the date palm (see page 42), a number of trees and shrubs have adapted to the climatic conditions of the Arabian Peninsula. Various strategies are used to survive, including the ability to shed leaves and remain dormant for several years during periods of drought. Deep roots allow such trees as *Prosopis cineraria (ghaf)* to obtain water at deeper levels, while the shrub *Haloxylon persicum* is able to catch moisture from the air. This moisture then falls to the ground as dew beneath the plants. Mountain regions and wadi beds support a wider range of species, and in some coastal areas mangrove trees provide a unique habitat for wildlife.

DESERT ADAPTATION

The bushy perennial *Calligonum comosum* (pictured right) is one of a number of desert shrubs with much reduced leaves, which results in less exposure to moisture loss. The distinctive fruits consist of a red capsule covered with short, red bristles. The fruit and young shoots are edible, while the leaves and stems have been used in the treatment of toothache. The woody stems ate useful as animal fodder, as well as providing a smokeless fire when burned.

GHAF TREE

The *ghaf* tree *Prosopis cineraria* (left) is a drought-tolerant tree native to Arabia, India, Pakistan, Afghanistan and Iran. It forms characteristic groves known as '*ghaf* forests' (above). Young trees can establish themselves at some distance from the mother plant by means of root suckers. The hard wood of the *ghaf* is excellent as firewood and for making charcoal, as well as for construction purposes and in the manufacture of items such as tool handles and posts. The leaves and seed pods make nutritious fodder for goats, camels and donkeys. Both the bark and the flowers have been used medicinally.

TREES AND SHRUBS OF THE GRAVEL PLAINS AND FOOTHILLS

Gravel plains are a characteristic landscape near mountainous regions of the Arabian Peninsula. In the foothillls of mountain ranges, flat expanses of rocks, pebbles and gravel deposited from the surrounding highlands are often dominated by large stands of *Acacia tortilis*. These characteristically flat-topped trees often grow in association with thorny shrubs, such as desert thorn *Lycium shawii* (below left) and *Gaillonia aucheri*, along with the succulent *Euphorbia larica* and semi-succulent *Ochradenus arabicus* (left). The *ghaf* tree *Prosopis cineraria* (see previous page) may also be found growing on these **alluvial** plains. In some regions, considerable quantities of the toxic shrub *Rhazya stricta* (below right) occur, often alongside lesser numbers of more palatable plant species that have been overgrazed by animals.

POISONOUS SAP

Sodom's apple *Calotropis procera* belongs to the milkweed plant family. It grows on sandy gravel plains and is often found in areas where there has been a lot of human disturbance. This fast-growing tree contains a poisonous, milky **latex** sap, which can affect the heart if eaten.

MANGROVES

Mangroves are a vital part of some coastal ecosystems, providing food and shelter for a wide range of both terrestrial and marine species. The mangrove *Avicennia marina* is well-adapted to salt water and is able to withstand waterlogging and a reduced supply of oxygen due to its unique root structure. In order to avoid suffocation in **anaerobic** soil conditions, mangroves have developed modified aerial roots called **pneumatophores** (see photo at left). Special pores are located on the surface of the root, allowing the tree to breathe. Mangrove roots also provide structural support in the soft mud in which they grow.

are used to manufacture a wide range of products, including building materials, boats, fish traps, fencing, baskets and mats.

The date palm remains an important part of the Arabian economy, with technology playing a vital role in increasing the number of plantations, as well as the yield and quality of the dates. Tissue culture (above) is now the main method of reproduction, allowing farmers to select only the best trees. Every plant produced by this process is genetically identical to the parent tree.

Progress is also being made in the use of biological controls against the spread of the red palm weevil (opposite page, top left), a major pest that has destroyed large numbers of date palms.

The future is likely to see further developments in the use of the date palm as a primary source of food in Arabia, as well as the possibility that future generations may drive their cars on fuel derived from the date palm.

Known in Arabic as *nakhl*, the date palm *Phoenix dactylifera* has been a vital part of life for people of the Arabian Peninsula for 8,000 years. Perfectly suited to arid regions, where high temperatures and continuous daytime exposure to sunlight often occur from flowering to fruiting, the date palm provides nutritious, energy-laden food for both people and animals of the desert.

In addition to providing food, various parts of the date palm have been and still

Pollination of the date palm is a labour intensive process, because individual plants support either male or female flowers, but not both together. For the female flower to be fertilised, pollen must therefore travel between trees. If there are male trees nearby, wind-pollination is possible, but pollination by insects is thought to be rare. In palm gardens, 90 per cent of the trees are female, so it has been common practice since antiquity to pollinate date palms manually. This is complicated by the short period of less than two days during which the female flower is receptive to male pollen. The pollinator gathers the branchlets of pollen-bearing male flowers, then applies the pollen to the female flowers with a sponge or brush, by shaking the pollen directly onto the female flower or by tying the male flower on top of the female one.

MARINE PLANTS AND ALGAE

Seaweeds have been around for hundreds of millions of years. They grow in the sea and **brackish** water on intertidal and subtidal rocks, seagrasses, the breathing roots of mangroves, and on other seaweeds and animals, including dead coral skeletons. Unlike **vascular** plants, algae lack an internal system for circulating nutrients and fluids, but they share the ability to use sunlight to generate into food through **photosynthesis**. Nutrients are obtained directly from the surrounding water. Seaweeds are a basic part of the food chain, without which many other organisms could not exist.

Green alga Ulva flexuosa

GREEN ALGAE

Known collectively as Chlorophyta, green algae are found mainly in fresh water, but about 10 per cent of this large group are marine species. The remainder are found on land. Green algae are more closely related to the green **vascular** land plants than any other group of algae. Their green colouration results from the same two **chlorophyll** pigments that are found in the higher plants. Green seaweeds are most commonly found in the shallow intertidal zone because they require sunlight for **photosynthesis**. Some green algae consist of microscopic single cells, while others form simple or branched **filaments**, spongy mats, flattened fronds or tubes.

BROWN ALGAE

Brown seaweeds contain the green pigment **chlorophyll**, but the green colouring is masked due to the presence of other pigments, resulting in a range of colours from gold or olive green to dark brown. All brown algae are multicellular marine species, which range from a few centimetres to many metres in length. Most brown algae live in the intertidal or shallow subtidal zone, and are mainly restricted to temperate or cooler climates. Brown seaweeds vary greatly in form and include some that are slender, thread-like **filaments**. Others (e.g. *Sargassum*) have leaf-like appendages. Some grow to a considerable size and have a distinct holdfast, stipe and frond.

Coralline red alga Lithophyllum kotschyanum

RED ALGAE

Red algae or Rhodophyta make up the majority of marine algae species, and may be found not only grow in the shallow, intertidal zone, but also occur in deeper waters. They occur as single celled forms as well as multi-cellular species that reach lengths of up to 3 m. Many red seaweeds have a rubbery, elastic quality, but the pink coralline seaweeds are hard, due to the presence of strengthening calcium carbonate in the cell walls.

Brown seaweed Sargassum latifolia

The brown seaweed Cystoseira trinodis *forms slender branches almost 8 m long. It occurs with other large brown seaweeds, forming dense forests on shallow, submerged rocky platforms.*

A VALUABLE RESOURCE

- Seaweeds have been utilised by humans in many parts of the world for centuries. In Greek and Roman times, seaweeds were used in the Mediterranean region in herbal medicines and as animal fodder. The people of Japan and China have included seaweeds in their diet for over 2,000 years. Other historical uses for seaweeds included fuel and fertiliser.

- Seaweed ash was used as a source of soda by glassmakers in the Cherbourg region of France during the 18th century. In the 19th century, an army chemist discovered a new substance from seaweed ash, which he called iodine – an invaluable antiseptic in treating wounds, as well as an essential trace element in human nutrition.

- More recently, scientists have learned more about the nutritional and chemical properties of seaweeds, and this knowledge has led to seaweeds being used commercially in the food, cosmetics and pharmaceutical industries.

- Scientific research continues to discover new uses for this valuable and renewable resource in fields such as agriculture, horticulture, aquaculture, biomedicine, pharmacology and environmental monitoring.

SEAGRASSES

Seagrasses, as their name implies, usually have long, narrow, grass-like leaves, but they are not true grasses. They are, however, flowering plants with true roots, stems and leaves that contain vein-like conducting tissues. Their flowers are inconspicuous. Grass-like shoots arise at intervals from creeping **rhizomes** that are anchored in sandy or silty shallows. Seagrasses commonly form extensive beds or 'meadows' that help to stabilise the underlying sediment and provide important nursery grounds for fish as well as a major food source for marine animals including dugongs and turtles. Seagrass habitats are under threat in many places as a result of such human activities as:

- industrial and agricultural pollution
- sewage disposal
- dredging and trawling
- sediment disturbance by boat propellers

TRADITIONAL PLANT USES

Zizyphus spina-christi

FOOD

As recently as 50 years ago, desert people relied on native plants as an essential part of their diet. The fruits of *Zizyphus spina-christi* (*sidr*) are still eaten, and the succulent stems of *Caralluma arabica* are sold at local markets for food. *Cynomorium coccineum*, a parasitic perennial, is occasionally eaten when young, as are the thickened **taproots** of *Emex spinosa*. The slightly peppery-tasting leaves of *Rhanterium epapposum* were once used as a spice, and both the young leaves and pods of the *ghaf* tree were commonly eaten. The fruits of *Calligonum comosum* are edible, and young shoots were used in salads. Desert truffles are regarded as a delicacy, but due to development of the coastal zone where they occur, they are now uncommon.

Calligonum comosum

MEDICINE

A large number of native Arabian plants have been used for centuries to treat medical conditions and improve general well-being. There are plant remedies for digestive problems, parasites, muscular pains, skin disorders, burns and bruises, colds and coughs, fevers and headaches. Other plants are used in childbirth and still others as health tonics.

Lawsonia inermis *(henna)*

COSMETICS

A number of plants were used in the past for cosmetic purposes, including the following:

Arnebia decumbens	skin dye
Helichrysum makranicum	deodorant
	body perfume
Pluchea arabica	body perfume
Salvadora persica	teeth cleaning

Henna *Lawsonia inermis*, although not strictly a native tree, has long been cultivated in mountainous areas for the red dye that can be obtained from its leaves and which is still commonly used to apply intricate patterns to women's bodies, as well as to colour hair. The leaves are also used for various medicinal purposes.

TEXTILE DYES

Some plants have a long history of being used in some regions in the production of textile dyes. Examples include *Indigofera* spp. (indigo), *Acridocarpus orientalis* (yellow), *Pulicaria glutinosa* (yellow) and the pounded root bark of *Calligonum comosum* (purple).

Lawsonia inermis

CONSTRUCTION

As well as that of the date palm the timber of several tree species has been widely used for construction purposes, including *Avicennia marina*, *Moringa peregrina*, *Prosopis cineraria*, *Tamarix aphylla* and *Zizyphus spina-christi*. In earlier times, a number of desert shrubs were an important source of fuel. These included *Calligonum comosum*, *Haloxylon salicornicum*, *H. persicum* and *Rhanterium epapposum*. The scientific name of the desert shrub *Leptadenia pyrotechnica* is derived from the fact that the plant's numerous seeds have long silky hairs which, when dried, could be used for tinder.

LIVESTOCK FODDER

Plants remain a vital source of livestock fodder. However, due to over-exploitation of the vegetation and excessive groundwater extraction resulting in severe land degradation, there is an urgent need to intensify efforts to protect many plants and promote their sustainable use.

>> LEARN MORE : USEFUL WEBSITES

GENERAL INFORMATION ON PLANTS

http://www.biology4kids.com/files/plants_main.html – excellent educational site with information on plant structure, photosynthesis, flowering plants, ferns, mosses and more

http://www.kathimitchell.com/plants.html – a directory of links to websites dealing with plants of all kinds

http://waynesword.palomar.edu/trmar98.htm – fascinating website about terrestrial and marine plant diversity

http://www.ucmp.berkeley.edu/plants/plantae.html – a very large website with a comprehensive section on the plant kingdom: has excellent navigation and links

INFORMATION ON ARABIAN PLANTS

http://www.uaeinteract.com/nature/plant/index.asp – excellent information on plants growing in the United Arab Emirates and relevant to the Arabian Peninsula as a whole

http://www.arabianwildlife.com/archive/vol1.2/flw.htm – article on flowers of the Arabian mountains

http://www.enhg.org/bulletin/b36/36_17.htm – extensive information on the adaptation of plants to a desert environment

http://www.enhg.org/bulletin/b17/17_18.htm – an introduction to the natural vegetation of Abu Dhabi

http://www.enhg.org/bulletin/b21/21_02.htm – article on the vegetation of the Arabian Gulf coast of the UAE

LICHENS

http://www.ucmp.berkeley.edu/fungi/lichens/lichens.html – full of interesting information about lichens

MARINE PLANTS

http://seaweed.ucg.ie/Algae/ – useful website on seaweeds, including photographs

http://www.algaebase.org/ – a large database on seaweeds originating from the National University of Ireland, but with worldwide coverage of 124,276 species, including photographs

http://botany.si.edu/projects/algae/introduction.htm – information on marine plants from the Smithsonian Institute, Washington, DC

MANGROVES

http://www.arabianwildlife.com/current/mangrove.html – informative article on mangroves of the Arabian Peninsula

http://www.enhg.org/bulletin/b32/32_02.htm – information on the grey mangrove *Avicennia marina*

MEDICINAL PLANTS

http://www.geocities.com/eyeclaudius.geo/HERBALME.htm – online handbook of Arabian medicinal herbs

PLANTS GLOSSARY

alluvial: soil or sediment carried by streams and rivers and deposited some distance away from its original location

anaerobic: with absence of oxygen

angiosperm: meaning 'covered seed' – flowering plants that produce seeds enclosed in a fruit ovary

annual (plant): a plant that germinates, flowers and dies within the space of a single year

arid: having little or no water

biennial: a plant that lives for only two growing seasons, usually flowering and producing seed in the second year

brackish: water containing more salt than fresh water does, but less than sea water

caudex: enlarged woody stem, trunk or root, used for water storage

chenopod: a plant of the goosefoot family

chlorophyll: green pigment required in plants for **photosynthesis** to take place

corm: a short, thick, underground stem used by some plant species for food storage

cyanobacteria: (or blue-green algae), a type of bacteria that obtains energy by photosynthesis

dicot or **dicotyledon:** a plant that produces two seed leaves

filament: a structure in which single cells unite to form a chain or thread

fungi: immobile organisms lacking chlorophyll and feeding on organic matter

gametes: specialised reproductive cells such as eggs or pollen

gametophyte: phase of a plant's life cycle that produces **gametes** see FERNS, page 37

gymnosperms: plants having seed that is not enclosed in an ovary

haustorium: a modified root through which a parasitic plant obtains food from its **host plant**

host plant: plant that is used as a source of nourishment by a parasitic plant

lateral (root): a root that extends horizontally from the main root

latex: milky sap produced by plants such as members of the milkweed family Asclepiadaceae

monocot or **monocotyledon:** plant that produces a single seed leaf

nucleus (plural **nuclei**)**:** the part of a cell responsible for growth and reproduction

perennial: a plant that lives for more than two growing seasons

photosynthesis: process by which green plants use sunlight to make food

pneumatophore: a modified root that allows mud-dwelling trees and shrubs, such as mangroves, to breathe

prothallus (plural **prothallia**)**:** small heart-shaped plant that forms from a fern **spore**

rhizome: horizontal creeping, underground stem

salinity: the amount of dissolved salt in water

sori (singular **sorus**)**:** the part of a fern that makes **spores** (the fern equivalent of a flower)

spore: reproductive body produced and dispersed by ferns, mosses and fungi

squamule: scale-like structures that form a lichen

taproot: a long, tapering root that grows straight downwards

vascular: plants with a system of veins for the movement of water, minerals and food

animal world

ANIMAL WORLD

Scientists classify all living things into five groups that are referred to as kingdoms. Nearly two million species belong to the animal kingdom (Animalia), which is further divided into animals with a backbone (vertebrates) and those without a backbone (invertebrates). Over millions of years, animals have evolved into an enormous array of shapes and sizes, each species with its own particular features and lifestyle.

THE ANIMAL KINGDOM (simplified)

INVERTEBRATES animals without backbones	VERTEBRATES animals with backbones

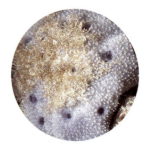

PORIFERA
sponges

CNIDARIA
jellyfish, sea anemones, corals

FISH

AMPHIBIANS

MOLLUSCA
bivalves, snails and slugs,
octopuses and squid

ANNELIDA
worms

REPTILES
turtles, lizards and snakes

BIRDS

ECHINODERMATA
starfish, sea cucumbers,
sea urchins

ARTHROPODA
arachnids, crustaceans, insects

MAMMALS

This simplified chart of the animal kingdom only contains those groups that are covered in this volume.

ANATOMY

Although members of the animal kingdom vary greatly in appearance, all animals have certain characteristics in common. Unlike members of the plant kingdom, animals cannot make their own food; instead they obtain their energy by consuming other animals or plants. The cells of animals, unlike those of plants, do not have rigid cell walls. Most animals can move around independently and spontaneously at some or all stages of development.

INVERTEBRATES

Invertebrates make up about 98 per cent of all life-forms. Lack of **vertebrae** (backbone) is the defining characteristic that separates them from other members of the animal kingdom. Some invertebrates, such as jellyfish, have a **hydrostatic skeleton** – a fluid-filled cavity surrounded by muscles, which enables the animal to move around. Others, such as insects and crustaceans, have a hard outer shell called an **exoskeleton**.

Jellyfish have a **hydrostatic skeleton.** *Composed of 95 per cent water, jellyfish have no heart, brain, eyes or bone. A simple nervous system known as a* **nerve net** *enables jellyfish to respond to light, touch, balance and food.*

Like most insects, the rhinoceros beetle has a protective outer covering known as an **exoskeleton.**

>> for further information on invertebrates, see page 60

VERTEBRATES

Vertebrates are animals with **vertebrae,** which form part of an internal bone skeleton. There are far fewer species of vertebrates than invertebrates, but their size, intelligence and ability to move around give them an advantage in nature. Vertebrates include fish, amphibians, reptiles, birds and mammals.

>> for further information on vertebrates, see page 118

The Arabian camel, like all vertebrates, has muscles and an internal skeleton, as well as an advanced nervous system.

ANIMAL SENSES

The animal world is full of fascinating ways in which both vertebrates and invertebrates have adapted to their surroundings by developing various sensory abilities. Humans have five main senses: taste, touch, smell, sight, and hearing. Some animal species have senses that are very different from those of humans.

ECHOLOCATION

Some animals are able to emit sound waves that bounce off objects and then return to the animal, allowing it to 'see' its surroundings through the information it receives. Returning sounds vary according to the size and position of the object.

Toothed whales, such as killer whales and dolphins, use **echolocation** to navigate and hunt for prey. The sounds they emit for echolocation often sound to us like high-speed clicks.

Many bats use **echolocation** to navigate in darkness, as well as to locate and identify food in the form of flying insects.

VISION

Vision varies greatly between different animal species. Some animals are able to do little more than distinguish between light and dark, while others see in great detail. Vertebrate eyes have a single lens, but many invertebrates have eyes made up of as many as 30,000 separate lenses (see below and page 61 for more information on compound eyes).

MAGNETIC SENSE

A number of animal species are able to navigate over long distances using the Earth's magnetic field as a guide. Animals that possess this ability include honey bees, migratory birds, eels, salmon, tuna, sharks and marine turtles.

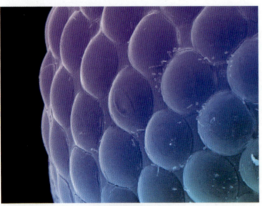

Ultraviolet and infrared vision >>

While some animals are unable to see a full range of colours, their eyes may be sensitive to wavelengths of light that are not visible to humans. Bees, for example, make use of **ultraviolet** vision to locate flowers, while snakes use **infrared** vision to locate prey at night.

<< Compound eyes

Most insects have **compound eyes** that consist of thousands of tiny sensory structures, each with its own lens, enabling the insect to see in all directions at the same time. **Compound eyes** cannot move or focus, so insects are short-sighted and can only clearly see objects that are close to them.

Binocular vision >>

Binocular vision allows an animal to see the same area from different angles, enabling it to estimate distances more effectively. Birds of prey have **binocular visio**n, which allows them to pinpoint small animals from thousands of feet up in the air.

<< Panoramic vision

Plant-eating animals that are hunted by predators usually have their eyes positioned on the sides of the head, with each having its own field of vision. This gives animals such as hares and gazelles the abilty to see predators approaching from any direction.

TASTE

The sense of taste is a fairly limited one and is often confused with the sense of smell. Humans are able to distinguish only five different tastes: salty, sweet, sour, umami (savouriness) and bitter. Taste buds, located mainly on the upper surface of the tongue, contain many **receptor cells**. When food is eaten, the saliva in the mouth dissolves the chemicals in the food, and the molecules enter the taste buds, setting off a process that results in the brain deciding that the item is either salty, sweet, sour, savoury or bitter.

Some animals have their taste **receptor cells** located on other parts of the body. Honey bees, for example, have taste receptors on their jaws, forelegs and **antennae**, while a butterfly has them on its feet.

SMELL

The sense of smell in humans is very limited compared to that of some other animals. Many rely on their sense of smell for finding food, for avoiding predators and for finding a mate. In some animals, such as bats, individuals use scent to pick out their own offspring from large groups. A highly-developed sense of smell allows many animals to follow the scent trails of other animals. This ability is not only useful in hunting for food, but also for avoiding territory belonging to other members of the same species.

Some insects, including butterflies, moths and ants, have a keen sense of smell. Unlike mammals, which smell through their noses, many insects sense odour through organs located at the tips of their **antennae**.

HEARING

Nocturnal animals often have a well-developed sense of hearing. Owls, in particular, are superbly adapted for hunting at night. Many owls have a dish-shaped disc of feathers surrounding each eye, which helps to channel sound to the large ear holes. In addition to being able to measure the difference in time that it takes for sound to reach each ear, the owl's brain can also determine the location of the sound, in part due to one ear hole being located slightly higher than the other. Sounds that are louder in the lower ear come from below, while those that are equally loud in both ears come from a source at eye level. According to some scientists, an owl's brain is able to form an image of the bird's surroundings based solely on the sound information that it receives.

FASCINATING FACTS: ANIMAL SENSES

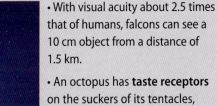

- Worker ants follow a trail of scented markers left by others from their colony in order to find their way back to the anthill.

- A scorpion can detect very faint air movements with the help of special hairs on its pincers.

- A polar bear can smell a seal that is hidden under snow or ice that is over a metre thick.

- Cells containing iron oxide (magnetite) in the abdomens of honey bees are thought to allow bees to detect changes in the Earth's magnetic field and to use it for navigation.

- Using **echolocation**, bats can find flying insects up to 5 m away and get information about the type of insect.

- Fish have a 'lateral line' on each side of their bodies containing sense organs that detect changes in water pressure and may be used to locate food and to aid navigation.

- Crabs have hairs on their claws and other parts of the body, which allow them to detect water currents and vibrations.

- The eyes of a dragonfly each contain 30,000 lenses.

- With visual acuity about 2.5 times that of humans, falcons can see a 10 cm object from a distance of 1.5 km.

- An octopus has **taste receptors** on the suckers of its tentacles, allowing it to remain hidden while it searches for food.

- Birds appear to have better colour vision than humans and they use colour to recognise others of their species as well as for courtship and protection.

FOSSILS

The story of Arabia's wildlife lies trapped in its rocks. Most of these cover three main periods: the **Miocene** (a geological time period from 5 million to 23 million years ago); the **Eocene** to **Oligocene** (23 to 55 million years ago) environment and the **Cretaceous** period (65 to 145 million years ago). Studies have also been carried out on some of Arabia's rare older rocks, on the 150-million-year-old fossils found in the Musandam region, and on some of the region's most recent rocks laid down in the last 1.8 million years or so.

DENTAL RECORDS

Fossil teeth provide evidence of animals inhabiting the Abu Dhabi region during the **Miocene** period. These include a tooth from an eight-million-year-old monkey (above); a molar tooth belonging to a **Miocene** elephant (centre) and the lower jaw of a hippopotamus (bottom).

LIFE IN AN ANCIENT MIOCENE LAND
Abu Dhabi 6–8 Million Years Ago

At this time, the climate of eastern Arabia was very different from that of today. Geological and palaeontological evidence from the Abu Dhabi coastal region shows that numerous channels, each about 10 m wide, formed a river system about 1 km across. The banks of the channels were formed of sandy gravels that had been deposited when the river was in flood.

Among the animals that inhabited this region were 4 m-long crocodiles, sabre-toothed cats, a primitive three-toed horse *Hipparion*, hyaenas and hippos.

ANCIENT SEAS

The Jebel Hafit Sea – 30 million years ago

The **Tethys** seaway stretched across southern Arabia linking the Indian Ocean with the Mediterranean and covering most of northern Africa, Jordan, Syria and Iraq. Parts of Turkey, the Balkans and part of Greece together formed an island and the Asian mainland (south-western Iran) was about 1,000 km from the Arabian coastline. At this time, the Hajar Mountains, stretching from the Emirates into Saudi Arabia, were an island and marine life flourished in the shallow tropical sea.

The Cretaceous Sea – 70 million years ago

In the late **Cretaceous**, a broad, shallow and warm sea lapped against the Hajar islands. The limestone sediments from this sea are now known as the Simsima Formation. Knowledge of the fossil record in these **carbonate sediments** is of particular interest to the oil industry, for they comprise the primary oil-bearing rocks of the Empty Quarter.

In exposed environments with high wave activity, pounding waves eroded the beach rocks to form large beds of boulders which had little in the way of marine life. In more protected bays, reefs and thickets of corals and **rudist bivalves** lived close to the shore, while sandy bays contained burrowing bivalves and marine snails.

*Among the **patch-reefs** and shallow rocky bottoms there lived a great variety of sea urchins. All are well-preserved although they have lost their defensive armament of spines.*

<< SEA URCHINS
In the nearshore sands a specialised community of burrowing sea urchins (*Faujasia eccentripora*) lived just beneath the surface and obtained their food by eating sediment grains and digesting microorganisms on them.

OYSTER
The carbonate succession indicates that the sea floor became progressively deeper through time. Towards the top of the succession the fauna becomes very much sparser and only a restricted number of forms are found. One of them is the oyster *Agerostrea ungulata,* pictured above.

AMMONITES >>
Although primarily open-water animals, occasional ammonite or nautiloid shells, like this *Deltonautilus* cf. *mermeti* were washed into the environment and are found in the basal beds of the succession.

EXTINCT ARABIAN WILDLIFE

Many Arabian mammals have suffered a severe decline in numbers in recent times, due to hunting, loss of habitat and the spread of human development. Some species, such as the Arabian leopard, Arabian oryx and Arabian tahr are the focus of intensive conservation programmes. Others have already become extinct in the region, including the cheetah, onager and Arabian ostrich.

LEGENDARY LONGEVITY

The onager *Equus hemionus* is an animal of the desert and arid plains. Once plentiful across a wide area that included much of Asia, Arabia and the Indian sub-continent, the onager, or Asiatic wild ass, is now extinct in Arabia and is classified as endangered on the IUCN Red List.

Onagers were highly regarded in Arabia since pre-Islamic times and were the subject of poetry and folklore. Many stories claimed that onagers had a life-span of as much as 800 years!

From ancient times, the onager was regarded as a game animal and was hunted for its meat, which was said to have a more delicate flavour than that of deer. Although noted for their ability to move at speed, the onagers' habit of remaining together in a group made them easy to hunt. It is not known whether they were ever fully domesticated, but there is evidence that they were used by the Sumerians to pull four-wheeled chariots until the arrival of the horse in Mesopotamia in the second millennium BC.

It is thought that the last Arabian onager was shot in 1927, near Lake Azraq in north Arabia. In spite of its legendary speed, the onager proved no match for the speed of the automobile or the power of modern guns.

'CAMEL BIRD'

The Arabian ostrich *Struthio camelus camelus* was known by the Chinese as the 'camel bird'. Like the onager, with which it was known to associate, the ostrich held a significant place in Arabian history and legend. A female ostrich, with numerous offspring, features in the rock drawings at Graffiti Rock, near Riyadh in Saudi Arabia. The ostrich is also known to have been a sacrificial animal in the Early Iron Age, and objects made from ostrich eggs were traded as far away as central Italy. Like the onager, the Arabian ostrich was hunted to extinction by the use of modern rifles and automobiles.

FASTEST ANIMAL >>

The Arabian cheetah *Acinonyx jubatus venaticus* was once distributed across much of Asia, including the Arabian Peninsula. Hunting and loss of habitat, together with the reduction in gazelles, on which it preyed, contributed to its decline and eventual extinction in Arabia.

>> LEARN MORE : USEFUL WEBSITES

GENERAL INFORMATION ON ANIMALS

http://www.arkive.org/ – one of the best websites for general information on a wide range of animals, with fact files, photographs and videos, and an emphasis on endangered species

http://www.kidport.com/RefLIB/Science/Animals/Animals.htm – useful information on the animal kingdom and classification of species

http://animaldiversity.ummz.umich.edu/site/index.html – a large website with extensive information about the animal kingdom

http://www.biologybrowser.org/animalguide.html – useful site for students and teachers; features a list of animal groups from protozoa to mammals with links to further detailed information

http://animals.nationalgeographic.com/ – alphabetical fact file on a wide range of animals from the National Geographic website

http://www.seaworld.org/animal-info/Animal-Bytes/index.htm – information on a range of vertebrates and invertebrate animals

http://www.earthlife.net/mammals/welcome.html – interesting information about mammals with links to further pages on mammals

http://www.earthlife.net/mammals/families.html – a checklist of mammal families of the world and their distribution

ANIMAL ANATOMY

http://webs.lander.edu/rsfox/invertebrates/ – advanced text material, but some very useful anatomical drawings of common invertebrates

http://www.earthlife.net/mammals/skeleton.html
http://www.earthlife.net/insects/anatomy.html
http://www.earthlife.net/birds/anatomy.html
http://www.earthlife.net/fish/anatomy.html
– excellent pages of information on anatomy from the Earth Life Web, an online encyclopedia of life on earth

ANIMAL SENSES

http://faculty.washington.edu/chudler/amaze.html – interesting facts about animal senses

http://marinebiologyoceanography.suite101.com/article.cfm/whale_echolocation_and_song – information on cetacean echolocation

http://www.earthlife.net/mammals/senses.html – information on the sensory world of mammals

FOSSILS

http://www.fossilmuseum.net/ – virtual fossil museum with good general information and images

http://www.fossils-facts-and-finds.com/ – information on fossils aimed at students and teachers

EXTINCT ARABIAN ANIMALS

http://www.arabianwildlife.com/archive/vol1.2/onager.htm – article on the extinct onager

http://www.qatarvisitor.com/index.php?cID=430&pID=1523 – article on the extinct fauna of Qatar

ANIMAL WORLD GLOSSARY

antenna (pl. antennae): segmented sensory organ; one is situated on each side of the head of an insect or crustacean

arthropod: group name for arachnids, insects, crustaceans, millipedes and centipedes

baleen: comb-like plates made of keratin, in the upper jaw of some whales, for filtering out food such as plankton from sea water

binocular vision: ability to combine the images received by the retina of each eye into a single, three-dimensional image

carbonate: a chemical compound containing oxygen and carbon, such as limestone

compound eye: visual organ in many arthropods, made up of a number of units each with its own individual lens

Cretaceous: geological time period in the Earth's history from 145 to 65 million years ago

echolocation: means by which an animal detects other animals or objects in its surroundings using reflected sound.

Eocene: geological time period in the Earth's history from 55 to 34 million years ago

exoskeleton: hard, outer covering that protects and supports the body of an invertebrate

hydrostatic skeleton: fluid-filled cavity surrounded by muscles, which are used to produce movement and to change body shape in some invertebrates, such as jellyfish

infrared: light radiated with wavelengths longer than those in the visible spectrum, but shorter than radio waves

lateral line: a sensory system consisting of pore-like openings along the sides of a fish, with which it detects water movement and vibration

Miocene: geological time period in the Earth's history from 23 to 5 million years ago

nerve net: simple nervous system found in some invertebrates, such as jellyfish

nocturnal: active during the night

Oligocene: geological time period in the Earth's history from 34 to 23 million years ago

patch-reef: an area of coral reef usually found in lagoons between the main reef-line and the shore

Pleistocene: geological time period in the Earth's history from 1.8 million to 10,000 years ago

receptor cells: cells within body organs that are sensitive to environmental stimulus, such as light receptors in the eye or taste receptor cells on the surface of the tongue in mammals

sediment: particles carried by water or wind and deposited on a land surface or at the bottom of a body of water, which may, over time, consolidate to form **sedimentary rock**

Tethys Sea: an ocean that existed between the ancient super-continents of Gondwana, in the southern hemisphere, and Laurasia in the northern hemisphere

ultraviolet: light radiated with very short wavelengths (but longer than those of x-rays) that are outside the visible spectrum

vertebrae: individual segments of cartilage that make up the spinal column in animal vertebrates

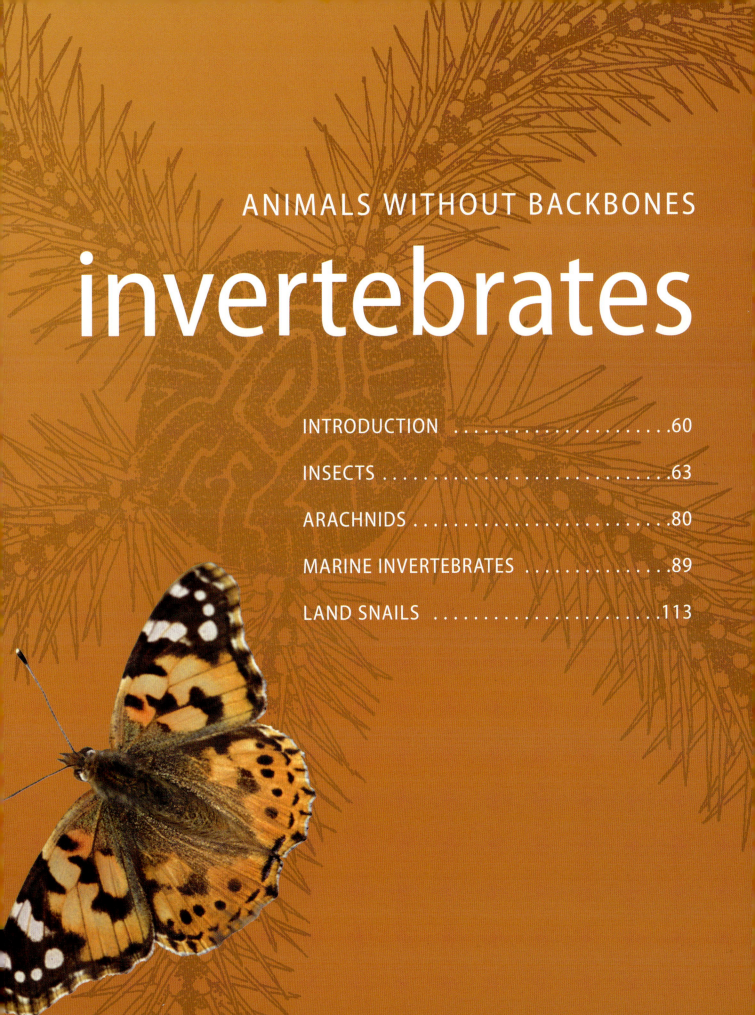

ANIMALS WITHOUT BACKBONES

invertebrates

INVERTEBRATES

Invertebrates are animals without backbones (vertebrae). More than 95 per cent of all animals on the planet are invertebrates. They are found in most terrestrial and aquatic habitats and play important roles in the Earth's ecosystems. There are many different types of invertebrates, which can be divided into five main groups: **cnidarians**, **annelids**, **echinoderms**, **molluscs** and **arthropods**, the latter being the most numerous, making up about 80 per cent of all invertebrate species. Methods of locomotion among invertebrates include flying, swimming, crawling, jumping and floating. Some invertebrates, such as sponges, remain in one place during their adult phase.

INVERTEBRATE SKELETONS – SPINELESS WONDERS

Whilst vertebrates keep their bodies stable by means of a bony skeleton, invertebrates have developed a number of other ways to support their body weight. Some invertebrates have an outer covering known as an **exoskeleton**; others have an internal system of support. Worms, jellyfish and sea anemones have a **hydrostatic skeleton**, which consists of a fluid-filled chamber that presses against the body walls to give the animal its shape. Many sponges contain a supportive network of calcium carbonate needles called **spicules**, along with a protein fibre called **spongin**, but others are supported by spongin alone.

Jellyfish have a flexible hydrostatic skeleton, a fluid-filled chamber surrounded by muscle fibre that contracts and expands to change the shape of the cavity, allowing the jellyfish to move rapidly through the water.

*Sponge **spicules** (above) may be arranged loosely or closely interlocked within a layer of spongin fibre. The **spicules** are different in each species and provide a means of identification for the many different types of sponges.*

*Many **molluscs** have a hard, outer skeleton in the form of a shell, but unlike the **arthropod exoskeleton**, the mollusc shell is made of calcium carbonate rather than **chitin**. Squid and cuttlefish have a hard internal skeleton, but in octopuses there is no hard skeleton present and the muscular system alone supports the body.*

*Arthropods make up by far the largest group of invertebrates and include crustaceans, insects and arachnids. They have a strong outer covering (exoskeleton) made of a material called **chitin**. This substance is a natural polymer (combination of elements) and is the subject of exciting medical research because of its healing properties.*

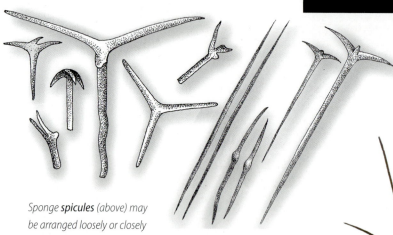

Radial symmetry

Bilateral symmetry

BODY SYMMETRY

Invertebrates have three basic symmetry patterns: asymmetric, bilateral and radial. The majority of invertebrates have a body plan that is bilaterally symmetrical with right and left halves that are essentially similar, and usually with definite front and back ends. Examples of this

Asymmetry

body plan are found in butterflies, beetles and worms. Some invertebrates have a circular body plan radiating out from a central mouth like the spokes of a wheel. This is known as radial symmetry and invertebrates with this type of body plan include sea anemones, starfish and sea urchins. Sponges are examples of invertebrates with asymmetric body patterns.

FASCINATING FACT

The head of an invertebrate may contain one or more pairs of eyes, along with organs that can taste, smell, or touch. However, in some invertebrates sense organs may be found on other body parts. Most grasshoppers and crickets, for example, have hearing organs on their legs or abdomen, while the leg bristles on some insects contain taste sensors.

THE IMPORTANCE OF INVERTEBRATES

Invertebrates have adapted to their ecosystems over many millions of years. As a result, they have become essential to the health of the planet's ecology, occupying a variety of niches in the food chain as consumers and decomposers, as well as being valuable sources of food for larger species. Invertebrates also perform other important roles in the environment, by helping in processes such as pollination and seed dispersal, soil aeration, reef-building and the decomposition of enormous amounts of organic matter.

INVERTEBRATE EYES

Most invertebrates have much less complex, but more varied eye structures than vertebrates. Some species, such as jellyfish and flatworms, only have groups of light-sensitive cells, which allow them to distinguish the direction and intensity of light.

Compound eyes are found in insects, centipedes, crustaceans and horseshoe crabs. These consist of many tiny units, each of which transmits light and colour information to the brain. These minute bits of information could be compared to the pixels on a computer screen, which combine to form an image. The quality of the image depends on the number of facets in the compound eye: the more facets, the better the image. Whilst grasshoppers have relatively few facets, dragonflies have a large number. Compound eyes do not give the same quality of vision as most vertebrate eyes, but they are especially good at detecting movement and seeing in many directions at once.

The cephalopods (octopus, squid and cuttlefish) are the only invertebrates with eyes that are superficially similar to those of vertebrates. The cephalopod eye contains a lens, retina, iris, and pupil. However, major differences between them indicate that the vertebrate and cephalopod eye evolved separately in a process known as convergent evolution.

This greatly enlarged view of the head of a fruit fly shows large compound eyes on each side of the head, which allow a wide field of vision.

Compared to most invertebrates, jumping spiders have excellent vision. This species is able to see in three ways using three sets of eyes.

Squid have very good eyesight, with a structure somewhat similar to the human eye.

>> LEARN MORE : USEFUL WEBSITES

INFORMATION ON ARABIAN INVERTEBRATES

http://www.uaeinteract.com/nature/insect/index.asp – information on the insects and arachnids of the United Arab Emirates

http://www.enhg.org – the website of the Emirates Natural History Group has numerous articles about Arabian invertebrates; specific subjects can be found using the excellent search facility on the site

http://www.breedingcentresharjah.com/Artropods.htm – information and photographs on desert invertebrates from the Breeding Centre for Arabian Wildlife, Sharjah

DIRECTORY LINKS TO INVERTEBRATE WEBSITES

http://www.dmoz.org/Kids_and_Teens/School_Time/Science/Living_Things/Animals/Invertebrates/ – open directory invertebrate page with links to numerous useful websites – a good starting point for research

http://www.google.com/Top/Kids_and_Teens/School_Time/Science/Living_Things/Animals/Invertebrates/ – another directory of websites about invertebrates for young people

KEYS AND IDENTIFICATION GUIDES

http://www.biokids.umich.edu/guides/invert_id – a downloadable PDF identification guide to invertebrates, arranged as an easy-to-use key

http://www.ento.csiro.au/education/key/couplet_01.html – interactive key to the invertebrates, leading to detailed information on various types of invertebrate; website also includes links to invertebrate glossary and numerous fact sheets; although this is an Australian website, much of the information is of general use

GENERAL INFORMATION ON INVERTEBRATES

http://www.earthlife.net/insects/six.html – excellent, comprehensive website on insects and arachnids, including an extensive glossary of insect terminology in language that is easy to understand

http://www.dmturner.org/Teacher/Library/5thText/InvTOC.html – an educational website with extensive information on invertebrates

http://www.biology4kids.com/files/invert_main.html – a good website for both general and specific information on invertebrates; designed specifically for schoolchildren

http://www.kidport.com/RefLib/Science/Animals/AnimalIndexInv.htm – well-organised introduction to invertebrates with sections on protozoans, annelids, molluscs, echinoderms and arthropods

http://www.earthlife.net/inverts/intro.html – the invertebrate section of a large educational website

www.msc.ucla.edu/oceanglobe/pdf/Invertebrates/Inverts_Intro.pdf – a downloadable PDF file containing an Introduction to Invertebrates

http://animaldiversity.ummz.umich.edu/site/index.html – this is a large website with excellent information on all animal species, with the invertebrates broken down into arthropods, insects, molluscs and echinoderms: fairly advanced, but well-written

http://nationalzoo.si.edu/Animals/Invertebrates/ – an interesting website from the Smithsonian National Zoo in Washington, DC (USA), which includes a gallery of photos and a variety of well-written articles

http://www.naturegrid.org.uk/biodiversity/invindex.html – a useful website with general information about invertebrates and their ecology

FOR YOUNGER CHILDREN

http://www.enchantedlearning.com/subjects/invertebrates/ – a useful website containing a large variety of information for younger children

USEFUL IMAGES

http://www5.pbrc.hawaii.edu/microangela/ – this website has many superb electron microscope images of invertebrate species: these copyrighted images may be downloaded for educational use

http://www.edupic.net/insects.htm & http://www.edupic.net/spiders.htm – an excellent photographic resource containing free images for teacher and student use

INVERTEBRATES GLOSSARY

annelids: animals with segmented bodies, including earthworms, leeches and numerous, mostly marine, worms called polychaetes

arthropod: invertebrates, such as insects, crustaceans, and arachnids, with jointed legs and segmented bodies

chitin: a fibrous substance, similar to cellulose found in the exoskeleton of arthropods

cephalopod: a member of the group of molluscs that includes octopus, squid, and cuttlefish

cnidarians: (from Greek 'cnidos' meaning stinging nettle) animals from the phylum Cnidaria, all of which have stinging cells; includes jellyfish, sea anemones and corals

compound eye: an eye, commonly found in many arthropods, that is composed of many individual lenses

convergent evolution: independent development, through natural selection, of similar characteristics in two unrelated species

echinoderms: marine invertebrates with tube feet and five-part radially symmetrical bodies

exoskeleton: supporting structure on the outside of insects and other arthropods

hydrostatic skeleton: a structure consisting of a fluid-filled chamber that gives support and shape to soft-bodied invertebrates

mollusc: an invertebrate with a soft, unsegmented body that is often, but not always, protected by a shell; includes snails, slugs, bivalves and octopuses

phylum: second highest grouping in taxonomy – e.g. kingdom: animalia, phylum: Cnidaria

spicules: hard, often needle-like objects that form the skeletal structure of most sponges

spongin: a fibrous material that binds spicules in the skeleton of a sponge

invertebrates/insects

/arachnids

arabian wildlife encyclopedia

DRAGONFLIES AND DAMSELFLIES

Although immature dragonflies are totally dependent on fresh water, adult specimens can be found in a variety of habitats, including offshore islands and inland sand dunes. The Arabian Peninsula has a remarkable and beautiful dragonfly fauna. Dragonflies and damselflies belong to the order Odonata, from the Greek meaning 'tooth', referring to the formidable jaw-like mandibles with which they kill their prey. In addition to their mandibles, these often colourful insects are characterised by a long, narrow abdomen, large **compound eyes**, and two pairs of transparent, veined wings.

Female emperor dragonfly Anax imperator

LIFE CYCLE >>

The immature stages of all dragonflies and damselflies are spent in fresh water. Eggs may simply be dispersed at random over water or the female may insert single eggs into slits cut into the stems of aquatic plants. After hatching, the **nymphs** may spend several years growing and developing in the water, before climbing out and becoming the mature winged insect in a final spectacular **moult**. Both young and adults are **carnivorous**.

Nymph

Adult

Two lesser emperor dragonflies Anax parthenope

The small, but striking damselfly Ceriagrion glabrum *has bright green eyes that contrast with the red and yellow colouring of its body.*

SINAI HOOKTAIL *Paragomphus sinaiticus*

Paragomphus sinaiticus was placed on the IUCN Red List of Threatened Species in 1988 and was listed as vulnerable in the IUCN 2005 assessment . Threats to this dragonfly species include human development, causing habitat loss and degradation; air and water pollution and drought.

GIRDLED SKIMMER *Orthetrum chrysostigma*

Males of this widespread and common dragonfly species have a distinct narrowing of the abdomen behind the wings. Females are smaller and brownish in colour, with an evenly tapered abdomen, but mature individuals may develop a bluish colour similar to that of the males.

GULLEY DARTER *Trithemis arteriosa*

This dragonfly is particularly common in mountain wadis of the Arabian Peninsula. Its colour varies according to locality. Due to its wide distribution in various habitats in Africa, southern Europe and the Middle East, this species is not considered to be under threat.

After butterflies and moths, dragonflies and damselflies are the most colourful group of insects in Arabia. Particularly colourful damselflies include the **endemic** powder-blue *Arabicnemis caerula* and the bright orange-red *Ceriagrion glabrum*. Blues and reds also predominate in the colours of Arabia's dragonflies. A striking example is the large and iridescent blue male emperor dragonfly *Anax imperator*, commonly found wherever there is water for it to patrol. The males of several other species have reddish-marked wings and bodies. Examples include the purple-blushed, gulley and orange darter dragonflies (*Trithemis annulata, T. arteriosa* and *T. kirbyi*, respectively).

The globe skimmer Pantala flavescens *is yellowish in colour, but males in Arabia can be quite red.*

GRASSHOPPERS AND CRICKETS

Orthoptera is one of the largest orders of insects that show **incomplete metamorphosis,** with over 20,000 species known worldwide. Most are moderately-sized or large insects, with nearly all having enlarged rear legs, modified for jumping. The hindwings may be very colourful, but are only seen in flight. Grasshoppers and crickets are common in well-vegetated, warmer regions of the world, but are also found in drier habitats, including deserts. Whilst there are relatively few different species present in Arabia, some of these may be so plentiful as to become pests.

ANATOMY

Grasshoppers have a three-part body (head, **thorax,** abdomen), which is protected by a hard **exoskeleton.** They breathe through holes called **spiracles** that are located along the sides of the **thorax** and the abdomen.

MAKING MUSIC

The mating song of a cricket is created by rubbing the front wings against each other. Male grasshoppers produce their characteristic mating songs by rubbing their hind legs against their bodies. Both grasshoppers and crickets have different kinds of songs for defending their territory and communicating with others of their own species.

LEAF-LIKE

Long-horned grasshoppers can be identified by their long **antennae** and usually green wings that make them resemble slender leaves. They are more closely related to crickets than to grasshoppers, and are also known as bush crickets.

antennae

compound eye

two pairs of wings

walking legs

long legs for jump

Gangling grasshopper Truxalis procera

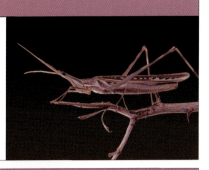

Truxalis longicornis

The rare and elegant grasshopper *T. longicornis* is known from the Hajar Mountains in the UAE and from an isolated population in the Air Mountains in Niger. Females of the species are considerably larger than the males. Both sexes have very long hindlegs and coloured hindwings.

Pseudosphingonotus savignyi

S. savignyi is one of a group of short-horned grasshoppers with brightly-coloured hindwings. This feature only shows when the insect is in flight. When it lands, the bright colours are hidden by the forewings and grasshopper's cryptic colouration makes it difficult to find against its surroundings

TREE LOCUST *Anacridium melanorhodon arabafrum*

One of the larger grasshopper species in Arabia, the tree locust is slender, greyish-brown in colour and has long tapered wings. Found in *Acacia* woodland and sand desert with *Zizyphus spina-christi* (sidr), *Acacia tortilis* or *Prosopis cineraria* (ghaf) trees. When numerous, can be harmful to crops.

CRICKETS

Compared to grasshoppers, there are few cricket species in Arabia. The bush crickets are represented by about five species, including *Decticus albifrons* (pictured above). True crickets include the tropical field cricket *Gryllus bimaculatus*, a stout black **nocturnal** insect common in cultivated areas. There are also several mole crickets *Gryllotalpus*, which are potential market garden pests, all of similar appearance and adapted for tunnelling just below the surface of damp soil.

LOCUSTS >>

Locusts and grasshoppers look alike but differ in behaviour. Locusts have two behaviour states, solitary and gregarious, whilst grasshoppers are generally solitary. When the locust population density is low, the insects behave like other grasshoppers, but when their numbers increase, they enter the **gregarious phase**. This is when they become a potentially dangerous pest as they form large swarms.

MANTIDS AND STICK INSECTS

Praying mantids derive their common name from the posture they adopt whilst waiting for prey. They are insects with **incomplete metamorphosis**, easily identified by their distinctive triangular head and long, slender **thorax**, large **compound eyes** and enlarged front legs. Usually brown or green in colour, mantises are well-camouflaged as they wait in the foliage to ambush a wide variety of insects, including other mantises. With their insatiable appetite for other insects, mantids are considered to be beneficial in limiting the populations of harmful pests. A total of 46 species of mantid are known from Arabia.

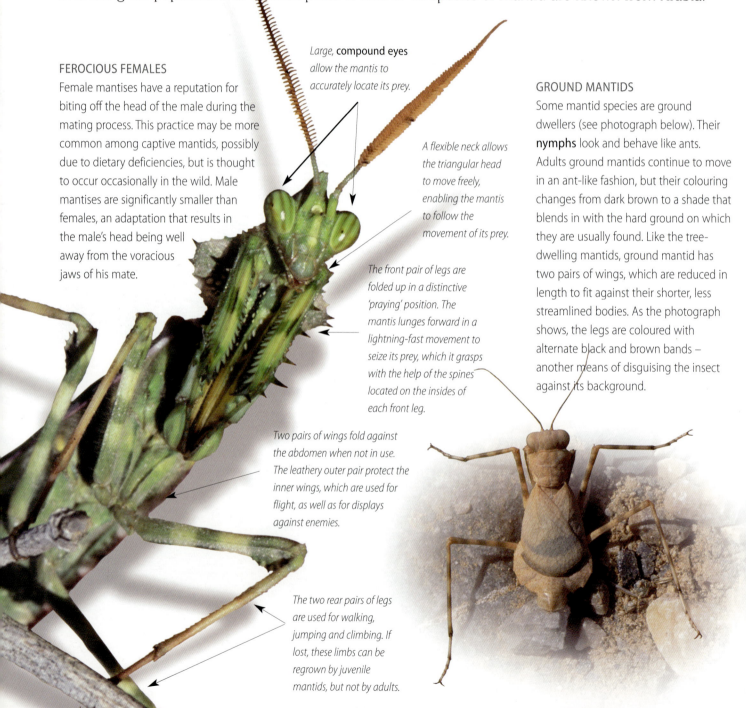

FEROCIOUS FEMALES

Female mantises have a reputation for biting off the head of the male during the mating process. This practice may be more common among captive mantids, possibly due to dietary deficiencies, but is thought to occur occasionally in the wild. Male mantises are significantly smaller than females, an adaptation that results in the male's head being well away from the voracious jaws of his mate.

*Large, **compound eyes** allow the mantis to accurately locate its prey.*

A flexible neck allows the triangular head to move freely, enabling the mantis to follow the movement of its prey.

The front pair of legs are folded up in a distinctive 'praying' position. The mantis lunges forward in a lightning-fast movement to seize its prey, which it grasps with the help of the spines located on the insides of each front leg.

Two pairs of wings fold against the abdomen when not in use. The leathery outer pair protect the inner wings, which are used for flight, as well as for displays against enemies.

The two rear pairs of legs are used for walking, jumping and climbing. If lost, these limbs can be regrown by juvenile mantids, but not by adults.

GROUND MANTIDS

Some mantid species are ground dwellers (see photograph below). Their **nymphs** look and behave like ants. Adults ground mantids continue to move in an ant-like fashion, but their colouring changes from dark brown to a shade that blends in with the hard ground on which they are usually found. Like the tree-dwelling mantids, ground mantid has two pairs of wings, which are reduced in length to fit against their shorter, less streamlined bodies. As the photograph shows, the legs are coloured with alternate black and brown bands – another means of disguising the insect against its background.

LAPPET MANTIS *Empusa hedenborgi*

This slender green and white mantis is named for the small, leaf-like appendages (lappets) on the upper third of the hind legs just above the joint. The family of mantises to which it belongs has a wide range spreading across Africa, Arabia, Asia and the Mediterranean.

PRAYING MANTIS *Mantis religiosa*

M. religiosa has a triangular head, which can be turned 180 degrees as the mantis searches for prey. The praying mantis has three simple eyes situated between two large, compound eyes. Its name comes from the two front legs, which are bent and held together in a manner that resembles a position of prayer.

IS IT A STICK OR . . .?

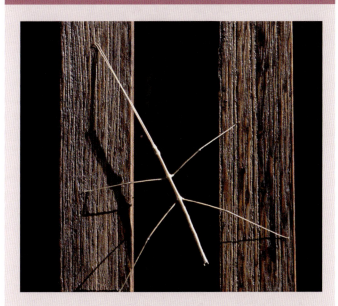

Stick insects, or phasmids, bear a remarkable resemblance to thin sticks as their common name implies. Like the mantids, most adult stick insects have two pairs of wings; a few species have none. Stick insects have thread-like **antennae**, which vary in length. They usually spend the daylight hours hanging upside-down and motionless on small plants or shrubs. When disturbed, they may sway back and forth, like a stick waving in the breeze, or alternatively, they may drop to the ground, where they will remain motionless, in an attempt to blend in with the background. They are usually green or brown in colour.

Stick insects are **herbivorous**, feeding at night on the leaves of plants. Males are usually much smaller than females and have larger wings. Stick insect eggs resemble small seeds and hatch into a wingless **nymph** stage. As they mature, stick insects go through a number of moults in which they shed their skin, often eating it for the protein that it contains.

DIMINUTIVE SIZE

The fairy mantis *Oxyothespis nilotica* (see photograph below) may be easily missed due to its tiny size.

BUTTERFLIES

Butterflies are divided into five families, all of which are represented in Arabia: Papilionidae (swallowtails); Pieridae (whites and yellows); Lycaenidae (hairstreaks, coppers and blues); Nymphalidae (danaids, nymphs and satyrs); and Hesperidae (skippers). Many butterflies are migrants and arrive in Arabia following rain when the vegetation is lush and their own populations are high.

FASCINATING FACTS

- From the time it hatches until it **pupates**, a caterpillar increases its body size by almost 30,000 times!

- Butterflies taste with sensors located on their feet.

- Butterflies are the second largest group of day-flying pollinators after bees.

- Butterflies prefer flowers that are red, yellow, pink or purple.

- Butterflies have no lungs. They breathe through tiny openings in the **thorax** and abdomen called **spiracles**.

- Butterflies can fly at speeds of up to 25 km/h.

- Butterflies are cold-blooded and only become active when the temperature reaches about 21° Celsius.

- Some butterflies migrate, flying thousands of miles.

- Butterflies are found on every continent except Antarctica.

- Unlike moths, butterfly caterpillars do not spin a cocoon. The outside protective layer of a butterfly **pupa** hardens to form a **chrysalis**.

BOLD AND BEAUTIFUL

One of the largest species occuring in Arabia is the lime butterfly *Papilio demoleus*. It is thought to be an introduction from western Asia as its food plants (*Citrus* spp.) do not occur naturally in Arabia. Its relative, the swallowtail *P. machaon muetingi* is an **endemic** species usually found in oases or similarly well-watered conditions.

SIPPING NECTAR

Butterflies are unable to chew their food. Instead, they sip liquids such as flower nectar or the juices of rotting fruits through their **proboscis**. This flexible, tube-like structure is well-adapted for reaching into the centre of a flower. When not required for feeding, the **proboscis** is coiled up like a spring on the underside of the head. When the butterfly feeds, the **proboscis** is extended and used rather like a drinking straw.

ON THE MOVE

Some butterflies migrate as part of their survival strategy. These nomadic species may travel long distances to take advantage of seasonal changes in the climate and vegetation. In the Arabian Peninsula, migrant species such as the plain tiger *Danaus chrysippus* and the painted lady *Vanessa cardui* may appear in wadis and other areas of vegetation after rain.

MICROSCOPIC MARVELS

The order to which butterflies belong is Lepidoptera, from the Latin meaning 'scale-wing'. Butterfly wings, made up of tiny overlapping scales, are attached to a thin, transparent membrane. These electron microscope photographs show the scales magnified many times.

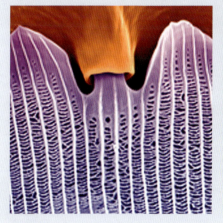

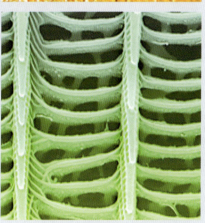

WINGS

Butterflies have four wings. These are relatively large and lightweight compared to those of other insects.

<< PAINTED LADY

The painted lady *Vanessa cardui* is one of the most widespread butterfly species in the world, being found on all continents except Antarctica. It is relatively unspecialised in its choice of food plants, which allows it to survive in a wider range of habitats and environmental conditions than many other species.

CAMOUFLAGE

Bright colours and markings on wings may warn predators that a butterfly has an unpleasant taste. Some butterflies simply mimic the markings of other species that taste bad in order to deter enemies. A number of species have large 'eye' markings on their wings, which scare predators by making a butterfly look like it might be part of a larger animal. The colours and markings on the underside of the wings are usually more muted to help butterflies blend in with their surroundings when they are at rest with the wings closed.

A female butterfly lays eggs on a leaf of the plant on which the caterpillars will feed. The eggs hatch into tiny caterpillars (larva).

THE LIFE CYCLE OF A BUTTERFLY

The caterpillar spends most of its time feeding. As it develops, the caterpillar sheds its skin several times in order to continue growing. When the caterpillar is ready, it will find a place to **pupate**, often on the underside of a leaf or branch.

The caterpillar next attaches itself by means of silken thread that comes out of a hole (**spinneret**) under its jaws. It then develops a hard outer layer (**exoskeleton**) called a **chrysalis** that protects it from predators. Its colouring is usually similar in colouring to that of its host plant. Inside the chrysalis, the caterpillar changes into a butterfly.

The outer covering of the pupa becomes transparent, and the colours and features of the butterfly may be seen inside. When the butterfly emerges, its wings are soft and crumpled until fluid is pumped into them from the butterfly's abdomen. Once the wings are hardened, the butterfly is able to fly.

PLAIN TIGER *Danaus chryssipus*

A large butterfly with burnt orange wings, usually, but not always, with black and white markings. Males more brightly coloured, but smaller than females, and have scent scales on hind wings to attract females. Food plants of caterpillars are poisonous milkweeds of the Asclepidaceae family.

SMALL SALMON ARAB *Colotis calais amatus*

A small butterfly, mainly found near coastal plains of UAE, Oman, Yemen and south-west Saudi Arabia. Often seen feeding in groups on the 'toothbrush bush' *Salvadora persica*. Sometimes travels long distances, but migration is not an essential part of its life cycle.

MEDITERRANEAN PIERROT *Tarucus rosaceus*

One of several species of tiny Pierrot butterflies found in Arabia. Upper side of the wings brilliant lilac-blue. Main food plant of this tiny species is *Ziziphus spina-christi*. This family of butterflies usually seek water on hot days. Larvae feed on only the green parts of leaves, leaving leaf membranes intact.

GIANT SKIPPER *Coeliades anchises jucunda*

Double the size of other Arabian skippers, with a stout body and pointed forewings. Larvae feed mainly at night, resting during daytime in a tent-like structure made from leaves of its food plant *Acridocarpus orientalis*. Caterpillar has a thin neck and distinctive reddish-orange and white stripes.

BLUE PANSY
Precis orithya, a common butterfly throughout most of Arabia, is often seen flying close to the ground. The muted tones of the undersides of the wings contrast sharply with the brightly-coloured upper sides.

FEMALE MIMICS

The diadem *Hypolimnas misippus* belongs to the same family as the plain tiger (see species description above). Males are black, with three purple-edged white spots, but females are a near-perfect copy of the poisonous plain tigers. This mimicry helps to protect the non-poisonous diadem female from predators.

MOTHS

Unlike butterflies, which all belong to just five families arranged in two superfamilies, the moths belong to numerous families and superfamilies. They range from tiny micro-moths, of which there are probably several hundred species in the Arabian Peninsula, to the large, and often strikingly beautiful hawk moths.

MOTH OR BUTTERFLY?

Moths differ from butterflies in a number of ways:

• Most butterflies are active during the day, whilst moths are generally active at night. However, there are also many species of moths that fly during the day, including some that occur in the Arabian Peninsula.

• Butterflies **pupate** above ground level, hanging from some type of support such as a leaf or branch, but moths pupate in a protective **cocoon** on or below ground.

• Moths open their wings and fold them over their back when resting, whilst butterflies hold theirs erect and closed, with the lower surfaces of the wings showing.

MICRO-MOTHS

Pachyzancla phaeopterus is an attractive moth that belongs to the Pyralidae family of micro-moths. This is a largely unstudied group of smaller moths. Several species from this family occur in the Arabian Peninsula, all of which fly during the day.

FASCINATING FACTS

• Caterpillars have about 4,000 muscles in their bodies compared to 629 in a human body.

• Caterpillars have many predators because they are a rich source of protein.

• Caterpillars are voracious feeders and some species resort to cannibalism if there is a shortage of food.

The recently-hatched larva and full-grown caterpillar of the death's head hawk moth Acherontia atropos *(top and centre images)* are good examples of the bizarre shapes and patterning found in the life stages of the hawk moths.

Adult death's head hawk moth
Acherontia atropos

HAWK MOTHS IN ARABIA

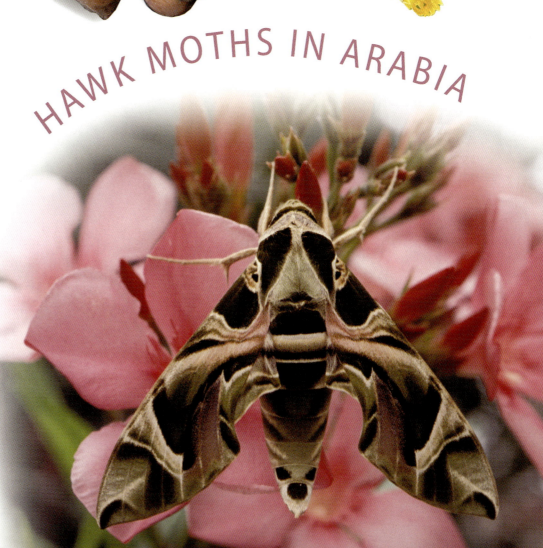

Hawk moths are medium to large moths with long, narrow wings that are well-adapted for rapid flight, as well as for hovering over flowers when feeding. Among the most spectacular of all moths, they have sturdy, cigar-shaped bodies and a well-defined head.

Caterpillars usually have stout, hairless bodies with colourful patterning. The last body segment generally has a prominent 'horn' at the end.

The oleander hawk moth *Daphnis netii* (pictured right) is a fairly common species in the Arabian Peninsula.

BEETLES

Beetles are surprisingly diverse and occupy all habitats from the intertidal zone of marine coastlines to the edge of permanent snowfields, including all types of freshwater habitat. This diversity, together with an ability to utilise a wide range of organic material as food, plus the protection offered by a pair of hardened forewings (**elytra**), is responsible for their success. In Arabia, beetles are a prominent group, including numerous large and relatively well-known insects, such as the domino ground beetle *Anthaxia duodecimguttata*, the rhinoceros beetle *Oryctes agamemnon arabicus*, the darkling beetle *Prionotheca coronata ovalis*, the longhorn *Anthracocentrus arabicus* and many others. As with other regions, in the Arabian Peninsula, spectacular beetles are far outnumbered by much smaller and often little-known species.

Domino ground beetle
Anthaxia duodecimguttata

RHINOS IN ARABIA

The rhinoceros beetles *Oryctes* spp. are named for the distinctive, rhino-like horns with which they challenge other males in disputes over desirable feeding locations. They are an important part of nature's recycling process since the larvae eat large quantities of rotting wood and compost. Adults eat small quantities of rotting fruit. However, in large numbers, rhinoceros beetles may become a pest in date palm plantations, where the larvae bore into the stems of dying or weakened trees.

YELLOW JEWEL

The sulphurous jewel beetle *Julodis euphratica* (left) is easily recognised by its bright yellow colouring. Jewel beetles have large eyes and a short head that fits closely in front of the **thorax**.

WARNING COLOURS

GARDEN HELPERS

The bright reds and yellows of ladybirds warn potential predators that these small beetles have a bitter taste, though, unlike the oil beetle (see below), they are not particularly poisonous. Most species, such as the seven-spot ladybird *Coccinella septempunctata* (pictured at right, feeding on aphids), are considered beneficial insects by gardeners and horticulturists. One exception is the large orange and black *Henosepilachna elaterii*, which feeds on plants belonging to the cucumber family and is classed as an agricultural pest in some regions.

OIL BEETLES

The colourful oil beetle is a common sight in the Arabian Peninsula, particularly after springtime rains. Unlike most beetles, it has a soft body and must rely on vibrant warning colours for protection. When it is handled, an oil beetle releases a highly toxic fluid that will produce severe skin blisters if it is not immediately removed with soap and water. Oil beetles are poisonous to lizards, birds and humans because they contain the deadly toxin cantharidin.

The female beetle lays a single egg inside each dung ball, which she forms from the original ball.

The larva hatches several days later.

The young dung beetle emerges from the dung ball and makes its way to the surface.

In a few weeks, the larva **pupates**.

RECYCLING MACHINES

Dung beetles belong to the family of scarab beetles, which also includes leaf-eating chafers. As their common name suggests, dung beetles feed on faecal matter. A number of Arabian species exhibit an interesting behaviour known as 'ball-rolling'. The balls usually consist of camel dung that has been chopped up by the beetle and re-formed into a spherical shape. The balls vary in size, depending on their purpose. Smaller ones are food for a single adult beetle, whilst larger ones are later divided into smaller lumps, into each of which a single egg is laid. The lump of dung will provide enough food for the white grub that hatches from the egg.

A beetle may roll a dung ball as much as 250 m by pushing it backwards using its middle and hind legs. Large balls may be rolled by two beetles, only one of which is likely to be a female. Once the beetle finds a suitable spot, it digs a shallow hole into which it buries the dung ball. Then it digs a tunnel, moving away from the ball. Once the tunnel is completed, the ball of dung is dug out of its temporary resting place and manoeuvred into the tunnel, which is then sealed. Larger balls are buried at greater depth, in readiness for the female to divide it into smaller lumps before laying her eggs.

UNDER ATTACK! DATE PALM PESTS

The red palm weevil *Rhynocophorus ferrugineus* (illustrated below) was introduced into the Arabian Peninsula in the 1980s, probably via imported ornamental plants. Females burrow into the crown of a palm tree where they lay an average of 260 eggs. Once the larvae hatch, they bore into the soft tissue of the palm, entering the trunk and digging tunnels, whilst feeding on the sap until they are ready to **pupate**. After tunnelling towards the surface, they locate the base of a palm frond, where they each build a **cocoon** using fibrous strands from the frond. A great deal of research, particularly in the United Arab Emirates, into biological control of these pests has resulted in a number of effective methods being developed.

The longhorn beetle *Jebusaea hammerschmidtii* (right) is a widespread pest that attacks palms. Whilst the damage caused by the red palm weevil quickly becomes evident, the boring activities of the longhorn beetle may go undetected until the damage is irreversible. As many as 500 larvae may bore tunnels inside the trunk of a date palm, opening the way for bacterial and fungal growth within the tree.

SCORPIONS

Scorpions are relatively common in the Arabian Peninsula in sand desert, gravel plains and mountains. Like other venomous animals they normally avoid humans and will only sting when threatened. Most stings occur when people inadvertently come into contact with scorpions, particularly during camping trips, when they are found hiding under rocks, stones, tents, clothing, debris and rubbish.

FASCINATING FACT

An interesting phenomenon concerning scorpions is the fact that they fluoresce when exposed to ultraviolet (UV) light. No one knows why this happens; it is just a natural property of the cuticle. However, it provides an easy way of detecting scorpions at night and is used by biologists to estimate their numbers without having to capture them. It is also an effective way of avoiding scorpions when camping, although in some desert locations it may be quite alarming to see just how many the UV light reveals!

TRUE DESERT DWELLER

The most common scorpion species in sandy areas is *Buthacus yotvatensis nigroaculeatus* (pictured above), which is mostly yellow but, unlike *Apistobuthus pterygocercus* (pictured below), it is black on the last segment of the tail and sting. Adults can reach up to about 75 mm in length. Its sting is seldom fatal, but it is essential to obtain medical attention as soon as possible after being stung.

FEEDING HABITS

Scorpions prey on other **arthropods**, particularly insects and arachnids, but they may also feed on small vertebrates. Species that have very large pincers do not always use their sting to kill prey, but may simply rely on the crushing power of their claws. Scorpions are able to survive for a long time without water, making them ideally suited to life in the desert.

THICK-TAILED SCORPIONS

Scorpions having a tail that is thicker than the pincers, like the Arabian thick-tailed scorpion *Androctonus crassicauda* (pictured right), usually have a more toxic venom than those with thinner tails. When threatened a scorpion holds its tail over its abdomen, ready to strike with the sting. However, it will only attack if provoked, since it requires considerable energy to produce venom. The scorpion *Orthochirus* sp. in the photograph below has itself become a victim, trapped in the web of the poisonous spider *Latrodectus* sp..

FIRST AID

Scorpion venom contains powerful and dangerous **neurotoxins**. Victims of stings feel a sharp pain followed by numbness, drowsiness and itching in the throat. This can be accompanied by excessive saliva and the tongue becomes sluggish with the jaw muscles contracted. If large amounts of venom have entered the blood system, difficulties in co-ordination arise and body temperature increases while the production of saliva and urine are reduced. Touch and sight can be affected, with sensitivity to strong light. There may also be haemorrhages and convulsions with increasing severity.

Primary first aid for scorpion stings is to reassure the victim, who will be suffering from shock. Clean the wound with cold water. If possible, keep the site of the sting cold with an ice pack or iced water. This will help in reducing pain and inflammation. Although fatalities are very rare, do seek medical help, particularly in the case of small children and invalids, who are most at risk.

CAMEL SPIDERS

Camel spiders, also known as wind scorpions or solifugids, are among the fastest running arthropods. They are not true spiders, being more closely related to scorpions. Like all arachnids they have four pairs of legs and a pair of **pedipalps**, which are held up in front of them and used in a similar manner to the **antennae** of insects. They have very long, silky hairs (**setae**) and are constantly moving in order to locate prey. Despite their fearsome appearance and strong bite, solifugids are unlikely to harm humans. In the past they were considered venomous and extremely dangerous, but it is now thought that the only risk of injury resulting from them is caused by shock or infection following a bite. There is no evidence of them having venom.

Camel spiders are nocturnal predators of other **arthropods**, including scorpions, and are voracious feeders. Some species kill and feed on lizards and it is speculated that others kill mice and birds. They rely solely on their speed and stealth to catch their prey. In desert areas they are often attracted to lights at night in search of food and their appearance can cause alarm if they enter tents. It is rare to see them during the winter months in the Arabian Peninsula and they are thought to hide or hibernate during cold periods.

Despite their conspicuous appearance and size, little is known about these creatures. The largest species is probably *Galeodes arabs* (main picture) which is particularly hairy and bulky. It is most frequently seen in sandy areas. Other species probably occur in mountain regions.

SPIDERS

True spiders of many kinds are found in Arabia. They are found in houses, on the banks of mountain streams, on all types of vegetation, under stones and debris and in burrows in mountain terrain, gravel steppe and sand dunes. From the tiny crab spiders to the large hunting species, spiders play a very important role as predators in the food chain. Without them, populations of other invertebrates would explode, resulting in damage to crops and food shortages for humans.

SPIDER WEBS

• Each web begins with a single thread, which the spider releases from one of the spinnerets at the end of its abdomen. This single silk thread is the beginning of the framework around the outside of the web.

• Once the outer structure has been established, the spider lays out radial threads from the centre of the web to the outer frame. Neither the outer frame nor the radial threads are sticky, so that these can be used by the spider to move around the web without getting stuck to it. Within this framework, the spider lays out a spiral of sticky threads, which forms the body of the web.

• If an insect gets caught in the web, the spider feels vibrations in the radial threads and moves towards its prey. Sometimes the spider may wait in a separate nest area, monitoring the web by means of a connecting signal thread.

• Orb-web spiders can distinguish between vibrations made by prey insects and those caused by foreign objects such as leaves or by dangerous insects, such as wasps.

• When the web deteriorates, many spiders recycle the silk by eating the threads.

COLOURFUL JUMPERS

Jumping spiders belong to the largest family of spiders, Salticidae, a name that comes from the Latin word *salto,* meaning to jump or dance. They are active hunters during daylight hours. Unlike many spiders, they have excellent vision, which allows them to distinguish colours and easily locate their prey. Small and relatively short-legged, a jumping spider can leap large distances and then return to its original location. This ability is due to the line of silk which the spider releases as a tether when it jumps. Although they do not make webs, jumping spiders also use their silk to make pouch-like nests in which they lay their eggs and hide during cold weather. Many species of jumping spider are brightly coloured and some mimic insects such as ants and beetles, whilst others are camouflaged to blend in with their surroundings.

BLACK WIDOW

FASCINATING FACTS

- Spiders seldom bite humans.
- All true spiders have some type of venom, most of which is harmless to humans.
- Spider silk is liquid until it comes in contact with the air.
- Spider silk has a tensile strength that is equal to high-grade steel of similar thickness.
- Depending on how wet it is, spider silk can stretch between 30 and 300 per cent of its length before breaking.
- Scientists are using spider silk to solve the problem of creating hollow optical fibres that are only 2 nanometres in diameter – 50,000 times thinner than human hair.
- Spiders' webs were once used to stop bleeding and as a dressing for wounds.
- Spider legs are covered with hairs that can pick up vibrations and smells from their surroundings.
- Most spiders have eight eyes, but some species have four or six.

Legs have an oil coating to prevent the spider becoming ensnared in its own web

Chelicerae – jaws with fangs that inject venom

Pedipalps (feelers) used mainly to hold prey while the spider injects venom

Abdomen

Spinnerets – silk-spinning glands at the base of the abdomen

Black widow spiders *Latrodectus* spp. are found in many parts of the world, including Arabia. The photograph (right) shows a female, with its characteristic red hour-glass marking on the abdomen. Females are larger than the males and sometimes kill and eat their mate, giving rise to the common name 'black widow. Although these solitary spiders are venomous, they are not aggressive. They are active at night, usually spending daylight hours inside the central tunnel of their web. Black widow spiders feed on insects and other **arthropods**, including many regarded as pests.

WOLF SPIDERS

Wolf spiders have characteristically long, stout legs and sturdy bodies, which are always carried low to the ground. Their bodies vary in length from about 2 mm up to almost 40 mm. They have eight eyes, two of which are large and forward-facing, and situated in the middle of the face. Two more large, upward-facing eyes are located farther back, whilst a row of four smaller eyes are positioned below. Wolf spiders have good eyesight and can locate prey, potential mates and predators approaching from any direction. They use their front legs to seize prey, then bite and crush it with strong, jaw-like appendages called **chelicerae**.

The hunting strategies of wolf spiders vary widely. Many hunt by day on the ground and in vegetation, but others hunt at night. Some live and hunt in aquatic environments, walking on the surface of the water or on submerged vegetation. Some species dig burrows in which they lie in wait for their prey. Some species' burrow entrances include a trap door.

Female wolf spiders lay their eggs in a large sac, which they carry, attached to the body, until the eggs hatch. Newly-hatched spiderlings climb onto their mother's back, where they remain until they are big enough to disperse.

OTHER ARACHNIDS

In addition to spiders and scorpions, the arachnids include some less well-known but equally interesting subclasses, which vary widely in appearance and lifestyle. These include the solifugids or camel spiders (page 82), the amblypygids and acarids, amongst others.

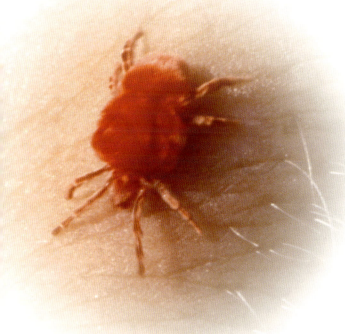

MITES AND TICKS

Acarids, commonly known as mites or ticks, are the smallest arachnids but are also the most numerous worldwide in terms of species. Adults have four pairs of legs while juveniles have three pairs. They include both parasites and predators. They generally live on other animals or inside plants, although some live in the soil.

Tick bites can be painful and irritating, and severe cases of multiple tick infestation on a single animal can result in anaemia, toxic reaction and paralysis. Although man is only an incidental host and their natural hosts are wild animals, some of the tick species present in Arabia can transmit human diseases. Many potentially infected ticks are accidentally imported along with foreign livestock. Although cases of tick-borne human disease are rare, there is an element of risk.

The tiny red velvet mite (pictured left) is only seen above ground following rain. Eggs are laid in the soil and the larvae attach themselves to other arachnids or insects as blood-sucking parasites.

SCORPION OR SPIDER?

Commonly known as a whip spider or tailless whip scorpion, *Phrynichus jakari* is really neither a scorpion nor spider. It is an amblypygid, from a different subclass of arachnids. Like all arachnids it has eight legs. The first pair are modified as long, whip-like sensory organs, which may be several times the length of the body. The **pedipalps** are large, with pincer-like claws for grasping prey. The head and **thorax** are wide and flattened. Unlike spiders, whip spiders have no silk glands. In spite of their appearance, these mainly nocturnal creatures are quite harmless.

>> LEARN MORE : USEFUL WEBSITES

ARABIAN INSECTS & ARACHNIDS

http://www.arabianwildlife.com/archive/vol3.2/buttr.htm – article on some common species of Arabian butterflies

http://www.arabianwildlife.com/nature/insect/index.html – information on insects and arachnids of the Arabian Peninsula

http://www.arabianwildlife.com/current/spiders.html – information on Arabian spiders, including jumping spiders and black widow spiders

http://www.arabianwildlife.com/archive/vol2.3/spider.htm – an article on the life and times of an Arabian spider

GENERAL INFORMATION ON INSECTS

http://www.earthlife.net/insects/six.html – excellent, comprehensive website on insects and arachnids, including an extensive glossary of insect terminology in language that is easy to understand

http://www.backyardnature.net/2arthrop.htm – interesting material on arthropods including spiders, centipedes and millipedes – insects are featured in a separate section of the website (see next listing)

http://www.backyardnature.net/2insect.htm – large section of a useful natural history website for children, including topics such as life cycles, metamorphosis and insect anatomy

www.enhg.org/trib/V08N2/TribulusV08N2p09-15.pdf – an illustrated checklist of damselflies and dragonflies found in the UAE

http://www.st-andrews.ac.uk/~wjh/jumping/ – a series of web pages showing how a grasshopper jumps; includes animated drawings

http://animals.nationalgeographic.com/animals/printable/praying-mantis.html – printable fact sheet from National Geographic

http://phasmid-study-group.org/content/phasmid-faqs – a website full of information about stick insects and leaf insects (phasmids)

http://stephenville.tamu.edu/~fmitchel/insects/Butterfly/index.htm – photo galllery of butterflies, including excellent emergence sequences

http://animaldiversity.ummz.umich.edu/site/accounts/information/Lepidoptera.html – information on butterflies and moths, including images

http://butterflywebsite.com/resource/index.cfm – the Butterfly Website lists numerous internet resources dealing with butterflies and moths

http://www.zin.ru/Animalia/Coleoptera/eng/all_fama.htm – part of an online atlas of beetles, this page contains superb illustrations of 189 families of beetles, with links to further illustrations

http://www.bbc.co.uk/nature/wildfacts/factfiles/498.shtml – dung beetle fact sheet

GENERAL INFORMATION ON ARACHNIDS

http://www.tooter4kids.com/Spiders/facts.htm – facts about spiders

http://www.arachnology.org/Arachnology/Pages/Latrodectus.html – long list of weblinks for *Latrodectus* spp. black widow spiders

http://www.xs4all.nl/~ednieuw/australian/wolfspiders/Wolfspiders.html – information about wolf spiders with numerous photographs

http://www.ub.ntnu.no/scorpion-files/scorpion_anatomy.jpg – excellent page on the anatomy of a scorpion, with labelled images

http://www.ub.ntnu.no/scorpion-files/faq.php – frequently asked questions about scorpions; part of a website with extensive information about scorpions

INSECTS AND ARACHNIDS GLOSSARY

antennae: flexible, jointed, sensory appendages on the head of an insect

carnivorous: an organism that feeds mainly or exclusively on meat

chelicerae: in arachnids, a pair of pincer-like appendages with two segments, located in front of the mouth, and used for feeding

chrysalis: hard protective covering of a pupa

cocoon: protective casing surrounding an insect pupa, produced by the larva prior to pupating

elytra: modified, hardened front wings of a beetle, which protect the rear, flight wings

endemic: native to a particular place or region

exoskeleton: supporting structure on the outside of insects and other arthropods

gregarious phase: period when usually solitary insects gather together as a group or swarm

herbivorous: feeding on plants

incomplete metamorphosis: refers to the three part life cycle – egg, nymph and adult – of insects such as grasshoppers and mantids

moult: shedding of the exoskeleton to allow for body growth

neurotoxin: a poisonous substance that affects the central nervous system

nymph: middle stage of incomplete metamorphosis

pedipalps: modified appendages in arachnids that serve a similar purpose to antennae in insects

proboscis: hollow, tube-like mouthparts, used for feeding by some insects, such as butterflies and moths

pupate: to enter the stage between larva and adult in the life cycle of an insect

setae: hair-like sensory structures projecting from the body of an insect or arachnid

spinnerets: silk-spinning glands located at the base of the abdomen in spiders and under the jaws in butterfly caterpillars

spiracles: small openings along the sides of an insect's abdomen, through which it breathes

thorax: the central section of an insect's body, between the head and the abdomen, to which the legs and wings are attached

invertebrates/marine

arabian wildlife encyclopedia

MARINE INVERTEBRATES

The coastlines of the Arabian Peninsula border on the Arabian Gulf, the Gulf of Oman, the Arabian Sea and the Red Sea. Each of these has differences in climate and in physical and chemical characteristics of the water, as well as in the types of surfaces available for colonisation by marine life. This has led to differences in the assemblages of marine organisms found in each marine region, although all are of Indian Ocean origin.

PLANKTON – THE FOUNDATION OF OCEAN LIFE

Plankton are microscopic plants (phytoplankton) and animals (zooplankton) that float freely in bodies of water, carried along by currents and tides. The word 'plankton' is derived from the Greek word *planktos*, meaning 'wandering'. These micro-organisms are the foundation on which the rest of the ocean food chain depends.

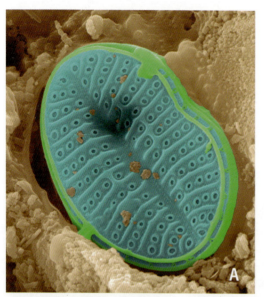

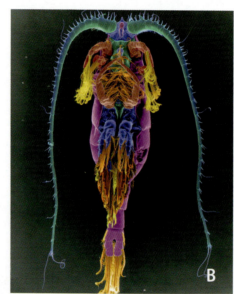

PHYTOPLANKTON

Phytoplankton use chlorophyll to convert sunlight, carbon and oxygen into energy, through the process known as photosynthesis. This energy is passed up the food chain as the phytoplankton is eaten by marine animals.

Most phytoplankton are diatoms (A), algae or blue-green algae.

(see page 37 for more on algae and blue-green algae)

ZOOPLANKTON

Zooplankton are microscopic animals that eat other plankton. Some zooplankton are early stages of larger animals, including fish and invertebrates such as crustaceans (C), molluscs, tubeworms (D), jellyfish and echinoderms.

Other zooplankton are single-celled animals, such as foraminiferans and radiolarians. The remainder (about 70 per cent of the total) are microscopic crustaceans. Among these are krill and copepods (B), which, unlike other planktonic species, are able to swim.

PORIFERA (Page 92)

Sponges

CNIDARIA (Page 93)

Hydroids, Jellyfish,

Sea Anemones and Corals

ANNELIDA (Page 100)

Worms

CRUSTACEA (Page 101)

Barnacles and Crabs

MOLLUSCA (Page 104)

Chitons, Gastropods

Bivalves and Cephalopods

ECHINODERMATA (Page 108)

Featherstars, Starfish, Brittlestars

Sea Urchins and Sea Cucumbers

CHORDATA (Page 111)

Sea Squirts

SPONGES

Sponges belong to the **phylum** Porifera. They are among the most primitive marine animals, having no mouth, nervous tissue, internal organs, circulatory or digestive systems. Varying considerably in size, shape and colour, some look like fans or have tree-like branches, others resemble barrels or simple tubes. They vary in size from a few centimetres to well over a metre. Most species attach themselves to a stable surface such as rocks or coral. A few are inadvertently able to move around by attaching themselves to the shells of hermit crabs.

SUSPENSION FEEDERS

A sponge feeds by drawing in water through its outer pores, filtering it and absorbing nutrients, such as plankton and fine organic matter, as well as oxygen. It expels waste water and carbon monoxide through an opening called the **osculum** on the top of its body.

FOULING SPONGES

Sponges and other invertebrates colonise underwater man-made structures such as jetty walls and pier piles. The blue sponge *Dysidea* (pictured above) is among the species found in such fouling communities. It is also the most frequently occurring sponge on dead coral reefs.

LEATHERY SURFACE

Chondrilla cf *nucuia* (pictured left) is a tough, leathery sponge that occurs on rocks below the tideline.

BORING SPONGES

Some sponges burrow into **calcareous** matter, such as mollusc shells and corals. Boring sponges can weaken the shells of molluscs, leaving them vulnerable to predators. Encrustations of boring sponges may also cause damage to limestone breakwaters. On the other hand, the ability of boring sponges to break down dead mollusc shells and corals plays an important part in the marine recycling process.

FASCINATING FACTS ABOUT SPONGES

- More than 5,000 sponge species are known worldwide.

- Many sponge species contain toxic substances, which may protect them from predators.

- Some bacteria and algae live in a **symbiotic** (mutually beneficial) relationship with sponges, providing food in return for protection.

- Sponges can reproduce asexually and sexually. Being **hermaphrodites** (possessing both male and female reproductive organs), sponges can produce both sperm and eggs.

- Some chemicals from sponges are useful in the pharmaceutical industry.

HYDROIDS

Hydroids include a very diverse range of marine animals, with body shapes and sizes that vary greatly. Most hydroids go through two stages as free-swimming **medusae** and as attached **polyps**. The majority of species live in large colonies containing thousands of polyps. Some colonies resemble corals, while others look like jellyfish and many are plant-like in appearance. Hydroid colonies work as a single entity, capturing animals by immobilising them with stinging cells called **nematocysts**.

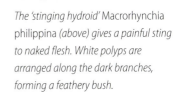

Clumps of the delicately branched hydroid Pennaria disticha *(left) occur on dead coral and subtidal rocks. The white polyps are arranged along one side of each branch.*

The 'stinging hydroid' Macrorhynchia philippina *(above) gives a painful sting to naked flesh. White polyps are arranged along the dark branches, forming a feathery bush.*

JELLYFISH

Ranging in size from a few millimetres to more than 2 m across, jellyfish are primitive invertebrates with a life cycle that includes a stationary **polyp** phase and a free-swimming **medusa** phase. They have no head, no skeleton, and no specialised respiratory system or digestive system. Food items and waste matter enter and exit through a single opening. Although a jellyfish is able to swim by rhythmically contracting its muscles, it is usually carried by ocean currents.

Catostylus mosaicus (above) has a translucent, dome-shaped bell, measuring up to 30 cm across. The eight conical mouth-arms contain no stinging cells. This edible jellyfish is considered a delicacy in parts of Asia.

*The tentacles of some jellyfish species may reach up to 10 m in length, and contain poisonous stinging cells (**nematocysts**), with which the jellyfish immobilises their prey. Some jellyfish stings are harmful to humans.*

Many species of jellyfish are solitary, but others, like the common moon jellyfish Aurelia aurita (pictured above) often travel in enormous shoals, which may cover many kilometres.

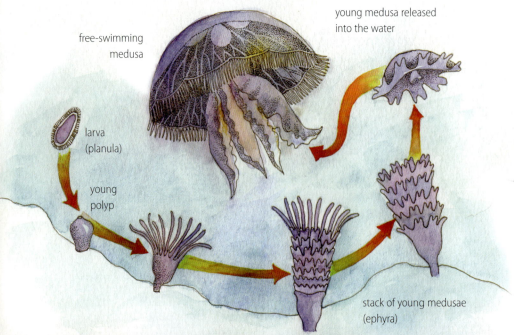

free-swimming medusa

young medusa released into the water

larva (planula)

young polyp

stack of young medusae (ephyra)

LIFE CYCLE

The life cycle of a typical jellyfish begins when sperm is released into the water column by the male. The sperm enter the mouth of the female and fertilises the eggs. The embryos develop into small swimming larvae (**planulae**), which exit from the mouth of the female and enter the water column. The larvae attach themselves to a suitable surface and form **polyps**. These polyps divide to form a stack of young **medusae** (**ephyra**). Each of these separates and is released into the water, where eventually it will develop into an adult **medusa**.

SEA ANEMONES

Sea anemones are closely related to corals. Both belong to the class Anthozoa, which comes from Greek words meaning 'flower' and 'sea'. Although many sea anemones look very similar to flowers, they are actually predatory animals, which range in size from a few centimetres to more than a metre across. Sea anemones immobilise their prey with stinging cells located in the tentacles, before pulling the food into the mouth, situated in the centre of the tentacles.

REPRODUCTION

Sea anemones reproduce in several ways. Some simply split into two new anemones. In other species, pieces of the adhesive foot break off and develop into clones of the original animal. Some anemones are **hermaphrodites**, producing both eggs and sperm; in others, the sexes are separate. In species that reproduce sexually, the eggs and sperm are released into the water, where fertilisation takes place. Fertilised eggs develop into larvae, which drift onto the seabed and grow into young anemones.

A SYMBIOTIC RELATIONSHIP

The clownfish *Amphiprion* sp. has a mucous coating that protects it from the stinging tentacles of the anemone. It lives and breeds among the anemone's tentacles, which provide a refuge from predators. In return, the anemone receives leftover food scraps.

THORNY CORALS, SOFT CORALS AND SEA FANS

Thorny corals, soft corals and sea fans are all colonial animals related to sea anemones and other corals. Thorny, or black, corals form tree-like colonies with numerous branches. The term 'black coral' comes from the colour of the internal skeleton. Soft corals are colourful, fleshy and bush-like in appearance. Sea fans are easily recognised by their brightly-coloured flattened branches, arranged in the shape of a fan.

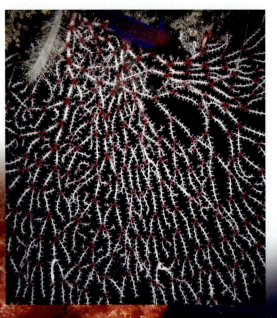

EIGHT-SIDED
Sea fans (left) and soft corals such as the *Dendronephthya* sp. below, are also known as octocorals. Unlike true coral **polyps**, which have a six-sided symmetry, the octocorals are eight-sided. The eight tentacles are branched, giving a feathery appearance.

The black coral Antipathes *sp. (above) has long, thorny branches with bright yellow polyps that do not retract. Black corals feed on zooplankton. They are slow-growing and live a long time if left undisturbed, providing an important habitat for other marine life.*

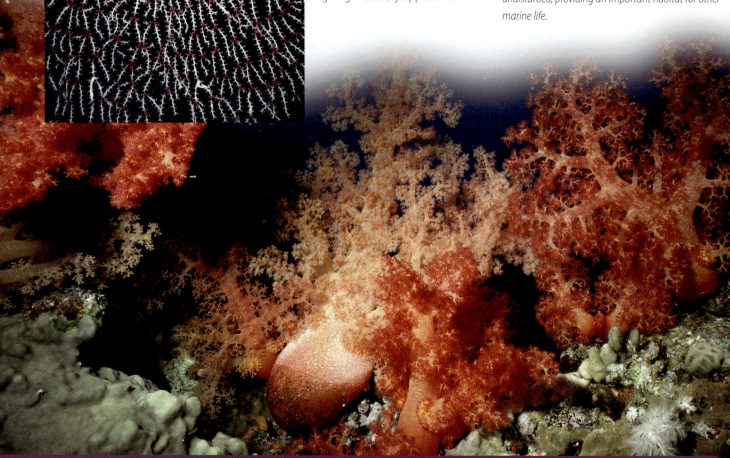

STONY CORALS

Corals are found in all of the waters surrounding the Arabian Peninsula. The diversity of coral species, however, depends on conditions within a particular body of water. The Arabian Gulf is a very shallow sea, averaging about 35 m in depth, and surrounded on all sides by very arid land. It is linked to the Gulf of Oman and the Arabian Sea by the narrow Straits of Hormuz, which limits the amount of water exchanged between these bodies of water. High evaporation rates and limited input of fresh water contribute to wide variations in salinity and water temperature, resulting in a relatively low species diversity. The deeper waters of the Gulf of Oman and the Arabian Sea create more suitable conditions for a wider variety of coral species. Although the Red Sea is also affected by high salinity and lack of freshwater input, it is much deeper than the Arabian Gulf, with a maximum depth of nearly 3,000 m. Coral reefs flourish in the warm, shallow waters of the Red Sea's narrow coastal shelf. Corals grow best in water that is low in nutrients that favour the growth of algae. Low-nutrient water is very clear, allowing **photosynthesis** to take place by the coral's **symbiotic** algae, the zooxanthellae.

BENEFICIAL ALGAE

Zooxanthellae are single-celled algae that live in **symbiosis** with reef-building corals. By using nutrients from the coral's waste products for **photosynthesis**, the algae produce enough food, in the form of simple sugar molecules, for themselves, as well as more than 80 per cent of that which is required by the coral. The **zooxanthellae** receive protection and a supply of nutrients from the host coral, whilst the coral benefits by having an efficient means of waste removal and a steady source of food, which ensures more rapid growth.

The presence of **zooxanthellae** gives corals their characteristic colours. If environmental conditions change, such as a sustained rise in temperature, the corals and **zooxanthellae** may be damaged. If the number of algae in the coral's tissues is reduced, the coral becomes pale. If most of the algae die, the coral loses its colour in a process known as 'bleaching'. If the source of environmental stress continues, the coral itself may die, but if conditions improve, the remaining **zooxanthellae** quickly multiply and the coral survives.

IMPORTANCE OF CORAL REEFS

Coral reefs are among the most diverse ecosystems on the planet, supporting more species (many of which are still undescribed) than any other marine habitat. Corals are also very important in controlling the amount of carbon dioxide in the ocean. Without coral, levels of carbon dioxide in the water would rise dramatically, which would affect all living things on earth.

Many reefs provide a barrier between the ocean and the coast, thereby preventing erosion and flooding resulting from wave action.

In addition to their environmental significance, coral reefs are also of huge economic importance. Significant amounts of money are generated by reef-based recreation and tourism. Fisheries at local, national and international levels depend on coral reefs to act as nurseries for large numbers of fish. Medicines developed from coral reef animals and plants are being used to treat diseases such as cancer, arthritis, and AIDS.

HOW DO CORALS REPRODUCE?

Coral reproduction varies according to species. Some corals produce both sperm and eggs at the same time. Others produce colonies in which all **polyps** are of the same sex. In such instances, at least two colonies are needed for reproduction to take place.

Fertilisation may occur inside a coral polyp when one polyp releases sperm, which then swims into the mouth of a polyp that has produced eggs. The sperm and egg combine to produce a larva known as a **planula**. Once the **planula** has matured, it is expelled into the water through the mouth of the **polyp**.

Other corals reproduce by releasing eggs and sperm into the water in a process called spawning. Spawning is synchronised so that polyps release vast quantities of eggs and sperm into the water at the same time, increasing the probability of fertilisation.

The coral larva moves to the ocean surface, where it floats as part of the plankton for several days or weeks, before settling on the seabed. There it attaches itself to a hard surface and develops into a **polyp**, which then divides many times, producing clones of itself, which fuse together to form a colony. When the colony is mature, the polyps produce eggs and sperm and the life cycle begins again.

CORAL POLYP

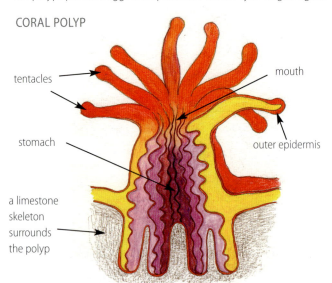

tentacles

mouth

stomach

outer epidermis

a limestone skeleton surrounds the polyp

HOW DO CORALS GROW?

The **polyps** of most stony corals are only a few millimetres across, but colonies may become very large and weigh several tonnes. Corals can grow into many different shapes, even within a single species. In strong currents and heavy wave action, corals are inclined to be short and sturdy, while the same coral may form a more delicate structure in a less exposed position.

Coral polyps secrete a hard, protective skeleton of calcium carbonate (limestone). As the coral colony grows it produces more skeletal material and eventually forms a coral reef.

THREATS TO CORALS AND CORAL REEF SYSTEMS

- PREDATION: Other species, such as the crown-of-thorns starfish *Acanthaster planci* (see page 109), as well as fish, molluscs and worms, eat **polyps** or bore into corals.

- GLOBAL WARMING: Rises in sea temperature will result in increasing incidents of coral bleaching (see page 97).

- CORAL DISEASES: Disease in corals appears to occur as a result of environmental stresses, such as increased temperature and deterioration of water quality.

- WATER POLLUTION: Oil spills, toxins, and heavy metals, as well as nitrate and phosphate pollution from agriculture and sewage, can cause algal blooms, resulting in degradation or even the death of a coral reef. Sedimentation from agriculture and industrial development cuts out sunlight and the corals' **symbiotic** zooxanthellae cannot photosynthesise.

- CLIMATE CHANGE: Violent storms can damage corals, especially large table corals, which are anchored by narrow stalks.

- HARMFUL FISHING PRACTICES: Bottom trawling, using explosives and over-fishing all have a harmful effect on corals.

- BOAT ANCHORS: Dropping anchor over reefs may damage corals, especially if the anchor is dragged over the corals.

- SPORT DIVING: Trampling on corals crushes the polyps. Harvesting corals as souvenirs damages and depletes the reef.

DAISY CORAL *Goniopora lobata*

The elongated **polyps** of the daisy coral are always extended during the day, giving the coral a flower-like appearance as they sway back and forth in the current. If disturbed, the polyps are retracted to reveal the coral's surface. *Goniopora* corals belong to the same family as *Porites* (see box on right).

Porites nodifera

This coral forms clusters of vertical columns, often squared off at the tips. This species, which is considered to be particularly tolerant of highly saline conditions, often occurs as part of *Porites* dominated patch reefs in shallow water. *Porites* species are important frame-building corals of many reefs.

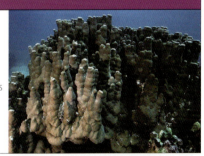

BRAIN CORAL *Platygyra daedalea*

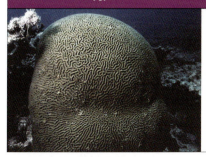

Brain corals usually form large, rounded colonies with winding, flat-topped, straight-sided walls, giving the coral a distinctive, brain-like appearance. This species occurs in a wide range of habitats in Arabian waters, from the reef-top down to at least 30 m. It is an important frame-building coral.

Acropora pharaonis

Acropora species are among the most common reef-building corals. Growth forms vary considerably, even within a single species. *A. pharaonis* is a sturdy, branching coral with a broad base, usually found in areas where there is a fast current. Some *Acropora* species also form large plates or tables.

WORMS

Polychaete worms are found exclusively in underwater environments, but are closely related to earthworms and leeches. Roughly 8,000 species have been described worldwide, and it is estimated that about 6 to 12 per cent of these known species occur in the seas bordering the Arabian Peninsula. Some species are sedentary, whilst others, such as ragworms, are able to move around freely. Sedentary worms live inside a tube or a burrow and feed on particles suspended in the water. Free-moving species are carnivorous and actively hunt for food.

FASCINATING FACTS

- Polychaete bodies are divided into segments, each of which has a pair of flaps with tiny bristles, which have given rise to their common name, bristleworms.
- Polychaetes play an important ecological role, with some preying on small invertebrates, while others provide food for larger invertebrates, fish and birds.
- Although most bristleworms are solitary, some species of tubeworms may form large colonies.
- Polychaete worms generally have highly developed sensory organs, which include tentacles, eyes and feelers for tasting food.

FLAMBOYANT FANWORMS

This group of sedentary polychaete worms get their common name from the often colourful crown of feathery tentacles that extend from the tube in which the worm lives. The tentacles are covered with minute hairs called **cilia**, and are used for collecting food, breathing and sorting sedimentary material for maintaining their tubes.

Fan worms are filter feeders. A mucous covering on the tentacles traps tiny food particles from the water. The food is then passed to the mouth, which is situated in the centre of the tentacles.

BARNACLES

Barnacles are members of the crustacean subphylum of animals, but unlike most of their relatives, such as crabs, shrimps and lobsters, they usually remain fixed to hard surfaces, except during the juvenile stages, in which they are free-swimming. Barnacles are the most abundant fouling organisms in the sea. In addition to settling on rocks in the intertidal zone, they commonly attach themselves to the undersides of boats and other man-made objects, resulting in the need for costly anti-fouling measures.

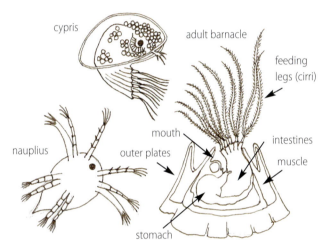

LIFE CYCLE

Barnacles are **hermaphrodites** and fertilisation takes place when sperm from one barnacle is received by a neighbouring one. The eggs hatch into minute **nauplius** larvae, which swim as part of the plankton. After going through six **nauplius** stages, the larva moults and enters the **cypris** stage, in which the larva finds a place to settle. This is followed by metamorphosis into a barnacle, which adheres to the chosen surface by means of a powerful cement secreted by special glands.

Tetraclita squamosa *is a distinctive acorn barnacle found in Arabian waters.*

Goose (stalked) barnacle

FASCINATING FACTS ABOUT BARNACLES

- There are two types of barnacles: stalked or goose barnacles (centre photo), usually found in the open sea, hanging upside down from pieces of timber and ship hulls, and acorn barnacles (top and bottom photos), which are commonly seen attached to rocks on the seashore.

- An acorn barnacle stands on its head and uses its legs to feed on plankton from within a protective casing of overlapping **calcareous** plates. The legs can be retracted through a hole in the top of the shell, which can be closed by a set of smaller plates.

- Some barnacles live attached to whales, while others attach themselves to the shells of molluscs and crabs. Still others may be found growing on mangrove roots.

- The glue produced by a barnacle, with which it adheres to an object is able to withstand extremely high temperatures, as well as most corrosive substances. A very thin layer is capable of supporting a weight of several tonnes.

- Barnacles are being used effectively to measure levels of heavy metal pollution in harbour waters.

Euraphia withersi *(above) is a small barnacle found on rocky shores. It may be confused with other species with six wall plates.*

CRABS

Crabs are among the most diverse, abundant, and ecologically-important groups of marine invertebrates. Many crabs are small, camouflaged, or spend much of their time in burrows or under rocks. Other, larger and more conspicuous species occur only in deeper water. Although crabs come in a great variety of shapes and sizes they all have the same general body structure, which includes a hard outer shell called a **carapace**, eight walking legs and an additional pair, which end in pincers, used for grasping food and for defence.

Walking legs

Chelipeds (first pair of legs, used for defence and feeding

Carapace

Swimming legs

GHOST CRABS

The fast-moving ghost crab *Ocypode* sp. is found on clean, sandy beaches, where it inhabits burrows, from which it emerges to scavenge at dusk. A typical burrow and accompanying tower is pictured above.

This crab has a serrated strip on one claw, over which the crab rubs the other claw, effectively 'playing a fiddle'. This produces quite a loud, characteristic call, thought to be associated with mating.

SWIMMING CRABS

These crabs with characteristic, paddle-like hindmost legs, are adapted for swimming. Swimming crabs are commercially important, and species such as *Charybdis* sp. (pictured above) and *Portunus pelagicus* are often seen in souqs.

SURVIVING THE WAVES

Grapsus albolineatus (above) is a herbivorous crab, which feeds on small algae, scraped off rocks in breaking waves. It survives the wave action by clinging to the rock surface with its spiky legs and having a smooth, disc-like body, which offers little resistance to the waves. The precarious habitat of *Grapsus* gives protection from potential predators, which are unable to operate easily in these conditions.

AT HOME IN A SHELL

Hermit crabs are not true crabs. Commonly found in the intertidal zone, these rather comical crustaceans find protection for their soft bodies inside empty gastropod mollusc shells. Shells are periodically replaced as the crab becomes bigger. Strong competition may develop between hermit crabs over 'ownership' of suitable shells.

CRABS IN THE MANGROVES

The largest mangrove crab in the world is *Scylla serrata* (pictured above). Large burrows in the mud indicate the presence of this edible crab, although the animal itself is rarely seen. *Scylla*'s diet consists mainly of fish and invertebrates, such as molluscs, which the crab crushes with its large pincer claws.

Fiddler crabs *Uca* spp. (below) are often seen amongst mangroves at low tide, waving their white claws. In some areas, such as Khor Liwa in Oman, they are particularly abundant, with as many as almost 200 burrows in a single square metre. The one oversized white claw is held aloft as they scuttle across the mud to their burrows and disappear completely from view on the approach of would-be predators. The claw then acts like a trap door to the burrow, from behind which the crab will cautiously re-emerge once danger has passed.

MOLLUSCS

Molluscs comprise one of the largest groups of invertebrates in the world. Although they come in many shapes and sizes, most molluscs have certain features in common. They have a head, a soft body containing the organs, and a muscular foot, as well as a **mantle** – a sheet of tissue covering the body. The mantle secretes the **calcareous** outer shell common to most molluscs. Gills, when present, are in the **mantle** cavity, which is a space between the mantle and the body. Some molluscs, such as the cuttlefish, have internalised their shell, and others do without one altogether. Molluscs are divided into four main groups: chitons, gastropods, bivalves and cephalopods.

CHITONS

Also known as coat-of-mail shells, chitons do not have a **calcareous** shell like most molluscs. The back is protected by eight overlapping plates. A chiton is flattened and elongated, and well-adapted to life in areas of strong wave action. It is able to cling tightly to a rock, using its strong, muscular foot. If it becomes separated from the rock on which it is situated, the chiton is able to roll up in a ball, rather like a hedgehog or woodlouse, in order to protect its body. Chitons feed by scraping algae from rocks using a tongue-like organ called a **radula**.

SNAILS AND SEA SLUGS

Gastropods are a large group of molluscs, found worldwide in marine, freshwater and terrestrial habitats. The soft body of a gastropod is often protected by a shell, into which it can retreat for protection. Snails with spiral shells, such as those pictured above and below, are able to close off the shell opening with a 'door' called an **operculum**. Other gastropods, such as limpets (left), have a cone-shaped shell and no operculum. Instead they are able to cling tightly to rocks, using a muscular foot. Still others, such as nudibranchs (sea slugs), have no shell at all.

MOLLUSCS

CHITONS SEA SLUGS AND SNAILS BIVALVES CEPHALOPODS

NUDIBRANCH (SEA SLUG) FACTS

- Nudibranch means 'naked gill' and some of these often brightly coloured molluscs frequently have feathery gill tufts prominently situated on the **dorsal** surface (back) of their soft bodies.

- Other species of nudibranch have soft finger-like projections called cerata on the back, through which the sea slug breathes.

- Nudibranchs are carnivores and may graze on a variety of other marine invertebrates, such as sponges, corals, hydroids, sea anemones, bryozoans, barnacles, and even other nudibranchs!

- Nudibranchs usually have both male and female sex organs, which increases the possibility of finding a mate. Once fertilised, nudibranchs lay egg masses that look like a length of ribbon wound in a spiral.

- Eggs hatch into minute larvae, which float in the plankton until environmental conditions indicate that it is time to settle, at which time the larva changes into an adult nudibranch.

- Never pick up a nudibranch if you find one, as their soft bodies are vulnerable to damage.

SEA SLUG *Hypselodoris infucata*

This carnivorous sea slug, shown here with its eggs at bottom left, is one of the few found in the southern Arabian Gulf. It is about 4 cm long with a semi-translucent body with blue and yellow spots. Usually found on sponges under rock slabs and boulders along shoreline.

SPANISH DANCER *Hexabranchus* sp.

The bright red colouring fringed with white, and graceful, undulating swimming method of this species has given rise to the common name of Spanish dancer. It is relatively large at up to 15 cm in length. Often found in association with the shrimp *Periclimenes imperator*.

Onchidium peronii belongs to the group containing land-dwelling and air-breathing snails, but is a marine species that emerges at night during low tide to graze on films of algae found on rocks.

HOODED OYSTER *Saccostrea cuccullata*

This oyster is very variable in form. The fluted edges of the valves fit together when the shell is closed. This species occurs along the shoreline, often forming a distinct band. It may also be found on the breathing roots and trunks of mangroves, as well as on pier piles.

Tridacna sp.

Tridacna clams have large, solid shells, in which each valve has radiating ribs, resulting in an undulating form. They are frequently found among corals. Like corals *Tridacna* sp. gets much of its food from single-celled algae (zooxanthellae), embedded in the mantle.

HOW OYSTERS MAKE PEARLS

The formation of a pearl begins when a piece of foreign material gets lodged in between the **mantle** and the shell of an oyster, causing an irritation. The oyster tries to get rid of the irritant by covering it with layers of the same substance that the **mantle** secretes in order to create a shell. These layers build up and eventually form a pearl.

Trapezium sublaevigatum (below) belongs to a family of oblong clams that attach themselves to hard surfaces by means of byssal threads.

BIVALVE FACTS

- Bivalves have two-sided, symmetrical shells, hinged together by a ligament. Each side of the shell is called a valve. Familiar bivalves include mussels, clams and oysters.

- Unlike many molluscs, bivalves do not have a **radula** (a tongue-like organ used in feeding). Instead, they are filter feeders. Water is drawn into the gills where tiny pieces of organic matter become caught in the gill mucus. This process also allows the animal to take in fresh oxygen.

- Bivalves have a variety of lifestyles. Some can swim by contracting the muscles that close the two valves, resulting in a jet of water being expelled, which propels the mollusc through the water. Others, such as clams, have a muscular foot with which they move and many dig burrows into sand, rock or wood. Mussels and other sedentary bivalves attach themselves to rocks and other underwater surfaces by means of fine filaments known as **byssal threads**.

- Burrowing species take in food and oxygen by means of a tube called a siphon or neck, which can be extended to the surface while the mollusc remains hidden, away from predators.

- Most bivalve species reproduce by releasing large quantities of eggs and sperm into the water, where fertilisation takes place. After hatching, bivalves go through a free-swimming larval stage before changing into their adult form.

OCTOPUSES, SQUID AND CUTTLEFISH

Cephalopods (the collective name for octopus, cuttlefish, squid and nautilus) differ from most molluscs because, with the exception of the chambered nautilus, they have either a much-reduced shell located within the body, or in the case of the octopus, have no shell at all. They have well-developed eyes that allow them to see in low light conditions.

With the exception of squid, which often occurs in large shoals, these predatory carnivores usually hunt alone, feeding on fish, as well as other molluscs and marine invertebrates. After crushing the prey with their hard beak-like jaws, they inject a venom that paralyses the prey and softens the flesh, making it easier to digest.

CUTTLEFISH REPRODUCTION

After mating, the female deposits her eggs in rocky crevices, while the male stays nearby to prevent other males mating with her.

COLOUR CHANGES

Cephalopods have special cells in their skin called **chromatophores** that enable them to quickly change the colour and pattern of their skin. This allows them to blend in with their surroundings. Squid can also hide themselves from predators by ejecting a dark cloud of ink.

OCTOPUS

An octopus may range in size from a few centimetres to several metres. It has three hearts, two of which pump blood to the two gills and the third that pumps blood to the rest of the body. Each of the eight arms has two rows of suckers on the underside. The lack of a hard skeleton allows the octopus to squeeze through very small openings.

SQUID

With their streamlined bodies, squid are built for speed. They usually travel backwards, propelled by water jets. Squid have eight arms, and two tentacles with flattened, spatula-like ends with suckers on them. The arms have suckers along the entire length. Squid have an internal shell, which supports the **mantle**. As a defence against predators, squid can eject a dark cloud of ink.

CUTTLEFISH

Cuttlefish are active at night, remaining hidden in crevices during the day. Like squid, they have eight arms and two tentacles, but cuttlefish keep their tentacles hidden in a pouch under the eyes.

ECHINODERMS

This group of invertebrates is exclusive to the sea and contains animals with bodies consisting of five equal parts, each of which has a set of internal organs. Many also have calcareous skeletons. The word 'echinoderm' comes from the Greek, meaning 'spiny skin'. Included in this group are featherstars, brittlestars, starfish, sea urchins and sea cucumbers.

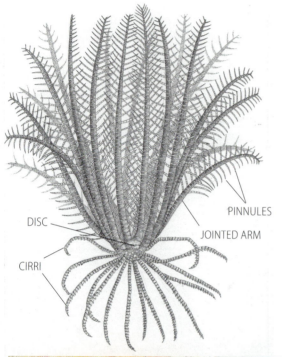

DISC
PINNULES
JOINTED ARM
CIRRI

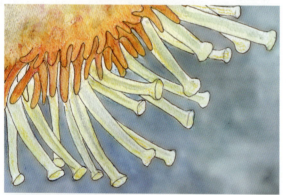

FEATHERSTARS

Featherstars (or crinoids) are ancient invertebrate life forms that first appeared on the planet nearly 500 million years ago, during the early Ordovician, a geological time period known for its large variety of marine invertebrates. Like all echinoderms, featherstars have tube feet, located on the **pinnules** (see drawing, above left) of each arm. However, unlike most echinoderms, the featherstar does not use its tube feet (see illustration, left) for locomotion, but for feeding. This is done by directing small particles of food, such as other invertebrate larvae that are suspended in the water, towards the food transport system, which begins at the pinnules and goes to the mouth on the upper surface of the central disc. Each of the segmented **cirri** (see diagram) ends in a small claw, with which the featherstar clings to rocky surfaces.

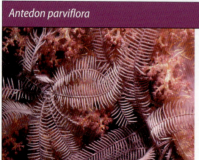

Antedon parviflora

These small, ten-armed featherstars are often associated with soft corals *Dendronephthya* spp., and other invertebrates that colonise underwater caves and crevices. Large numbers of these featherstars may be found hanging from the roof of such caves.

Tropiometra sp.

This featherstar is characterised by its ten arms with distinctively upright and stiff pinnules. It frequently occurs at depths between 5 m and 20 m in holes in regions of coral rock, as well as on some reef-flats.

ECHINODERMS

FEATHERSTARS STARFISH BRITTLESTARS SEA URCHINS SEA CUCUMBERS

STARFISH

Starfish have arms radiating out from a central disc, the underside of which contains the mouth. Each arm has several rows of tube feet, which the animal uses for locomotion. Species that live on rocky surfaces have suckers on the tips of the tube feet that may be used for maintaining a grip on the rock, as well as for securing prey. Starfish that live on sand have longer tube feet without suckers.

Most starfish are carnivores, living on other invertebrates, sometimes including other starfish. A few are scavengers or feed on the films of algae found on rocks.

Some starfish, such as this Linckia sp. (top right) may discard one or more arms, which it has the ability to regrow, often giving the starfish an irregular shape.

Culcita schmideliana (left) is a 'cushion' star, which feeds on corals. It has a pentagonal shape and no obvious arms.

CROWN-OF-THORNS STARFISH

The crown-of-thorns *Acanthaster planci* is a large starfish with as many as 20 sharp spines, which are highly toxic. The crown-of-thorns feeds on live corals, which are left white and dead after having been grazed. From time to time, crown-of-thorns population explosions occur, and entire areas of coral reef are wiped out. The causes of such events are still uncertain, but it does appear to be a naturally occurring phenomenon, although human activities may also play a role. Eventually, coral reefs recover, but may not have the same diversity of species.

STRANGE TABLE MANNERS

A starfish feeds by pushing its stomach out through its mouth to envelop the food object. After secreting digestive juices in order to liquify the prey, the starfish then sucks in the stomach, along with the digested food.

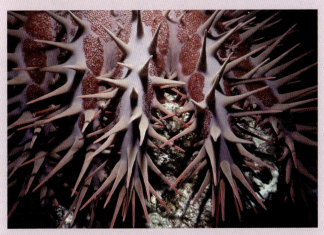

BRITTLESTARS

Brittlestars belong to the class Ophiuroidea, meaning 'snake-like'. Most brittlestars have five long, flexible arms, radiating from the central disc, which contains the mouth and internal organs.

Brittlestars usually feed on plankton and decaying matter, but some may eat small invertebrates. Like the starfish, brittlestars push out their stomach and release digestive juices, in order to digest their food, after which the stomach is drawn back into the disc.

In order to escape predators, brittlestars are able to shed their arms, which will regrow. Unlike starfish, brittlestars do not use their tube feet for locomotion. Instead they use their flexible arms to move around with a rowing, or snake-like motion.

SEA URCHINS

Unlike the flexible skeletons of other echinoderms, those of sea urchins are composed of closely interlocking plates, which form a rigid shell called a **test**. The body of a sea urchin is covered with movable spines that are attached to **tubercles** in the test. Spines vary in length and thickness, depending on the species. Some species have spines containing poison.

In common with other echinoderms, sea urchins have tube feet, arranged in five paired rows between the spines. Sea urchins use their tube feet for both locomotion and feeding.

Urchins feed mainly on algae and other plant matter that they scrape off rocks or the sea bottom. They do this using their five claw-like jaws, which make up the Aristotle's lantern, located at the base of the body. Some species feed on dead fish, as well as small invertebrates.

Diadema setosum has long, needle-sharp spines.

Pencil urchin
Heterocentrotus sp.

ARISTOTLE'S LANTERN

The mouth parts of a sea urchin were described by the Greek teacher, Aristotle, over 2,000 years ago. He compared the chewing structure, with five jaws, to the five-sided lanterns made from animal horn that were in use in those days. This name is still used today.

SEA CUCUMBERS

Sea cucumbers differ from other echinoderms in having a soft body wall, rather than a **calcareous** one; a largely horizontal symmetry, with the mouth and anus at separate ends of the body, rather than the entirely radial symmetry of other echinoderms; and no arms. In spite of these differences, sea cucumbers still conform to the five-part symmetry common to all echinoderms. Running along the sides of the leathery body are five rows of tube feet, tipped with small suction cups, that are used to cling to rocks or move around the seabed.

A sea cucumber's mouth is surrounded by a ring of branched tentacles that are used to trap food particles. Sea cucumbers feed mainly on algae, microscopic organisms and waste materials.

Sea cucumbers have two distinctive methods of defending themselves. When threatened by predators, some species eject a sticky, stringy substance to trap the attacker. Others are able to disgorge their internal organs by means of powerful muscle contractions. Organs lost in this manner can be quickly regrown.

CORAL REEF RECYCLERS

Sea cucumbers are important members of the coral reef ecosystem. It has been estimated that they are responsible for moving 150 tonnes of sand per hectare per year. They do this by ingesting sand with food particles, and later discharging the indigestible material as tiny faecal pellets.

SEA SQUIRTS

Sea squirts, or ascidians, are known most commonly as fouling organisms that colonise natural and man-made surfaces. However, sea squirts are of great interest to scientists because the tadpole larvae have a primitive spinal cord known as a notochord, which is a forerunner of the backbone found in all vertebrates. Unlike the tadpoles of frogs, these larvae do not go on to develop a backbone. This unusual attribute puts sea squirts in a special group called urochordates, making them more closely related to vertebrates such as fish, birds and humans than to invertebrates.

The photograph on the left shows various colonial sea squirts fouling the surface of a buoy.

In addition to fouling man-made structures, Didemnum spp. often form colourful encrusting sheets on the undersides of rocks and boulders. They are also among the first colonisers of dead coral.

>> LEARN MORE : USEFUL WEBSITES

GENERAL INFORMATION ON MARINE INVERTEBRATES

http://www.arabianwildlife.com/marine_invertebrates

http://www.oceanicresearch.org/education/wonders/lesson.html – educational site with informative text and excellent photographs

http://www.seasky.org/reeflife/sea2.html – attractive website with information and photographs on marine life of the coral reef

http://oceanlink.island.net/biodiversity/ask/ask.html – 'Ask a Marine Scientist' information on marine life in question and answer format

http://www.ucmp.berkeley.edu/help/topic.html – index page for marine biology topics from the University of California Museum of Palaeontology

http://www.pbs.org/kcet/shapeoflife/animals/index.html – information on marine and terrestrial invertebrates

http://www.seaweb.org/home.php – conserving the oceans; excellent links to other relevant websites in resources section

www.uaeinteract.com/uaeint_misc/pdf/perspectives/14.pdf – A Survey of the Habitats, Invertebrate Fauna and Environmental Sensitivity of the Mainland Coast of the UAE, with Information on Status and Distribution of Crustaceans (Emirates Natural History Group)

SPONGES

http://www.vliz.be/Vmdcdata/porifera/porifera.php?p=search – useful database where you can look up sponges by species name

http://www.enchantedlearning.com/subjects/invertebrates/sponge/coloring.shtml – information and diagrams from educational site aimed at primary-level children

CORALS, JELLYFISH AND SEA ANEMONES

http://www.enhg.org/bulletin/b09/09_06.htm – article on the corals of Abu Dhabi from Emirates Natural History Group

http://www.saudiaramcoworld.com/issue/197806/coral.in.the.gulf.htm – article on corals in Arabian Gulf from Saudi Aramco World

http://www.oceanservice.noaa.gov/education/kits/corals/coral01_intro.html – excellent information on all aspects of corals and coral reefs

http://www.bishopmuseum.org/research/pbs/Oman-coral-book/ – online book 'Corals of Oman' – extensive material on corals found in Arabian waters

WORMS

http://www.mesa.edu.au/friends/seashores/worms.html – informative text, diagrams and photos related to marine worms

CRABS

http://www.museum.vic.gov.au/crust/crabbiol.html – biology of crabs

MOLLUSCS

http://www.enhg.org/bulletin/b35/35_21.htm – Marine Molluscs and the Arabian Peninsula – article from Emirates Natural History Group

http://www.enhg.org/bulletin/b16/16_31.htm – an article on sea shells from Emirates Natural History Group

http://www.thecephalopodpage.org/ – website dedicated to information on squid, octopuses and cuttlefish

ECHINODERMS

http://www.starfish.ch/reef/echinoderms.html – information and photos on a variety of echinoderms

http://animaldiversity.ummz.umich.edu/site/accounts/information/Echinodermata.html – fairly advanced, but useful for second-level students

http://phylogeny.arizona.edu/tree/eukaryotes/animals/echinodermata/echinodermata.html – Tree of Life website – quite advanced, but useful for secondary school students; arranged taxonomically

MARINE INVERTEBRATES GLOSSARY

autotomy: ability of an organism to discard an appendage when injured or under attack

budding: outgrowth of an organism, which breaks off to form a new individual without sexual reproduction taking place

byssal threads: strong protein threads by which a bivalve mollusc attaches itself to the surface on which it lives (sometimes called **byssus thread**)

calcareous: having a mineral structure based on calcium carbonate, such as corals do

carapace: hard outer covering of a crab's body

chromatophore: pigment cells that enable an organism, such as a cephalopod, to change colour

cilium (pl. **cilia**): fine, hair-like structure

cypris: non-feeding larval stage in barnacles that follows the nauplius stage and is characterised by two shell-valves

dorsal: upper side or back of an organism

ephyra: last larval stage of jellyfish

hermaphrodite: having both male and female reproductive organs

mantle: protective layer of skin in molluscs, which secretes calcium carbonate to form the shell

medusa: free-swimming, umbrella-shaped stage of a cnidarian, for example a jellyfish

nauplius: first larval stage of some crustaceans, with unsegmented body, three pairs of appendages for swimming, and a single eye

nematocyst: stinging cell found in hydroids, sea anemones and jellyfish

operculum: flap or lid-like disc covering the shell opening in some molluscs

osculum: an opening in a sponge from which water is discharged

phylum: second highest taxonomic classification after kingdom

pinnule: side branch on arm of featherstar

planula: free-swimming, flattened larva of jellyfish

polyp: stationary form in life cycle of cnidarians such as corals

radula: rough, tongue-like structure found in most molluscs, and used for feeding

regeneration: ability of an organism to regrow a body part that has been lost

sessile: attached or immobile, such as a barnacle

symbiosis: close relationship between two different species in which both species benefit

test: hard, rigid shell of a sea urchin

tubercle: small projections on the surface of an animal (for example, on a sea urchin test)

invertebrates/land snails

arabian wildlife encyclopedia

LAND SNAILS

Most molluscs live in the sea, but some gastropods (snails and slugs) have adapted very successfully to living in fresh water and on land. Tens of thousands of species of land snails exist today worldwide. Among other adaptations, they have exchanged gills for lungs, and for this reason they are called **pulmonates**. They are most numerous and diverse in moist or humid environments, but even the arid Arabian Peninsula has somewhat more than 70 species, although most of these are concentrated in the relatively wet regions of south-western Arabia and Dhofar.

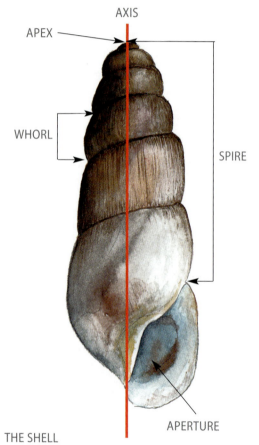

AXIS

APEX

WHORL

SPIRE

APERTURE

THE SHELL

The shell protects a snail against predators. The outer layer of the shell is coloured to provide camouflage. A snail's shell, which is composed mainly of calcium carbonate, is built by the **mantle** – a membrane-like organ around the **aperture**. The shell is connected to the body by a strong muscle attached to the **columella** – the internal central column of the shell. By contracting this muscle, the snail can withdraw into its shell and seal the **aperture** with a plug of mucus. This protects the snail during periods of drought.

Most land snails have four projections on the fronts of their heads (see photograph above). Although these look a little like the antennae of insects, they are in fact **tentacles**. Light-sensitive eye spots are found at the tips of the two longer ones. The shorter tentacles feel, taste and smell the surroundings, allowing the snail to search for food and water and to remain alert to danger.

A snail's mouth is on the bottom of its head, near the short **tentacles**. Snails eat by means of a specialised tool, the **radula**, located inside the mouth. The **radula** is similar to a rough tongue with thousands of tiny, sharp teeth. Snails eat by using the **radula** to scrape small particles from leaves and other vegetation.

Mordania omanensis (above and below) is a land snail that has been found at relatively high elevations in the Jebel Akhdar region of Oman and the Jebel Bani Jaber south of Muscat, as well as in the crevices of a steep, north-facing limestone cliff in the Ru'us al-Jibal in the UAE. The only other representative of the genus *Mordania* is found in the mountains of north-western Iran.

ALIEN INTRODUCTIONS

A number of terrestrial mollusc species have been introduced to the Arabian Peninsula by extensive public and private landscaping and agricultural activities using imported plants, soil and fertiliser.

Among these is the flat African slug *Laevicaulis alte* (pictured above) and the disc-shaped Florida native *Polygyra cereolus* (below right). These two species are present in pest proportions in some lawn and garden environments. A record size *L. alte* (ca. 90 mm) was recovered from the nostril of a racehorse in Abu Dhabi, having been accidentally inhaled with a morning meal of fresh alfalfa from a well-watered fodder farm!

FASCINATING SNAIL FACTS

- Some snails have been known to live up to 15 years, but in the wild they generally live from one to seven years, depending on the species.
- Snails are hermaphrodites, which means that they have both male and female reproductive organs.
- Snails rely mainly on their sense of touch and smell to find food because they have very poor eyesight.
- Shells increase in size as the snail grows, creating growth lines on the shell.
- Snails can crawl upside-down due to the suction created by their slime.
- Snails are more active at night than by day.
- Most land snails move at about 58 cm per hour.
- The largest land snail is the giant African land snail, which may reach more than 30 cm in length.
- Slugs need moist conditions in order to survive and rarely exist in the aridity of desert habitats.

USEFUL WEBSITES

http://www.uaeinteract.com/uaeint_misc/teanh/018snai.pdf – information on land snails of the Arabian Peninsula in pdf format

http://www.backyardnature.net/2mollusk.htm – useful material on slugs and snails

http://www.sciencenewsforkids.org/articles/20070808/Feature1.asp – scientific article on slug slime written in child-friendly language

http://www.lawrencehallofscience.org/foss/fossweb/teachers/materials/plantanimal/landsnails.html – general information about land snails for schools and teachers

http://members.tripod.com/arnobrosi/evo.html – information on the biology of snails

LAND SNAIL GLOSSARY

aperture: opening in the shell through which a snail emerges

columella: central internal column of a snail shell

gastropod: a type of mollusc that has a single shell, (which is sometimes reduced or even absent) and a muscular foot

mantle: membrane-like structure around the aperture that builds the shell

pulmonates: snails that breathe with lungs

radula: rough, tongue-like organ covered with tiny, sharp teeth used to rasp away at leaves and other food

tentacles: sensory projections on the head of a snail (two pairs)

whorl: a full spiral coil of a snail shell

MOVING LIKE A SNAIL

Land snails move by gliding on a single flat foot located on the underside of the body. A series of muscular contractions in the foot create a kind a wave-like movement that pushes the snail forward. A special gland in the front of the foot produces a slimy mucus, which enables the snail to move over sharp or rough surfaces.

ANIMALS WITH BACKBONES
vertebrates

VERTEBRATES

Vertebrates are animals that have a backbone or spinal column. In almost all species the backbone consists of a series of **vertebrae** (bony, ring-like segments). These protect and support the delicate spinal cord, an essential part of the animal's nervous system, which sends messages from the brain to other parts of the body. Other vertebrate characteristics include the presence of muscles, an internal skeleton, a brain enclosed in a **cranium** (skull), a closed **circulatory system**, and a heart. These features allow vertebrates to move around and to perform complicated tasks. Vertebrates are divided into five categories: reptiles, amphibians, fish, birds and mammals.

REPTILES are a varied group of **cold-blooded**, egg-laying vertebrates with a scaly skin. Unlike amphibians, which lay their eggs in water, reptiles lay theirs on dry land. >> see page 121

AMPHIBIANS are **cold-blooded** vertebrates that usually live on land as adults. Young amphibians live in water, using gills to breathe in much the same way as fish. The name 'amphibian' means 'double life'. >> see page 151

FISH are vertebrates that live in water and breathe using gills. Most fish can be divided into two categories: bony and **cartilaginous**. >>see page 155

BIRDS are **warm-blooded** vertebrates that have wings, a beak, no teeth and feathers. Flying birds have strong, hollow bones and powerful flight muscles. Most birds have the ability to fly, but some species, such as the ostrich, are flightless. >> see page 171

MAMMALS are **warm-blooded** vertebrates that usually have body hair and whose young are fed on milk from the female's **mammary glands**. Human beings are **mammals**. >> see page 193

ON THE MOVE. . .

Vertebrate animals move around in order to find food and water, protection and other animals. Their physical structure is designed to enable them to move in the environment in which they live, and differs considerably, depending on whether they live on land, in water or in the air.

IN THE WATER

Moving poses many challenges for animals that live in an aquatic environment. Fish and marine mammals generally have long, thin, streamlined bodies, which enable them to move through the water at speed. Amphibians and aquatic birds have webbed feet, which help them to push against the water. Sea mammals such as dolphins and seals have flippers, which help them to steer through the water.

IN THE AIR

The most common flying animals are birds. The bird skeleton is lightweight and strong. Weight is kept down by the bones being hollow. Many bones, which are separate in mammals, are joined together (fused) in birds. Strong muscles help to move the wings. The only true flying mammals are bats.

A DIFFERENT SOLUTION

Snakes have no legs, so they slither along the ground, making use of their scales and muscles. A snake has long chains of muscles along its backbone, which are connected to the ribs and vertebrae. Skin muscles allow the ribs to pull the belly scales backwards and forwards, in order to help the snake to move. Snakes use four types of movement. For more information on snake locomotion >> see page 141.

ON LAND

Land animals have many ways of moving, usually by using either two or four legs. People and birds run, jump and walk on two legs, while animals such as horses, oryx, leopards, tortoises and lizards use four legs to move around. Some animals, including gazelles and hares, have very powerful back legs for bounding or leaping.

>> LEARN MORE : USEFUL WEBSITES

INFORMATION ON ARABIAN VERTEBRATES

http://www.uaeinteract.com/nature/ – information on the wildlife of the United Arab Emirates

http://www.uaeinteract.com/uaeint_misc/pdf_2009/The-Emirates-A-Natural-History/ – this volume on UAE natural history can be viewed online and contains extensive material on Arabian vertebrates

http://www.enhg.org – the website of the Emirates Natural History Group has numerous articles about Arabian vertebrates; specific subjects can be found using the excellent search facility on the site

http://www.breedingcentresharjah.com/ – on vertebrates of the Arabian Peninsula from the Breeding Centre for Arabian Wildlife, Sharjah – includes photographs

GENERAL INFORMATION ON VERTEBRATES

http://www.biology.uc.edu/faculty/jayne/videos.htm – excellent web page containing a number of short, downloadable videos showing movement characteristics of snakes and lizards

http://magma.nationalgeographic.com/ngexplorer/0703/articles/main article.html – article about animal locomotion on the National Geographic website directed at children

http://www.kidport.com/RefLib/Science/Animals/AnimalIndexV.html – well-organised basic introduction to vertebrates with links to other relevant websites

http://www.ucmp.berkeley.edu/vertebrates/vertintro.html – a more advanced introduction to vertebrates, including a large glossary

http://www.earthlife.net/begin.html – an educational website with with large sections on mammals and fish, including sharks

http://animaldiversity.ummz.umich.edu/site/accounts/information/Vertebrata.html – this is a large website with excellent information on all animal species; fairly advanced, but well written

http://www.naturegrid.org.uk/biodiversity/galindex.html – a useful website with general information about vertebrates and their ecology

http://www.big-animals.com/Vertebrates.html – 'The Longest, Largest, Tallest, Heaviest and Biggest in the Animal Kingdom' – fact-filled website with useful, easy-to-understand information on vertebrates; other sections deal with invertebrates

FOSSIL VERTEBRATES

http://www.palaeos.com/Vertebrates/default.htm – extensive website on vertebrates, including fossils; fairly advanced, but contains a large number of useful images including skeletal drawings

http://www.kidsciencelink.com/paleontology/index.html – large directory of links to palaeontology websites for young people

http://www.ucmp.berkeley.edu/vertebrates/vertfr.html – information on fossil vertebrates from the University of California Museum of Paleontology; easy to navigate

http://www.nhm.ac.uk/nature-online/life/index.html – this section of the British Museum of Natural History website contains a large amount of information on both vertebrates and invertebrates

http://animals.nationalgeographic.com/animals – numerous articles on vertebrates, including informative fact files on many species

http://www.bbc.co.uk/nature/animals/ – information about many vertebrates, including Arabian species such as oryx, dugong and turtles

FOR YOUNGER CHILDREN

http://www.enchantedlearning.com/subjects/invertebrates/ – a useful website containing a large variety of information for younger children

USEFUL IMAGES

http://nationalzoo.si.edu/Animals/AnimalIndex/ – the website of the Smithsonian National Zoological Park has many photographs of vertebrate species, as well as factual information and webcams

http://www.edupic.net – an excellent photographic resource containing free images of wildlife for teacher and student use

http://www.arkive.org/ – videos, images and fact files on a large number of animal species worlwide; new material added regularly

VERTEBRATES GLOSSARY

cartilage: strong, flexible tissue found in vertebrates – much of which is replaced by bone as the animal develops (in sharks and rays the cartilage remains throughout the animal's life)

cartilaginous: consisting of soft cartilage, rather than bones

circulatory system: the system that moves blood around the body by means of blood vessels, providing nourishment and oxygen to cells, removing waste products and fighting infection

cranium: the part of the skull that encloses and protects the brain in vertebrates

cold-blooded: referring to vertebrates that are incapable of maintaining a stable body temperature internally, relying on their surroundings to warm up or cool down

mammals: warm-blooded vertebrates that usually have body hair and sweat glands and give birth to live young that are fed with milk from the mother's **mammary glands**

mammary glands: milk-producing organs in female mammals by means of which the young are fed

warm-blooded: animals that are capable of maintaining a constant body temperature that is regulated internally, enabling the animal to cool down or produce more body heat as required

vertebrae: bony segments that collectively form the spinal column in vertebrates; often referred to as the 'backbone'

vertebrates /reptiles

arabian wildlife encyclopedia

REPTILES

The nearly 8,000 species of reptiles found worldwide are divided into four main groups: turtles; snakes, lizards and worm lizards; alligators and crocodiles; and tuataras (two species of ancient, lizard-like reptiles from New Zealand). Reptiles are found on every continent except for Antarctica, but only the first two groups listed above are still found in the wild in the Arabian Peninsula.

COLD-BLOODED

Reptiles are **ectotherms**, which means that they are unable to generate enough internal heat to maintain a constant body temperature. Their body temperature is regulated by their behaviour and surrounding conditions. Many reptiles bask in the sun in order to raise their temperature, but if it is too hot, they may burrow underground or look for a shady spot where they can cool down. If their surroundings are too cold, reptiles sometimes become lethargic and enter a hibernation-like state known as **brumation**.

SPITTING IMAGE

Young reptiles, like these recently hatched yellow-bellied house geckos, are tiny replicas of their parents when they are born. Amphibian offspring, however, look very different from adults of the same species.

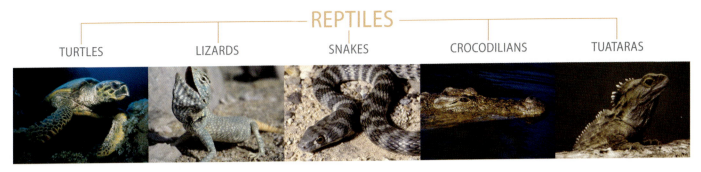

REPTILES

TURTLES LIZARDS SNAKES CROCODILIANS TUATARAS

NO NEED FOR A MOISTURISER!

Reptilian skin, with its waterproof scales, forms a barrier against evaporation. The scales are joined together by the outer layer of skin, and allow reptiles to retain moisture in their bodies and live in dry habitats, such as the desert. Reptile skin does not feel wet and slimy like that of fish or amphibians. Reptile skin is dry and scaly.

Reptile scales are composed of a protein called **keratin**, which is light, strong and flexible, and are similar to human fingernails.

The scales of snakes and lizards overlap for protection. Many snakes have wider, overlapping belly scales, which grip the ground and help them to move faster.

Turtles also have scales. The outer layer of the shell is covered with large horny scales called **scutes**. These form part of the turtle's outer layer of skin and make the shell stronger by overlapping the spaces between the shell bones. Some turtles, such as the leatherback, have no horny **scutes**. Instead they have shells covered with leathery skin. These shells are much lighter, allowing greater speed in the water.

As reptiles grow, they shed their scales and replace them with larger ones. Snakes generally shed their entire skin, but other reptiles may shed large patches of skin. In turtles and tortoises, an old scale often remains stuck to the larger new scale below it, so that their shells often show a series of growth rings.

MEET THE RELATIVES...

Dinosaurs were a varied group of reptiles that dominated the Earth for more than 150 million years. Many of them were no larger than a dog or cat. But others, such as this carnivorous *Spinosaurus*, grew to enormous proportions. Like today's reptiles, the dinosaurs had scaly skin and laid eggs. The term dinosaur means 'terrible lizard'.

TURTLES

Of the roughly 300 species of turtle worldwide, most live in ponds, lakes and rivers, while seven species make their home in the sea. Five species of sea turtle are known to occur in Arabian waters. These are the green turtle *Chelonia mydas*, the hawksbill *Eretmochelys imbricata*, the loggerhead *Caretta caretta*, the leatherback *Dermochelys coriacea*, and the olive ridley *Lepidochelys olivacea*, which is known to occur in Oman and is almost certainly a visitor to other Arabian waters. The most frequently occurring species are the green and the hawksbill, both of which nest on Arabian shores.

RUSH HOUR

About two months after the eggs are laid, tiny hatchling turtles emerge from the nest and make a dash towards the sea. Before they reach the relative safety of the open ocean, hatchlings must survive a dangerous journey across the sand and through shallow coastal waters. Many fail to escape from the armies of predators, including crabs, birds, foxes, fish and marine mammals, which prey on this periodic food source. A naturally low survival rate is reduced still further if turtle eggs are taken by humans.

EGG LAYING

Although marine turtles spend most of their life at sea, and mate at sea, they still lay their eggs on land. Females crawl out of the sea onto sandy beaches after sunset. They dig nests and lay a clutch of around 100 soft, rubbery eggs. Heat from the sand acts as an incubator and the eggs develop without the presence of either parent. Male turtles never return to land once they have left the beach where they hatched.

MAKING TRACKS

The tracks left by a nesting green turtle are easily recognisable: as the fore flippers are swept backwards together pulling the turtle along the beach, the right flipper leaves a distinct linear groove in the sand exactly opposite the left flipper, creating a series of parallel, horizontal tracks on either side of the body.

Unlike green turtles, hawksbills move along the beach by alternately sweeping the fore flippers backwards, much like a freestyle swimming stroke. The tracks left by each flipper either side of the body are therefore parallel (see photograph above), but not directly opposite each other as with the green turtle.

GREEN TURTLE *Chelonia mydas*

Smooth, rounded **carapace** (upper shell) up to 120 cm long, with four pairs of large plates (**costal scutes**) on either side; colour variable but generally dark brown with lighter patches. Head relatively small; beak blunt and rounded. Feeds on seagrass and algae.

HAWKSBILL TURTLE *Eretmochelys imbricata*

About 80 cm in length; narrow head with pointed, slightly hooked beak. Similar to young green turtle but has two pairs of plates between the eyes, compared to one in green turtle. Feeds on soft corals, sponges, ascidians and other soft-bodied animals.

LEATHERBACK TURTLE *Dermochelys coriacea*

Largest of the sea turtles. Soft skin covers shell with seven prominent ridges running length of **carapace**. Mostly black with white markings. Large, smooth head on thick, short neck; rounded beak. Feeds in open ocean, mostly on jellyfish and plankton.

LOGGERHEAD TURTLE *Caretta caretta*

Carapace usually less than 1 m. Five pairs of **costal scutes**. **Carapace** relatively flat, often light brown; leathery skin has orange tinge. Large broad head on a thick neck; beak sharply pointed but thick and solid. Feeds on crabs, shellfish and other reef animals deep on reef.

LONG DISTANCE TRAVELLERS

Many adult sea turtles migrate hundreds or even thousands of miles in order to reach feeding grounds, mating areas and nesting beaches. Relatively little is known about these ocean travels. However, satellite tracking in Arabia has shown that some of the green turtles in waters off Ra's al-Khaimah are part of a resident population, while others appear to migrate. A small number of hawksbill turtles in Abu Dhabi waters have also been tracked, and they appear to move within a generally small range within the Arabian Gulf.

LIZARDS

Lizards are the most common reptiles in Arabia. They are abundant in almost every habitat, from city to mountaintops. A wide diversity of species is represented in the Arabian Peninsula. Contrary to popular belief, none are poisonous. Most Arabian lizards are small, with the exception of the two species of *dhub* or *dhab* (spiny-tailed agamid) and the desert monitor.

Two species of dhub *or spiny-tailed lizard occur in Arabia.*

DISAPPEARING ACT

The colour and patterning of most lizards allows them to blend in well with their surroundings. For example, lizards living in the desert are often nearly the same colour as the sand, while those that live in the mountain regions may be greyish. Patterns such as stripes or spots act as a further means of blending in with the colours and textures of their habitat. This natural camouflage helps to protect them from predators.

SHOWING OFF

Some male lizards, such as the Sinai agama *Pseudotrapelus sinaitus* (left), are brightly coloured. Their colouring becomes even more intense when they are sexually aroused or angry. These lizards often take up a position on a large rock when they are defending their territory.

LIZARDS

CHAMELEONS AGAMIDS GECKOS WALL AND SAND LIZARDS SKINKS DESERT MONITOR

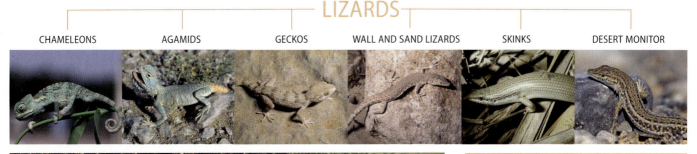

MONITOR LIZARDS

The desert monitor *Varanus griseus* is by far the largest Arabian lizard, sometimes reaching over a metre in total length. Young monitors have bold black and yellow bands, especially on the tail. Adults are more subdued in colour, but the dark bands can still be seen amongst a pattern of cream spots and mottling. Monitors have a forked tongue, prominent yellow eyes and sharp, needle-like teeth. When threatened, they inflate their bodies, hiss and lash out with the tail. They can inflict severe bites, which may become septic. They are active hunters, sometimes covering 6–8 km in a day, and have been known to swim in an attempt to prey on chicks of wading birds. They also prey on other reptiles, small mammals, birds, insects and carrion. They either dig burrows with their powerful clawed legs or use those of other animals, and are most active in the morning and late afternoon, avoiding the hottest part of the day.

AMPHISBAENIANS

Zarudnyi's worm lizard *Diplometopon zarudnyi*, is rarely seen, although it is common in sandy habitats in Arabia. Its distinctive trail of alternate swirls, left as it moves fast on the surface, is more often observed.

The name **amphisbaenian** comes from the Greek, meaning 'to walk on both sides'. Zarudnyi's worm lizard has no distinct eyes and looks rather like a plump, pinkish earthworm. It spends the day buried deep in the sand, but at night may move several hundred metres over the surface seeking its prey of insects and geckos. It has excellent hearing and smell, and is an effective predator. Worm lizards have no venom and they are quite harmless to humans.

DRASTIC MEASURES

Many lizards are able to shed their tails as an escape strategy when attacked by predators. This ability is called **autotomy**. Smaller, fast-moving lizards are more likely to shed their tails than the larger species, which often rely on strong claws, powerful teeth and thicker skin for defence. Although losing its tail may save a lizard from being eaten by a predator, the loss may hinder the lizard when it comes to catching food or finding a mate. The lost tail is regrown but may be shorter and usually has smaller scales in a more irregular pattern than the original tail.

Short-snouted lizard, *Mesalina brevirostris*

CHAMELEONS

The veiled chameleon *Chamaeleo calyptratus calyptratus* is a native Arabian lizard found in inland wadis in Yemen and southern Saudi Arabia. This hardy reptile is able to tolerate extremes in temperature. Like other chameleons, it has developed a number of characteristics that allow it to survive its preferred habitat.

USEFUL HEAD GEAR

The 'veil' refers to the enlarged helmet-like **casque** on the chamaeleon's head. It is thought to aid in directing droplets of water towards the mouth for drinking, as well as being used in threat and mating displays.

UNIQUE EYES

Chameleons are the only animals with eyes that can rotate independently of each other, as well as swivel almost 180 degrees. This allows them to look in any two directions at once, without turning the head or changing their body position. Excellent eyesight assists the chameleon in hunting and catching food.

AN AMAZING TAIL

The chameleon's strong, **prehensile** tail is another useful aid in getting around, allowing it to hold on to branches as well as to move at speed on any surface. Males also use their tails in mating rituals and displays of aggression.

STRONG GRIP

Chameleon feet are split into two parts with two toes on one side and three on the other. This allows the chameleon to maintain a strong grip around branches, allowing it to climb trees with ease.

COLOUR CHANGES

Chameleons are known for their ability to rapidly change colour. Although this characteristic allows them to blend in well with their surroundings, it is primarily a way of communicating mood, state of health, temperature and breeding status. Males are more brightly coloured than females, with vivid green, yellow, brown and blue banding along the body.

WATCH THAT TONGUE! >>

The tongue of veiled chameleons is remarkably engineered for catching prey from a distance. The **hyoid** bone launches the tongue from the mouth, then strong muscles inside the tongue propel it towards the target and back into the mouth. The sticky tip ensures that prey is securely fastened onto the tongue.

TINY REPLICAS

Female chameleons lay anything from 20 to 70 eggs, 20 to 30 days after mating. After digging a hole in moist sand, the female lays her eggs and then covers them. This is a heavy drain on her energy reserves, leaving her vulnerable to predators. As a result, females have a much shorter lifespan than males (a maximum of five years compared to eight years for males).

Baby chameleons usually hatch five to eight months after the eggs are laid. Just before hatching, the egg begins to 'sweat'. The moisture appears to send a hormonal message to the other eggs so that all the eggs hatch at the same time. The baby chameleon cuts a slit in the tough-skinned shell using a special 'egg tooth'. It may take 24 hours or more for all the baby chameleons in a clutch to emerge as tiny, bright green replicas of the adults.

AGAMIDS

Agamids, or chisel-teethed lizards, are a diverse family of lizards, superbly adapted to desert life. The family gets its common name from its specialised teeth, which are not set in sockets, as in other lizards, but are firmly fused to the jaws. Most species can change colour as part of their temperature regulation or behavioural repertoire. These lizards are active during the day.

SABKHA DWELLER
The spotted toad-headed agama *Phrynocephalus maculatus* (above) prefers hard sandy surfaces and is one of the few reptiles associated with **sabkha**.

<< ARABIAN TOAD-HEADED AGAMA
The Arabian toad-headed agama *Phrynocephalus arabicus* (see photograph below) is a small lizard of sandy habitats. It prefers warmth and is active in all but the hottest hours of the day. On cold winter days it may remain dormant. Highly adapted to life in loose sand, toad-headed agamas have fringes of long scales to keep the sand grains out of their eyes, fringes on their longest toe, and no external ear opening. The head is short with a deep forehead and snub nose. On hot days they stand high on extended legs, and limit contact with the sand by balancing on their heels and tips of their toes, using the tail as a prop. They are variable in colour with a pattern of black, white and reddish-brown markings and tend to match their background, with lizards from pale coastal sands being much paler and less patterned than those from red, inland sands. The underside of the tail has a black tip, which becomes a highly visible signal when the tail is lifted and curled.

Toad-headed agamas can sink into the sand (see photograph above) by rapidly vibrating their bodies, a process sometimes called 'shimmy burial'.

FASCINATING FACTS: LIZARD TONGUES

Many lizards, for example monitor lizards, smell with their tongues. The lizard sticks out its tongue to catch tiny particles in the air, then retracts its tongue and places the end in a small cavity in the roof of its mouth. This cavity is known as **Jacobson's organ** and contains special sensory cells that provide information about food, other lizards, or potential dangers.

SINAI AGAMA >>
The colourful Sinai agama *Pseudotrapelus sinaitus* is an inhabitant of the mountains and foothills. Males may be completely sky-blue, or can have a blue head and throat with a brown body. The ear opening is large and round. This species does not have a throat pouch.

TREE-TOP LOOKOUT

The yellow-spotted agama *Trapelus flavimaculatus* and Sinai agama *Pseudotrapelus sinaitus* are agile climbers with a 'sit and wait' hunting strategy. In the photograph above, a yellow-spotted agama watches for prey from its vantage point in an acacia tree.

This agama is easily distinguished from the Sinai agama by its heavier build, rougher scales and the presence of a throat pouch (**gular sac**), which is darkened and inflated as a threat display (see right). Like the Sinai agama, the yellow-spotted agama can develop blue colouration on the back and head, but this is mottled with cream scales, and the tail is orange.

▶▶ FOCUS ON **SPINY-TAILED LIZARDS**

Spiny-tailed lizards or *dhubs* are the largest agama lizards in Arabia. These ancient-looking reptiles, which resemble small dinosaurs, live in colonies and require firm sand, soil or soft rock in which to dig their extensive and deep burrow systems. Originally thought to be the same species throughout Arabia, there are now two species recognised, the Egyptian spiny-tailed lizard *Uromastyx aegyptia* and Thomas's spiny-tailed lizard *U. thomasi*. *Dhubs* bask at the burrow entrance, slowly changing colour from black to white and yellow as they warm up. Once warm, they may take a circular walk from the burrow, visiting shrubs to browse. They are far more active in the summer. On cooler winter days they remain inside their burrows.

SCIENTIFIC NAMES: *Uromastyx aegyptia; Uromastyx thomasi*

ARABIC NAME: *dhub*

HABITAT: gravel plains and firm sandy areas

STATUS: threatened

LENGTH: up to 65 cm

FOOD: mainly vegetation, grasses, leaves; occasionally insects

REPRODUCTION: mating takes place March–April. Eggs hatch August–September.

PREDATORS: birds of prey, foxes, desert monitor

SPOT THE DIFFERENCE

Juveniles are easy to distinguish, with *thomasi* being an overall dark grey, while *aegyptia* is lighter grey-brown with yellow bars and spots across the back.

WELL-ADAPTED

Dhubs have a very low metabolism and can survive several weeks without eating anything. These lizards may go through their entire lives without drinking a single drop of water. Most of their moisture needs are met by the rather dry and often salty plants that they eat.

REPTILE RESCUE

Dhubs have recently come under increasing pressure from development. An environmental impact study carried out in early 2005 revealed a large colony of Thomas's spiny-tailed lizards lived in the desert area proposed for expansion of the Abu Dhabi International Airport, in the path of the new runway. This survey indicated that this species was distributed over a much larger area than had previously been recognised.

Project management consultants for the airport set to work to capture the *dhubs*, in order to relocate them away from the planned development. With help from the Environment Agency Abu Dhabi (EAD), a resident ecologist and a group of volunteers, around 200 animals were trapped.

A number of radio-tagged lizards were released in the safety of a desert oilfield and their progress followed. Later, EAD arranged for most of the other animals to be released near Remah, between Abu Dhabi and Al Ain, where others of the same species were already known to be present. It is also hoped that some will be reintroduced back into protected areas within the new airport, once construction work has been completed.

GECKOS

Geckos are small lizards with broad, flattened heads and large eyes. They are well adapted to living in a variety of habitats, and can be found in tropical regions worldwide. Many geckos produce chirping or clicking sounds, and the name 'gecko' comes from the sound made by the tokay gecko from South-east Asia. Most gecko species are nocturnal (active at night). They feed on insects. Some species of gecko live close to humans, and may be seen hunting for insects on walls and under the eaves of buildings.

<< STICKY FEET

A gecko's toe pads do not use suction. Instead the undersides of the toes have special scales called **scansors** covered in up to 150,000 fine hair-like **setae**, which allow geckos to stick to surfaces. This enables them to walk on trees and steep rock faces and even to hang upside down.

The toes of leaf-toed geckos each have a pair of scansors that project beyond the claws so that the toes appear heart-shaped.

<< SAND GECKOS

This dune sand gecko *Stenodactylus doriae* is the largest species of sand gecko. It lives on fine, wind-blown sands, where it walks slowly at night, raised high off the surface on its long legs. Sand geckos have flattened toes with projecting fingers of long scales to increase the amount of surface area in contact with the loose sand.

COMMON FAN-FOOTED GECKO *Ptyodactylus hasselquistii*

This gecko is found in the mountains. Its long legs and distinctive toes make it an excellent climber on cliffs. It can often be found during the day in caves, deeply-shaded overhangs or in ruined buildings. Fan-footed geckos lay two eggs, which they glue to the rock in caves.

BANDED GROUND GECKO *Bunopus spatalurus*

This ground-dwelling gecko can be found in the mountains and gravel outwash plains. It has prominent dark cross bars and **tubercles** arranged in six continuous fine lines down the back. The tail is shorter than in other gecko species. This species is active at night.

GULF SAND GECKO *Stenodactylus khobarensis*

The Gulf sand gecko lives on *sabhka*. Like its cousin, the east sand gecko *S. leptocosymbotes*, this species has rounded toes, an adaptation for walking on firm surfaces. *Stenodactylus* species show how the toes of geckos adapt to suit the environment in which they live.

ROCK SEMAPHORE GECKO *Pristurus rupestris*

Semaphore geckos are so named because they signal to one another using their tails. Signals include curling, wagging and flicking their tails. This common species is found in mountain areas, other rocky areas and in cities, where it may sometimes be seen on walls and in gardens.

ROUGH-TAILED BOWFOOT GECKO *Cyrtopodion scabrum*

The toes of the rough-tailed bowfoot are longer than those of other ground-dwelling geckos and are distinctly kinked. There are **tubercles** on the back, along with well-defined dark spots. This species is usually found in disturbed habitats, such as in towns, oil camps and desert farms.

GROUND DWELLERS >>

The skink gecko *Teratoscincus scincus* is a large gecko that makes burrows in the sand (see above). It occurs in areas of low, undulating sand dunes and on gravel plains. This gecko has large reflective eyes, which can be seen shining in a spotlight from over 150 m away. When disturbed, the skink gecko sometimes makes a loud hissing sound by rubbing its large back and tail scales together. The skin is very fragile and can be shed as an escape strategy.

WALL AND SAND LIZARDS

There are nine recognised species of wall and sand lizards (lacertids) in Arabia. They are usually small- to medium-sized, with enlarged scales on top of the head, long, fragile tails and square or rectangular belly scales arranged in well-defined rows. They are active during the day and generally very alert and very fast.

SHADES OF BLUE

Two species of Oman lizard are found in the northern Hajar Mountains. The blue-tailed Oman lizard *Omanosaura cyanura* (left) is smaller and less frequently seen than its larger cousin. The dorsal colour of adults may be entirely electric blue, or this colour may be restricted to the tail, with the body being uniform brown (see photo on right). Juveniles have a strong pattern of black and cream longitudinal stripes, though they too have a long blue tail. This species lays clutches of three eggs at intervals of roughly three weeks.

<< LARGE HUNTER

Jayakar's Oman lizard *Omanosaura jayakari* is easily identified by its large size (up to 200 mm long excluding the tail) and small blue or grey spots. It is an active hunter in mountain wadis and hillsides, where it is quite common.

Acanthodactylus haasi

A. haasi is a sand dweller with well-developed toe fringes. Its pale colours and markings provide excellent camouflage in the desert environment in which it lives. The tail is yellow in juveniles. This species is the only fringe-toed lizard that is known to regularly climb in small shrubs.

FRINGE-TOED LIZARDS

Arabia has a number of fringe-toed lizards, belonging to the genus *Acanthodactylus*. All of them are active during the day. Colour patterns are variable and tend to change with age.

BOSK'S FRINGE-TOED LIZARD *A. boskianus*

A relatively large (up to 95 mm) fringe-toed lizard, *A. boskianus* has a very rough appearance due to the raised scales on its back. Its colouring and texture make it inconspicuous among the gravel outwash plains from the Hajar Mountains, the habitat in which it has been observed.

SNAKE-TAILED FRINGE-TOED LIZARD *A. opheodurus*

The snake-tailed fringe-toed lizard is comparatively small (65 mm) with a particularly long tail. Its colouring is tinged with red when immature. Sightings have been reported from the hard sandy plains near Al Ain, where it is locally abundant. It is also known as the spiny-footed lizard.

Schmidt's fringe-toed lizard Acanthodactylus schmidti (main photo) is one of Arabia's commonest species of fringe-toed lizard. It is found in sand sheets and dunes, wherever there is enough vegetation to support its burrow systems and insect prey. It has highly-developed scale fringes on their toes to help it move on soft sand. Schmidt's fringe-toed lizard has a pattern of small pale spots, and never has longitudinal stripes, even when young.

HADRAMAUT SAND LIZARD *Mesalina adramitana*

Closely related to the fringe-toed lizards, the Hadramaut sand lizard is found on firmer sand sheets and gravel plains. The short-snouted sand lizard *M. brevirostris* (see photo on page 127, bottom right) is more mottled in appearance, and is found in coastal regions.

SKINKS

Skinks form one of the largest families of lizards, with over 600 species known worldwide. At least five species are recorded in Arabia. Skinks have very short legs and a cylindrical body covered with smooth, shiny scales. The head is cone-shaped with a pointed snout and small eyes. Skinks are extremely fast and capable of disappearing vertically into the sand.

BODY ARMOUR
Scales overlap strongly and are underlaid with bony plates, giving skinks' bodies protection from predators and a rigidity that suits their burrowing habits.

The tessellated skink Mabuya tessellata lives in the wadis and loose rocks of the Hajar Mountains and their foothills.

SNAKE EYES
The Asian snake-eyed skink *Ablepharus pannonicus*, (shown below) lives in the mountains. This small and secretive skink lacks eyelids and has slender, but well-developed limbs. It may have cream and dark longitudinal stripes down its body. It is usually only glimpsed as a silvery shape darting into dense cover.

<< SECRETIVE

The ocellated skink *Chalcides ocellatus* is a brown skink of gardens and farms, found mainly in coastal regions of Arabia. It has been recorded in inland localities in Oman and at Al Ain, although it may have colonised these areas with the spread of agriculture. Secretive, ocellated skinks burrow in leaf litter, but in suitable habitat they can easily be found by turning over rocks and bits of wood. They are typical skinks with shiny scales and small limbs. The back has a pattern of black and white scales forming the 'eyes' that give the species its common name.

DESERT SWIMMER >>

Perhaps best-known and most often seen skink is the aptly named eastern sandfish *Scincus mitranus*. This handsome lizard dives beneath the sand surface and 'swims' through the sand. When there is no perceived danger from predators, sandfish move across the surface of the dunes. Sandfish are superbly adapted to their habitat, with highly-polished skin and a streamlined, chisel-shaped snout to reduce drag. The body and tail base are thick and muscular. The mouth is recessed and the ear openings are small, although these lizards have excellent hearing, used to locate insects such as beetle larvae moving below the surface. Sandfish have a golden-pink colour, with each scale edged in black. A series of golden bars or crescents run down the sides of the back, with a further row of dark bars on the flanks.

SNAKES

Snakes are highly evolved reptiles that are found in a wide variety of habitats on every continent except Antarctica. There are around 50 species of snakes in Arabia (see page 148 for information on sea snakes). A number of these are dangerously venomous, while some others have relatively mild venom. Although cases of snake bite are rare, it is wise to remember that there are dangerous snakes in most parts of the region.

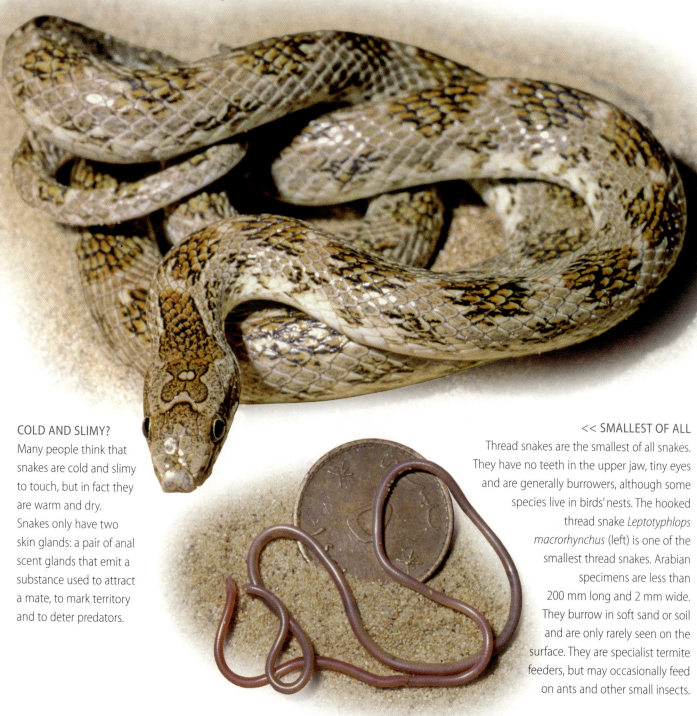

COLD AND SLIMY?

Many people think that snakes are cold and slimy to touch, but in fact they are warm and dry. Snakes only have two skin glands: a pair of anal scent glands that emit a substance used to attract a mate, to mark territory and to deter predators.

<< SMALLEST OF ALL

Thread snakes are the smallest of all snakes. They have no teeth in the upper jaw, tiny eyes and are generally burrowers, although some species live in birds' nests. The hooked thread snake *Leptotyphlops macrorhynchus* (left) is one of the smallest thread snakes. Arabian specimens are less than 200 mm long and 2 mm wide. They burrow in soft sand or soil and are only rarely seen on the surface. They are specialist termite feeders, but may occasionally feed on ants and other small insects.

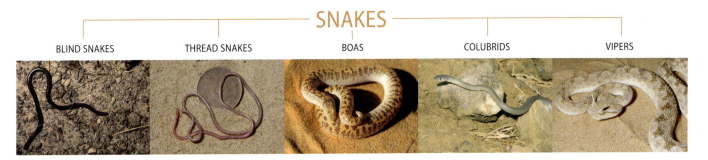

SNAKES

| BLIND SNAKES | THREAD SNAKES | BOAS | COLUBRIDS | VIPERS |

LOCOMOTION

Although snakes have no legs, they are able to move with amazing speed, using their muscles and scales. There are four basic ways in which snakes move around:

a) **Serpentine:** the most common form of movement allows the snake to move at maximum speed. The snake's muscles relax and contract to produce an 's' shape.

b) **Side-winding:** a method used to move across loose, hot sand. The snake contracts its muscles to lift and fling its body, creating an 's' shaped sideways movement.

c) **Rectilinear:** a slower type of movement in which the snake contracts its body in up and down curves rather than side to side, using its belly scales to push against the ground.

d) **Concertina:** a method used for climbing. The snake grips the surface using the belly scales and contracts the muscles to form a series of horizontal loops; the body then straightens and springs forward.

a

b

c

d

A REPRODUCTION RARITY

BLIND SNAKES are small, harmless reptiles that look more like dark, shiny earthworms than snakes. Unlike earthworms, blind snakes ares not segmented and cannot increase or decrease their body length. The eyes are small, dark dots, with a covering of semi-transparent scales.

No male blind snake has ever been recorded. Females lay small clutches of unfertilised, thin-shelled eggs that hatch into miniature snakes, all of which are females. This way of reproducing is called **parthenogenesis** and also occurs in some species of lizards.

The blind snake *Ramphotyphlops braminus* has probably been introduced into Arabia in imported garden soil. It is also known as the 'flowerpot snake' due to its habit of burrowing in soft, moist garden soil.

SNAKE EGGS

Most snakes lay eggs that have soft and leathery shells. Unlike birds' eggs, which have a hard, relatively watertight shell, snake eggshells allow liquids and gases to pass through, making the eggs susceptible to drying out.

Some snakes keep their eggs inside the body in a string of membranous sacs until they are developed enough to hatch. Although this method lessens the dangers of exposure to predators and fluctuating temperatures for the babies, it is more difficult for the mother. With a larger body, her movements become slower and more awkward, making her more vulnerable to predation.

Most female snakes abandon their babies shortly after hatching, but those that give birth to live young may remain with their offspring for a time.

When they are ready to hatch, baby snakes use their egg tooth to break out of their shell, after which this special tooth falls off. A baby may stay in its shell for several days before moving to another location.

<< SHEDDING

Since snakes continue to grow throughout their lives, they periodically shed their skin. Prior to shedding, a snake will become less active, the skin appears dull and the eyes cloud over as a layer of fluid builds up under the old skin. The snake may rub against a rough surface to help the shedding process, which begins at the head and progresses to the tail.

<< GROOVED FANGS

The Schokari sand racer *Psammophis schokari* has a pair of non-venomous fang-like teeth in the upper jaw near the front edge of the eye, and one or two pairs of strongly enlarged and grooved venomous fangs at the rear edge of the eye. Lizards, small birds, rodents and other snakes are caught, chewed to inject with the venom, which immobilises them, and then swallowed head first. The venom is not considered dangerous to humans.

PILING ON THE PRESSURE

Since they lack venom, members of the boa family kill their prey by constriction. This sand boa is coiling its body around a gecko. When the lizard exhales, the boa tightens its grip so that its victim cannot take another breath.

The sand boa Eryx jayakari is the only true constrictor in Arabia. Active at night, this snake is seldom seen, but its tracks are a common sight in areas of sand sheets and dunes. Its shape is suited for burrowing and moving through soft sand, the chisel-shaped snout, recessed mouth, protected nostrils and highly-polished scales all reducing friction under the sand. With its eyes located on top of its head, the sand boa can remain submerged in the sand and still observe surface prey, which includes geckos and possibly worm lizards.

EXPANDABLE JAWS

A snake's jaws are specially adapted to enable the animal to swallow prey that is larger than itself. In mammals, the upper jaw is fused to the skull and cannot move independently. In snakes, however, the upper jaw is attached by ligaments, muscles and tendons, allowing much greater movement. The upper and lower jaw are connected by means of a quadrate bone, which provides a double hinge, allowing the lower jaw to open very wide when swallowing large prey. The sides of the jawbones are connected by muscle tissue rather than being fused together at the front, resulting in even more flexibility.

CAMOUFLAGE

As this photograph of the Persian horned viper shows, the colouration and texture of many snakes provide superb camouflage in their natural surroundings.

COLUBRIDS

The colubrid family is by far the largest of the snake families, including about 70 per cent of all snake species. Most species, including those found in Arabia, are harmless to humans. Colubrids with venom are rear-fanged, and inject venom using a pair or cluster of teeth around the middle of the jaw. Some species found in Arabia have mildly toxic venom.

<< COBRA-LIKE BEHAVIOUR

The hooded malpolon *Malpolon moilensis* is a fast-moving snake with a chequered pattern and large, hooded eyes with round pupils and orange or red irises. The head has a pointed snout, that protrudes over the mouth. There are poison sacs and one or two very large grooved fangs situated just behind the eye, but this snake is not considered dangerous to humans. When disturbed the hooded malpolon lifts the front third of its body off the surface, holds it at an angle of 45° to the ground and spreads a hood, giving rise to reports of 'cobras' being seen. Found in gravel and stony deserts, sandy coastal regions and cultivated areas, it is apparently absent from pure sand deserts and mountains.

FAST MOVER >>

The Schokari sand racer *Psammophis schokari* is a thin, fast-moving snake that is active during the day. It is relatively common in well-vegetated areas, especially among trees and shrubs. An excellent climber, it is able to catch birds in trees. It is also found in sand and gravel areas with low shrubs and grasses, and occurs from sea level to mountain summits.

SCHOKARI SAND RACER *Psammophis schokari*

Up to 150 cm long, with a distinct neck. Large eye with round pupil surrounded by pale yellow ring and golden-brown iris. Body pattern is variable but generally longitudinal cream and dark stripes on olive or tan background. Venom from this species is not considered dangerous to humans.

WADI RACER *Platyceps rhodorachis*

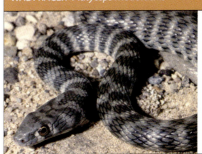

Up to 1 m. Highly variable in colour, from dark greenish-grey with black speckling, giving a banded appearance, to almost unmarked dull tan. In all colour phases, dark markings become indistinct towards tail. Cream coloured bars in front of and behind eyes in both patterned and unmarked individuals.

ARABIAN CAT SNAKE *Telescopus dhara*

Widespread in Arabia. Up to 113 cm long. Large eyes with vertically elliptical pupil and opaque greenish-grey or reddish-brown iris. Overall colour is pinkish brown with highly-variable dark markings. Excellent climber. Hunts at night, preying on birds, bats and geckos. Mildly poisonous.

DIADEM SNAKE *Spalerosophis diadema cliffordii*

Usually less than 1 m. Heavier body than other racers. Back has a series of dark olive spots, often edged in white, on paler sandy-beige base. Usually has dark band (the diadem) running across the head between eyes. Voracious feeder on rodents; young ones feed on small lizards. Has no venom.

WADI RACER >>

The range of the wadi racer includes North Africa, Arabia and south-western Asia. Though usually found in wadis with permanent water, it can also live in dry desert regions and on mountain-sides. It is fast, agile and are able to climb with ease on to near-vertical rock faces. Wadi racers have no fangs, but their saliva may have a mildly toxic effect. In wet wadis, these snakes are often semi-aquatic and hunt for fish and tadpoles. A favourite retreat is in small crevices just above the water level. In Oman, they have been observed feeding on fish on rocky seashores.

VIPERS

The vipers are a major group of venomous snakes, which are found worldwide, with the exception of Madagascar, Australia and Antarctica. Vipers have a pair of shortened upper jaw bones, each of which has a single, long, hollow fang. There are usually one or more replacement fangs on each side, which move into position when the originals are broken or shed. Viper venom affects the blood and blood vessels.

   In the Arabian species, the upper side of the head is covered with small, overlapping scales, and the pupil contracts to a vertical slit in bright light. They are usually active at dusk and during the night. Heavier-bodied than the other snake families, vipers rely on various ambush techniques and a lightning-fast strike to catch their prey. Once envenomed, the prey is usually released to die. The viper then follows the scent trail to its meal.

CARPET VIPER *Echis coloratus*

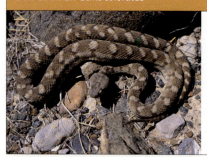

Maximum 70 cm in length; slightly stockier and a little more colourful than *E. carinatus* (see bottom of page). A separate species within the same complex, *E. omanensis*, has only recently been recognised as occurring in the rocky mountain wadis and hillsides of the UAE and northern Oman.

PERSIAN HORNED VIPER *Pseudocerastes persicus persicus*

Widespread in Iraq, Iran and Pakistan. Restricted to higher altitudes in northern Oman mountains and also reported from Jebel Hafit and Ru'us al-Jibal in the UAE. Will sometimes climb into small bushes. Medium-sized, with thick body and prominent multi-scaled horns above the eyes.

POWERFUL POISON

Although small (up to 60 cm long), the Sind saw-scaled viper *Echis carinatus sochureki* (see picture below) is a dangerous snake with powerful venom. It strikes quickly with very little provocation. When threatened, it forms a series of c-shaped coils that are rubbed against each other in opposite directions, producing a loud rasping warning hiss. Its preferred habitat is sand or sandy gravel plains, but it also occurs in cultivated areas.

   In Arabia, the Sind saw-scaled viper is confined to northern Oman and the northern lowlands of the UAE, as far south as Abu Dhabi.

<< SIDE-WINDING TRACKS

The Arabian horned viper *Cerastes gasparettii gasparettii* (top right) is found throughout the sandy deserts of Arabia from the eastern edge of the Sinai peninsula, and north-eastwards to Iraq and western Iran. Its distinctive tracks are more often seen than the animal itself. Some individuals bear a pair of 'horns' made of single, enlarged scales above the eyes. The keeled lateral scales (top left) can be rubbed together to create a loud, rasping warning. Although nocturnal, horned vipers may bask on winter days. They feed on rodents, lizards and birds.

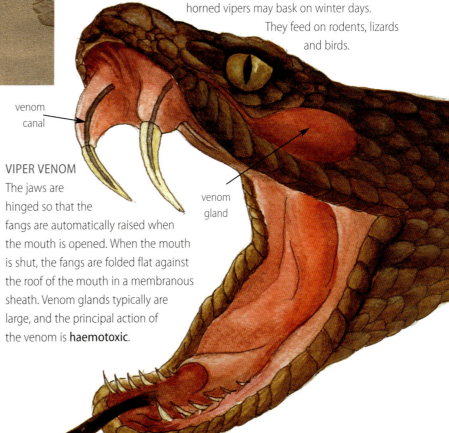

venom canal

VIPER VENOM
The jaws are hinged so that the fangs are automatically raised when the mouth is opened. When the mouth is shut, the fangs are folded flat against the roof of the mouth in a membranous sheath. Venom glands typically are large, and the principal action of the venom is **haemotoxic**.

venom gland

FIRST AID NOTES

Viper bites are rarely fatal in Arabia. In exceptional cases where death has occurred, this has resulted from delayed or inappropriate medical intervention. The recommended first aid advice is to reassure the patient, immobilise the bite site (usually a leg or arm) with a firmly applied bandage and splint, and take the victim to the nearest hospital. Do NOT cut or suck the wound, apply a tourniquet, or give aspirin or spirits. Attempting to kill the snake is not recommended as this may result in further injury. Vipers, striking defensively, often do not inject venom.

SEA SNAKES

Sea snakes occur throughout the Arabian sea area in both the Arabian Gulf and the Gulf of Oman. Nine species have been recorded. They are excellent swimmers and the laterally flattened tail makes them easily recognisable and distinguishes them from eels, such as the harmless yellow and black banded snake eels that often feed in sandy seabeds, but are rarely seen on the surface alive. Sea snakes are most abundant in the warm, shallow seas of the Arabian Gulf, where they are frequently seen resting motionless on the sea's surface.

STRANDED

The unique colouring of the yellow-bellied sea snake (above) is easily recognised: a dark brown back with pale yellow sides and underside. The tail is black with a bold, diamond-shaped pattern. This species is most plentiful in clear, warm, shallow water in both the Arabian Gulf and the Gulf of Oman.

Sea snakes do not cope well out of water and, since the skin provides insufficient waterproofing, stranded sea snakes may die from dehydration.

WHICH SNAKE IS WHICH?

The striking bright yellow and black bands of the Arabian Gulf sea snake *Hydrophis lapemoides* (opposite page, lower right) has a seemingly unmistakable appearance, but in fact it can easily be confused with a number of other species. The annulated sea snake *H. cyanocynctus* (pictured above) is very similar and both the yellow sea snake *H. spiralis* and Shaw's sea snake *Lapemis curtus* (below) could be mistaken for either. The first two are generally fairly large and bulky, reaching lengths of more than 1 m, but not as large as the yellow sea snake, which can easily exceed 2 m. Confusingly, the colour varies among them from yellow to green to grey and the black banding is also variable in extent and shade. In Shaw's sea snake the bands often take on a rough diamond shape, thicker over the spine and converging to points on the sides.

ARE THEY DANGEROUS?

Sea snakes are the most venomous of the world's snakes. One drop of sea snake venom is reputed to have the potency to kill five men. This high toxicity enables them to disable their cold-blooded prey, such as fish, crabs and squid, on which they feed. Even young sea snakes, which are born live at sea, have a venom as potent as any adult.

People are rarely bitten by sea snakes, which appear to be very docile. Fishermen are sometimes struck, having unintentionally angered a sea snake by hauling one into a boat in a fishing net. One of the first signs of the venom acting on a victim is a difficulty in breathing and swallowing, aching muscles and drooping eyelids. Although undoubtedly very dangerous, sea snakes, like all snakes, do not necessarily inject venom at each bite and symptoms of shock are often misidentified as serious snake bite cases.

BABIES GALORE

All sea snakes give birth to live young and generally produce clutches of between three and nine relatively large babies. The beaked sea snake *Enhydrina schistosa* is an exception, producing larger clutches averaging about 18, but sometimes up to 30 offspring. The photograph above shows two beaked sea snakes mating.

ADAPTED FOR LIFE UNDER WATER

Sea snakes are the most completely marine of all reptiles existing today. They never voluntarily come out of the water, and live, reproduce, feed and die at sea. Like terrestrial snakes, all sea snakes have scales, but they lack expanded belly scales and the ability to move on land. Sea snakes have valved nostrils, which close when the snake is under water. Their body form is variable. Fish-eating species usually have a shape similar to that of terrestrial snakes, but those that feed on burrowing eels have small heads and forebodies, with large, deep hind bodies up to ten times the diameter of the head and neck.

>> LEARN MORE : USEFUL WEBSITES

GENERAL INFORMATION ON REPTILES

http://www.stlzoo.org/animals/abouttheanimals/reptiles/ - reptile section of the website of St Louis Zoo

http://www.whozoo.org/ZooPax/ZPScales.htm – interesting information on reptile scales from Fort Worth Zoo

http://animal.discovery.com/guides/reptiles/reptiles.html – information on reptiles from the Discovery Channel website

INFORMATION ON ARABIAN REPTILES

http://www.uaeinteract.com/nature/reptile/index.asp – descriptions of snakes and lizards found on the Arabian Peninsula

http://www.uaeinteract.com/uaeint_misc/pdf_2009/The-Emirates-A-Natural-History/ – online version of *The Emirates – A Natural History* including extensive section on Arabian reptiles, beginning on page 229

http://www.enhg.org/bulletin/reptiles.htm – information from the Emirates Natural History Group

http://www.enhg.org/alain/resources/articles/uae_snakes/uae_snak.htm – *Land Snakes of the UAE and Surrounds*, article from the Emirates Natural History group

http://www.alshindagah.com/march99/arabianwildlife.htm – article on snakes found in the UAE and the Arabian Gulf region

http://www.wildlifeextra.com/go/news/seasnakes_abudhabi.html#cr – article about sea snakes in the Abu Dhabi region, including interesting general facts on sea snakes

TURTLES

http://www.seaturtle.org/mtn/ – Marine Turtle newsletter

http://www.worldwildlife.org/turtles/ – series of informative pages from the WWF; includes conservation and species details. See also: http://www.panda.org/what_we_do/endangered_species/marine_turtles/

http://www.mcsuk.org/marineworld/turtles/the+marine+turtles info – information on all turtle species from the Marine Conservation Society

http://www.arkive.org/green-turtle/chelonia-mydas/video-09e.html?movietype=rpMed – excellent BBC video footage of green turtles hatching (a number of other videos of turtles are also available at the Arkive website)

http://www.mcsuk.org/marineworld/adopt-a-turtle/turtle+adoption – Marine Conservation Society's adopt-a-turtle page

http://www.starfish.ch/reef/marine-turtles.html – descriptions and drawings of the seven species of marine turtle

LIZARDS

http://www.arabianwildlife.com/current/dhub.html – article from Arabian Wildlife magazine

http://ladywildlife.com/animal/howlizardslosetheirtails.html – detailed information on how lizards lose their tails – part of a larger website on endangered wildlife

SNAKES

http://animal.discovery.com/guides/reptiles/snakes/anatomy.html – information on snake anatomy and physiology from the Discovery Channel website

http://www.arabianwildlife.com/archive/vol3.1/snake.htm – article on the more common Arabian snakes

rah-orac.org/yahoo_site.../Venomous_Crawlies.31142107.pdf – single page, downloadable PDF on first aid for venomous snake bites

SEA SNAKES

http://www.seasnakes.info/ – website dedicated to information on sea snakes (Australia-based, but of general interest)

IMAGES

http://www.starfish.ch/collection/reptiles.html – photos of sea snakes and marine turtles

http://www.arkive.org – use the search facility on the home page of this extensive website to find numerous still images and videos of marine reptiles

REPTILES GLOSSARY

amphisbaenian: from the Greek meaning 'to walk on both sides' – worm lizard; a worm-like, usually legless relative of lizards and snakes

autotomy: from Greek *auto* meaning 'self', *tomy* meaning 'severing' – ability to shed various body parts, including skin, when attacked

brumation: state of semi-hibernation in some reptiles, brought about by cold temperatures

carapace: hard, upper shell of a turtle, which is made up of fused bony plates

casque: helmet-like crest protruding from the top of the head of some chameleon species

ectotherm: a cold-blooded animal that is unable to regulate its own internal body temperature

gular sac: throat pouch present in some lizard species (see agamids on page 131)

haemotoxic: containing a toxin that destroys red blood cells

Jacobson's organ: sensory organ in the roof of the mouth of some vertebrates, including snakes, that allows the animal to smell and taste

keratin: tough, fibrous protein found in hair, nails, horns, hooves and reptile scales

parthenogenesis: a form of reproduction in which an egg develops without having been fertilised by a male

sabkha: flat, salt-encrusted desert

scansors: special **setae**-covered scales on the undersides of gecko toes that allow the animals to stick to vertical surfaces or even to hang upside down

scute: one of the bony plates making up a turtle's shell

setae (singular seta): from Latin for 'bristle'; hair-like structures found on gecko footpads

vertebrates/amphibians

arabian wildlife encyclopedia

AMPHIBIANS

Amphibians include frogs, toads, newts, **salamanders** and
. The name 'amphibian' means 'dual life'. Most
amphibians lay their eggs in fresh water, where the
juvenile stage (tadpole) develops. Since the skin of most
amphibians provides little protection against drying out,
the majority live in or near ponds, streams or other moist
places. Some, however, have adapted to drier, more
seasonal habitats. In the Arabian Peninsula, only frogs and
toads are present and nine species are known, of which
six are found only in Arabia.

MALE CHORUS >>
Male toads 'sing' to
attract females during
the mating season by
inflating a sac in the
throat like a balloon and
forcing air across the
vocal cords.

WHAT'S THE DIFFERENCE?

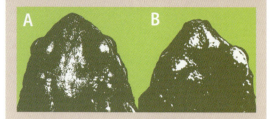

A   B

The Arabian and Dhofar toads are very similar
in appearance but they can be reliably
distinguished by careful attention to several
features:

a) The eardrum (**tympanum**) of the Dhofar
toad is large and prominent. It is nearly the
size of the eye socket. In the Arabian toad it
is only about half or two-thirds the
diameter of the eye and less prominent.

b) From above, the snout of the Arabian toad
(A) is more rounded than that of the Dhofar
toad (B). The Dhofar toad has a broader
nasal bridge and more vertical 'cheeks' than
the Arabian toad.

c) Viewed from the side, the front edge of the
Arabian toad's snout is vertical or rounded,
whereas the snout of the Dhofar toad slopes
backwards from the tip, just below the
nostrils, to the lower jaw.

d) The staccato *kra-kra-kra* mating call of the
Dhofar toad is easily distinguished from the
prolonged *krrraaaa* of the Arabian toad,
which has been compared to the sound of a
creaking hinge.

<< DHOFAR TOAD
The Dhofar toad *Bufo dhufarensis* is
less commonly observed than the
Arabian toad *B. arabicus*. Its
distribution in habitats that are some
distance from water suggests that
it must be able to breed
successfully even in
puddles and potholes.

AMPHIBIANS

FROGS   TOADS   NEWTS   SALAMANDERS   CAECILIANS

LIFE CYCLE

In or near permanent water, breeding occurs year round, as shown by the presence of black, pearl-like strings of toad eggs in rocky pools, cisterns and *falaj* channels. Both the Arabian and Dhofar toads lay large numbers of eggs on the chance that at least a couple will reach adulthood and breed again.

Toad eggs develop into tadpoles, which live exclusively under water and breathe through gills instead of lungs.

The Arabian toad Bufo arabicus *is normally found in or near water. Although it is active by day as well as by night, it seeks shelter in damp, shady spots in the heat of the day.*

Tadpoles change into small toads in a process called **metamorphosis***, during which they develop legs and lungs, and lose their tail. In places where pools dry up quickly, tadpoles must develop rapidly.*

FROGS AND TOADS – WHAT'S THE DIFFERENCE?

Toads and frogs belong to the same order or group of amphibians and have many characteristics in common. Toads are, in fact, frogs that belong to one particular family called Bufonidae or 'true toads'. There are a number of ways in which true toads usually differ from other frogs:

FROGS	TOADS
moist, smooth skin	dry, bumpy skin
live mainly in or near water	live mainly on land
slender body	wide, stocky body
long hind legs	short hind legs
webbed hind feet	hind feet not webbed
eggs laid in clusters	eggs laid in strings

AMPHIBIANS: FASCINATING FACTS

- Amphibians evolved more than 350 million years ago. As the first land vertebrates, amphibians form an evolutionary link between fish and reptiles.

- Unlike most land vertebrates, which respire (breathe) only by means of lungs, the majority of amphibians also respire through their skin.

- The skin of amphibians is **permeable** (allows water to pass through), making them susceptible to dehydration, particularly in hot, arid habitats, such as deserts.

- Many amphibian species use camouflage to blend in with their surroundings as a means of defence.

- A few poisonous species are brightly coloured as a warning to predators.

- Amphibians are **ectotherms**.

- The amphibian diet is very varied and includes many types of invertebrates, such as slugs, insects and spiders.

>> LEARN MORE : USEFUL WEBSITES

GENERAL INFORMATION ON AMPHIBIANS

http://www.amphibiaweb.org/declines/ – information on the worldwide decline of amphibian species, the causes and what can be done to save them

http://www.sandiegozoo.org/animalbytes/a-amphibians.html – general amphibian information page with links to more specific information on frogs, toads, salamanders, newts and caecilians

INFORMATION ON ARABIAN AMPHIBIANS

http://www.geocities.com/jaffacity/Arabian_Amphibians.html – information about Arabian amphibian species found in Arabia's Wildlife Centre, Sharjah

FROGS AND TOADS

http://www.arkive.org/arabian-toad/bufo-arabicus/info.html – Arabian toad fact sheet and images

http://www.frogs.org/getinfo/index.asp – informative website on all types of amphibians, with links to other relevant websites

http://www.hamline.edu/cgee/frogs/science/frogfact.html – useful fact sheet about frogs

INFORMATION FOR YOUNGER CHILDREN

http://www.enchantedlearning.com/subjects/amphibians/frogs.shtml – information, diagrams, worksheets, activities and printouts on frogs and toads; good resource for teachers of younger children

http://www.zoomwhales.com/coloring/amphibians.shtml – lots of information, diagrams, printouts and activity pages

OTHER AMPHIBIANS

http://www.sandiegozoo.org/animalbytes/t-caecilian.html – informative page of facts about caecilians

http://www.sandiegozoo.org/animalbytes/t-salamander.html – facts and images of salamanders and newts

CONSERVATION

http://www.amphibianark.org/whoweare.htm – website devoted to the conservation of amphibian species worldwide

http://www.iucnredlist.org/amphibians – a global assessment of amphibians conducted by the IUCN, including lists of threatened species and major threats to survival

AMPHIBIANS GLOSSARY

amphibians: animals that begin life as larvae in water but live on land and in water as adults

tympanum: in frogs, the eardrum disc located behind each eye, with which the frog hears

caecilian: tropical amphibians with a worm-like appearance (not present in Arabia)

ectotherm: a cold-blooded animal; an animal that is unable to internally regulate its own body temperature

metamorphosis: the process by which frogs and toads change their appearance and body structure from that of tadpole to adult

salamanders: a group of amphibians that are characterised by short legs, a slender body and a long tail (not present in Arabia)

permeable: (in reference to amphibian skin) allowing substances, particularly fluids, to pass through with relative ease

ertebrates /fish

arabian wildlife encyclopedia

FISH

Fish form the largest group of animals with backbones, but they are divided into four classes that are only distantly related to each other: two classes of jawless fish (lampreys and hagfish) with sucker-like mouths, bony fish and **cartilaginous** fish. Fish are well-adapted for life in an aquatic environment and are found in both fresh water and salt water. The Arabian Peninsula is surrounded by bodies of water on three sides. The Arabian Gulf, the Gulf of Oman, the Arabian Sea, the Gulf of Aden and the Red Sea each have varying characteristics, such as **salinity** and water depth, which provide habitats for different species of fish.

FISH ANATOMY

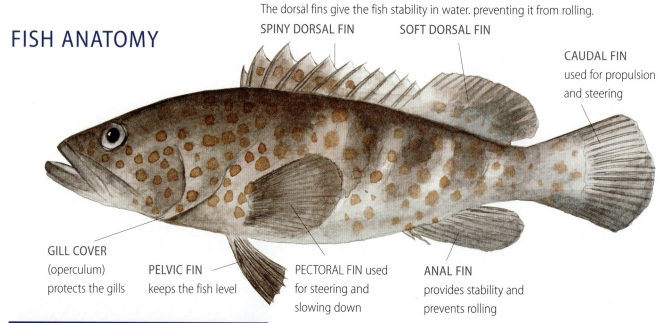

The dorsal fins give the fish stability in water. preventing it from rolling.

SPINY DORSAL FIN

SOFT DORSAL FIN

CAUDAL FIN
used for propulsion
and steering

GILL COVER
(operculum)
protects the gills

PELVIC FIN
keeps the fish level

PECTORAL FIN used
for steering and
slowing down

ANAL FIN
provides stability and
prevents rolling

HOW FISH BREATHE

Fish breathe by taking oxygen from the surrounding water. As the fish opens its mouth, the outer cover of the gills (**operculum**) closes, drawing water into the mouth. The water then passes through a filter system called the **gill rakers**, where food and other particles are removed. As the filtered water passes over the gills, oxygen from the water enters the blood circulating through the feathery **gill filaments** and **lamellae**, from where it is carried to the rest of the body. Waste carbon dioxide in the bloodstream – formed as the oxygen breaks down food for fuel – passes into the water and is carried out of the body through the gill slits.

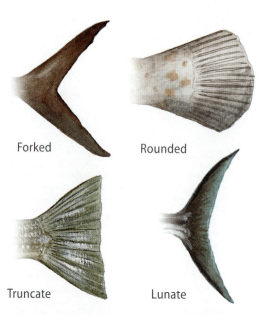

Forked

Rounded

Truncate

Lunate

TAIL SHAPES
The tail fin (**caudal fin**) helps fish to move through the water and the shape indicates how the fish moves. Fish with forked tail fins usually swim continuously, while those with a **lunate** tail fin are able to swim rapidly over long distances. Fish with **truncate** or rounded tail fins tend to move more slowly but have enough power to swim steadily over long distances.

COMPARISONS BETWEEN BONY FISH AND SHARKS

	BONY FISH	SHARKS
SKELETON	bones and cartilage	cartilage only
GILLS	gill cover over gill slits	gill slits but no gill cover
SKIN	smooth overlapping scales	rough, plate-like scales with thorny projections
BUOYANCY	gas-filled swim bladder	no swim bladder
REPRODUCTION	eggs usually fertilised in water	eggs fertilised within female's body

Some species look after their offspring after they hatch, such as these clownfish protecting their eggs from predators.

REPRODUCTION

BONY FISH

There is considerable variation in the way that bony fish reproduce. In most species there are male and female individuals, whilst some others are **hermaphrodites** (one individual produces both sperm and eggs). In a few species, individuals change sex at some stage during their lifetime.

Some females release their eggs into the water, where they are fertilised by a male, but in other species the male and female mate and the eggs are fertilised inside the female. The offspring may be released into the water as fertilised eggs, larvae, juvenile fish or, in some instances, as mature adult fish.

SHARKS

Fertilisation in sharks always take place within the female, but once the egg is fertilised it may develop in a variety of ways. Some remain in the mother's body, receiving oxygen and nutrients from her until she gives birth to a fully developed baby shark (**viviparity**). Others remain in the mother's body, but without direct nourishment from the mother, relying instead on the egg's yolk sac, or in some cases, on other eggs (**ovoviviparity**).

Other sharks lay eggs in tough leathery cases (see photo at right) and attach them to seaweed or rocks, where they remain until the baby shark hatches (**oviparity**).

BODY SHAPES

The shape of a fish's body influences how it moves in the water and how it catches food. Fish with a long, streamlined shape are fast swimmers and actively hunt their prey, whilst fish with shorter, stouter bodies usually lie in wait until the prey approaches.

Flat-bodied fish are ideally suited for life on a sandy seabed where they blend in with the surroundings while lying in wait for prey.

The sunfish Mola mola *has no scales.*

A MATTER OF SCALES

Fish scales are a form of body protection. The size and weight of them varies between species. Fast swimmers usually have smaller, lighter scales that allow greater freedom of movement. Fish with larger, heavier scales move more slowly, but have greater protection.

Most scales are flat and thin, but those of sharks and a few other cartilaginous fish resemble teeth and are called denticles. Flat-bodied cartilaginous fish such as rays and skates have far fewer denticles than sharks do.

Some bony fish, including the sunfish (left) have no scales at all, whilst others, such as the puffers and porcupine fish have moveable spines, which are actually modified scales. A few fish, such as the pipe-fish and the sea horses, have sacrificed speed and agility in favour of greater protection: their scales have become modified into armour-like bony plates.

SHARKS

There are more than 350 species of these ancient vertebrates in the world's oceans. Fossil records of their evolution can be traced back about 400 million years. More than 40 species are found in Arabian waters. Unlike bony fish, sharks have skeletons made of cartilage, a more elastic material than bone, which enables them to bend and turn with ease. They differ in other ways as well, including their reproductive methods, digestive system, sensory mechanisms, skin composition and ways of maintaining buoyancy in the water.

SHARK ANATOMY

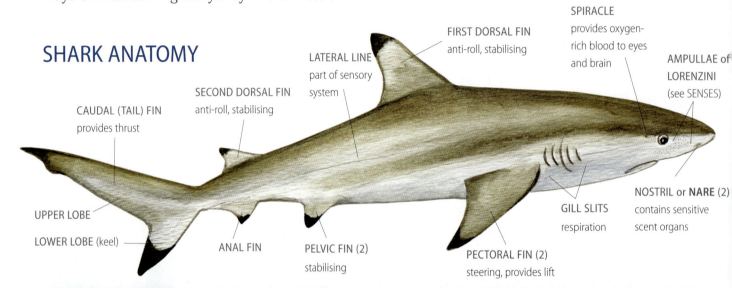

FIRST DORSAL FIN
anti-roll, stabilising

LATERAL LINE
part of sensory system

SECOND DORSAL FIN
anti-roll, stabilising

CAUDAL (TAIL) FIN
provides thrust

SPIRACLE
provides oxygen-rich blood to eyes and brain

AMPULLAE of LORENZINI
(see SENSES)

NOSTRIL or NARE (2)
contains sensitive scent organs

GILL SLITS
respiration

UPPER LOBE

LOWER LOBE (keel)

ANAL FIN

PELVIC FIN (2)
stabilising

PECTORAL FIN (2)
steering, provides lift

SENSES

SIGHT
Sharks have a reflective layer called the **tapetum lucidum** located behind the **retina** of the eye. This layer reflects light that passes through the **retina** back onto the **photo-receptors**, allowing the shark better vision in low light conditions. Since sharks feed mainly at dusk, during the night and at dawn, this is a very useful adaptation. Unlike bony fishes, sharks have eyelids, but they are unable to close them. Some sharks have a membrane below the eye that can cover the eye when the shark is feeding.

SMELL
Sharks have a very highly developed sense of smell that allows them to detect fish extracts in concentrations of less than one part per billion. Shark nostrils, or **nares**, are used only for smelling. Unlike the nasal cavities of other animals, those of sharks are not connected to the mouth and throat. Water flows into the nares, where minute quantities of dissolved substances come in contact with sensitive receptor cells that respond by sending a signal to the brain by means of an electrical charge.

HEARING
Sharks have no outer, visible ear, but they do have inner ears, located in the frontal skull. These help the shark to maintain balance, but it is uncertain whether sharks hear in the same way as us.

TASTE
When a shark bites into an object, chemicals are released by the object and picked up by sensory cells in the lining of the shark's mouth and throat. These cells send signals to the brain, which determines whether the object is suitable for eating.

ELECTRORECEPTION
Sharks have numerous large pores around the snout that have evolved into sensory organs known as **ampullae of Lorenzini**. Each of these contains cells that collect electrical signals emitted by objects in the surroundings and then send them to the brain. Sharks appear to rely on this sense more than sight and smell when they are close to an object. Some sharks, such as the hammerheads, can also detect weak electrical signals given off from prey that is hiding motionless on the seabed.

Slender hammerhead shark
Eusphyra blochii

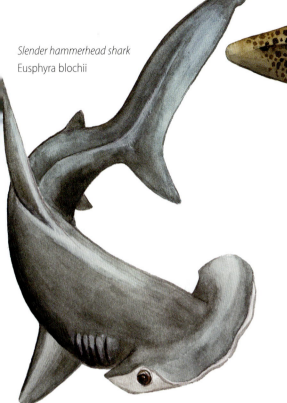

Zebra shark Stegostoma fasciatum

THICK-SKINNED

Shark skin is composed of small, hard, tooth-like scales or **denticles** that give the skin a rough surface that feels like sandpaper. The structure of these scales is similar to that of teeth (see SHARK TEETH below). Unlike the scales of other fish, which increase in size as the fish grows, shark scales remain the same size and the shark simply grows more of them.

Most sharks have a light-coloured underside, to blend in with light from above, while the top of the body is darker, allowing the shark to blend in with the darkness below it. Bottom-dwelling sharks, such as the zebra shark (pictured above) have mottled colouring that helps them to blend in with the seabed.

Arabian smoothhound Mustelus mosis

SHARK TEETH

Although sharks' teeth have a similar structure to those of other animals, they are actually modified scales that have developed a pulp cavity in the centre, surrounded by dentine and an enamel exterior. Sharks' teeth are arranged in rows, with those in the front being the largest and descending in size to the back row. When a tooth in the front row is damaged or lost, a tooth from the next row replaces it.

Shark teeth come in various shapes and sizes, depending on what the shark eats. Sharks such as the slender hammerhead (pictured above) that do not chew their food, but swallow it whole or tear it into pieces, have very sharp, wedge-shaped teeth with a jagged edge. Bottom-dwelling sharks, such as the nurse shark (pictured below), have thick, conical or flattened teeth at the back of the mouth for crushing crabs and molluscs.

SALTIER THAN THE SEA

Sharks do not drink water in the same way as bony fish. The blood and body tissue of **cartilaginous** fish, including sharks, contain very high amounts of **urea** and other salts. As a result, sharks are more salty than the sea itself. This characteristic helps sharks to absorb water by **osmosis**: a process by which water moves from an area where the concentration is higher to one where it is lower, in an effort to equalise the concentration. In sharks, sea water flows into the body through the gill tissues.

Nurse shark (Ginglymostomatidae)

WHALE SHARK

Whale sharks are the largest living fishes in the world. They are found in tropical and temperate waters of the Atlantic, Pacific and Indian Oceans. Reaching up to 16 m in length, these extraordinary fish are found near the surface of open waters, where they feed mainly on plankton. Satellite tracking has shown that whale sharks travel thousands of kilometres over periods of weeks or months, following blooms of planktonic organisms and changes in water temperature. Whale sharks have been observed in Arabian Gulf waters, in the Arabian Sea and off the north-east coast of Oman. The IUCN Red List classifies the whale shark as 'vulnerable'.

FEEDING HABITS

The whale shark is one of four species of **cartilaginous** fish that filter feed. It moves very slowly, sucking water containing plankton, small fish, crustaceans and squid into its huge mouth. The **gill rakers** (see also page 156) filter out any organisms over 2–3 mm in size and the remaining liquid passes back out through the gills.

The whale shark Rhincodon typus *is a gentle, solitary shark, seldom seen in groups, except where there are large amounts of plankton.*

REPRODUCTION

Until recently, it was thought that the whale shark was, like most fish, **oviparous**, laying eggs that are then fertilised outside the female's body by the male and hatched on the seabed. However, it is now known that female whale sharks are **viviparous** – they give birth to live young that are about 60 cm in length.

*The whale shark has a narrow mouth (when shut) that extends right across the wide, flattened head, at the end a rounded snout. It has small eyes located far forward on the head and five long gill slits that extend above the **pectoral fins**.*

RAYS AND SKATES

Known collectively as batoids, rays and skates are **cartilaginous** fish, like the sharks from which they are thought to have evolved. There are about 500 species worldwide. Although some species, such as manta and eagle rays, swim in the open ocean, the flattened bodies of the batoids are primarily adapted for life on or near the seabed and differ considerably from those of sharks. Many rays have venomous spines on the tail and some have thorn-like scales, both of which are used as a defence against predators. Electric rays are capable of producing short bursts of electricity as strong as 200 volts for defence and catching prey. Most rays and skates feed on fish, crustaceans and worms, but a few, such as the manta ray, eat plankton. Like sharks, rays and skates are intelligent fish.

ANATOMY

In contrast to the short, thick **pectoral fins** of sharks, which are joined to the body behind the head, those of rays and skates are enlarged and joined to the head to form the characteristic disc-shaped body. In most species, the **dorsal** and **caudal fins** are either small or missing completely. The eyes are located on the top of the head rather than on the sides, in order to provide a good view of the water above. Two sets of five gill slits are situated on the underside of the body.

Large pectoral fins are used like wings when swimming in open water

WHITE-SPOTTED EAGLE RAY

The white-spotted eagle ray *Aetobatus narinari* grows to at least 3.5 m wide and 9 m in length, including the long whip-like tail, and can weigh over 200 kg. It has a flat, rounded snout and a thick head with a prominent brow. The large pectoral fins form a disc that is bluish-black with numerous white spots on the upper side and white on the underside.

Whip-like, flexible tail has a long, venomous spine located behind dorsal fin

STINGS AND SHOCKS

Swimmers and divers may occasionally encounter rays, especially when the fish are motionless on the seabed. When wading, it is a good idea to prod the sand in front with a stick and shuffle one's feet rather than taking large strides. In the event that a swimmer receives a sting or an electric shock from a ray, it is wise to administer first aid immediately, followed by further medical attention as soon as possible.

Despite its small size the electric ray Nardine sp. (right) can deliver a real electric shock to divers who disturb it underwater.

MORAY EELS

Moray eels are common on coral reefs and in rocky areas of shallow tropical seas. From hiding places in holes and crevices, the moray ambushes passing fish and other prey, but may emerge at night to hunt over a wider area. There are about 100 species of moray eels worldwide.

THICK-SKINNED

Unlike most fish, moray eels do not have scales. Their thick skin is patterned to provide camouflage and is covered with a protective mucous coating. Most morays lack **pelvic** and **pectoral fins**, but have a **dorsal** fin that runs along the back and joins seamlessly with the **caudal** and anal fins, giving the fish a snake-like appearance. The eyes are small, but morays have a keen sense of smell with which they seek out prey.

JAWS

Moray eels are unable to swallow food in the same manner as other fish. Instead, they have a second set of toothed jaws, located in the throat. These are called **pharyngeal jaws.** When feeding, morays project these jaws into the mouth cavity, from where they drag prey into the throat and down into the digestive system. Moray eels are the only animals known to use **pharyngeal jaws** to actively capture and restrain their prey.

SEA HORSES

There are over 30 species of sea horses worldwide, belonging to a single family, Syngnathidae. Sea horses are specialised bony fish with a head that resembles that of a horse. This is held at a 30° angle to the body, as the sea horse moves upright through the water. Due to the bony plates beneath its skin, a sea horse cannot swim fast and spends much of its time hidden amongst seagrass or seaweed, anchoring itself with a flexible, **prehensile** tail. Sea horse habitats include seagrass beds, coral reefs and mangroves.

A female thorny sea horse
Hippocampus histrix

FAITHFUL MATES

Sea horses are **monogamous**: a pair will remain together for life, producing several broods of offspring each year. Whilst the males of many fish species play a role in caring for eggs after they are laid by the female, the male sea horse is the one who becomes pregnant after the female deposits her eggs in his pouch, where they are fertilised. The length of the pregnancy varies from about ten days to six weeks, depending on the species and on the water temperature.

MASTERS OF DISGUISE

Sea horses use camouflage to hide from predators. As well as being able to change colour, sea horses can grow skin filaments and tendrils that match the texture of the habitats in which they live. Colour changes may also occur after mating.

GAME FISH

Recreational fishing is popular in Arabian waters. Informed management of the fisheries and the enforcementt of sustainable levels of fishing are vital for maintaining species diversity and ecosystem stability. Government bodies such as the UAE's Environment Agency – Abu Dhabi (EAD) have set up various programmes, including a system of permits and licences for recreational fishing, along with the tagging and live release of certain species in order to better understand and manage this valuable resource.

Kingfish Scomberomorus commerson

Orange-spotted trevally
Carangoides bajad

SPECIES

Among the most popular species with recreational anglers are the pickhandle barracuda *Sphyraena jello*, cobia *Rachycentron canadum* and jacks and trevallies such as the Talang queenfish *Scomberoides commersonnianus*, orange-spotted trevally *Carangoides bajad* (left), golden trevally *Gnathanodon speciosus* and giant trevally *Caranx ignobilis*. By far the most favoured group is the tuna and tuna-like species, which includes kingfish *Scomberomorus commerson* (above), longtail tuna *Thunnus tonggol* and, to a lesser extent, yellowfin tuna *T. albacares*, as well as the Indo-Pacific sailfish *Istiophorus platypterus* (below right).

Cobia Rachycentron canadum

SAILFISH TAGGING >>

The sailfish *Istiophorus platypterus* (right) is known for its speed and jumping ability. It is a popular game fish wherever it is found.

To preserve stocks, catch and release and tagging are widely practiced by anglers and charter operators. In the United Arab Emirates, the Environment Agency – Abu Dhabi (EAD) has distributed tags to fishermen. This has permitted study of the migratory movements and growth patterns of sailfish in the Arabian Gulf.

CORAL REEF FISHES

Coral reefs are among the planet's richest ecosystems and provide shelter for many marine animals, including a large number of fish species. The wide diversity of species is due mainly to the complexity of this unique habitat, which provides fish with many different ways in which to live, hunt, eat and reproduce. Many species of fish on coral reefs are brightly coloured and have distinctive patterning. For some this may provide camouflage, For others it is a means of identifying members of the same species or a way of warding off predators.

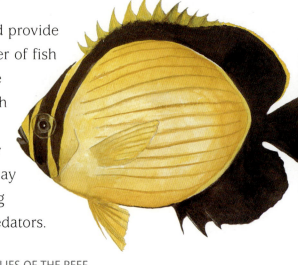

BUTTERFLIES OF THE REEF

Butterflyfishes belong to a single family that contains over 100 species worldwide. With an amazing array of colours and patterns, they are among the most common fish found on coral reefs.

Butterflyfishes can be recognised by their flattened, disc-shaped bodies. Some, like the black-spotted butterflyfish *Chaetodon nigropunctatus* (pictured left) have quite dull colouring, but many others, such as the Arabian butterflyfish *C. melapterus* (above) exhibit distinctive dark patterns against a vividly coloured background. A number of species have dark bands that extend over the eye, while others have eye-like spots, usually situated towards the rear of the fish. These markings help to confuse predators.

Most butterflyfish feed during daylight hours, then seek out safe hiding places among the corals where they spend the night. Some species feed on coral polyps and zooplankton, while others graze on algae growing on the corals. While resting, the bright colours tend to fade and the dorsal spines are held erect for protection.

Butterflyfishes are present in all Arabian waters, but the largest number of species are found in the Red Sea. Here there are 12 species in all, six of which are not found elsewhere. Best known of these is the unmistakable masked butterflyfish C. semilarvatus *(left), known locally as* tabag *(saucer). With its yellow body and bluish-greyish eye mask, this species is commonly seen motionless on the reef – a characteristic that has made it one of the most photographed fishes in the Red Sea.*

CLOWNFISH

Brightly coloured clownfish are found in the warm seas of the Pacific and Indian Ocean as well as in Arabian waters. All clownfish species live in a close **symbiotic** relationship with sea anemones on coral reefs. The tentacles of sea anemones contain stinging cells that are lethal to most fish that come into contact with them. Clownfish, however, have a thick layer of mucus on their bodies that allows them to live amongst the tentacles, which provide them with protection from predators. In return, the clownfish feeds on undigested matter that might otherwise be harmful to the anemone.

Most clownfish live in small groups around a single anemone. These groups consists of one breeding pair and a number of smaller males. When the female dies, her mate changes sex and becomes a female. All clownfish begin life as males.

Surgeonfish or sohal
Acanthurus sohal

<< SURGEONFISHES

These colourful residents of inshore reefs are so-called because of their ability to slash at other fish aggressively with the sharp, scalpel-like spines located in front of the caudal fin.

The surgeonfish or sohal *Acanthurus sohal* is one of the most common reef fishes found in Arabian waters. It is easily observed inshore in the intertidal surf zone on shallow reefs, where it works the marginal rocks, scraping algae with its sharp teeth. Surgeonfish can be inquisitive and aggressively defend their home range.

TRIGGERFISHES >>

Triggerfishes are small to medium-sized fish with high foreheads and eyes placed very high above a longish pointed snout. They move by propelling themselves with their second dorsal and anal fins, which they beat in an undulating motion, and only use their tails when under threat. The aptly-named Picasso triggerfish *Rhinecanthus assasi* is particularly colourful, with a vertical dark brown stripe with blue edges from eye to gill cover, preceded by a yellow bar lined with a pale blue stripe. It feeds on zooplankton, crabs and molluscs.

Picasso triggerfish
Rhinecanthus assasi

<< CLOWNFISH COUSIN

The Indo-Pacific sergeant *Abudefduf vaigiensis* belongs to the damselfish family Pomacentridae – the same family as the clownfish (see above). As adults, these colourful fish live on inshore reefs, as well as on the upper margins of outer reef slopes. Juvenile fish may be found amongst floating seaweed. Like the clownfish, the sergeant is territorial. It feeds on zooplankton, small invertebrates and algae on the sea floor. Eggs are laid on the sea floor, where they are aggressively guarded by the male.

Indo-Pacific sergeant
Abudefduf vaigiensis

VENOMOUS FISH

The underwater world is a competitive place in which to live, and like other marine life, fish have developed many different ways of defending themselves against predators. These defences can pose dangers not only to other marine life, but also to unwary humans who come into contact with them. In some species of fish, these defences are combined with superb camouflage that makes potential danger difficult to spot.

SYMPTOMS & TREATMENT

SYMPTOMS
In addition to pain and swelling, symptoms of a venomous fish sting can include a rise or fall in blood pressure, nausea and vomiting, a change in heart rate, shortness of breath, muscle weakness and paralysis, seizures, delirium, and loss of consciousness.

FIRST AID
Seek immediate medical attention.
Whilst waiting for assistance, elevate the wounded area, clean the wound and soak in the hottest water the victim can stand without scalding. Scorpionfish anti-venom, antibiotics and anti-tetanus vaccine may be administered if available.

HIDDEN DANGERS

Although some venomous fish advertise their presence with bright colours and spectacular patterns (like the lionfish, above), others are virtually invisible until they move. Among the latter are the scorpionfish (below left) and the stonefish (below right). Their peculiar camouflage allows them to blend in with their surroundings while waiting for prey to come along. Unwary humans who tread on these bottom-dwellers may receive a very painful sting from the venomous spines. In the case of the stonefish, a sting may be fatal. It is important to seek immediate medical attention after being stung.

COMMERCIAL FISH

Fishing has been important in Arabian waters since ancient times and still provides an important source of income, food and recreational opportunity. Recent decades have seen a substantial increase in commercial fishing, leading to concern about sustainable use of this valuable resource. Commercial fisheries involve many species and species groups and employ different types of fishing equipment and methods, deployed from various types and sizes of fishing vessels.

Silver grunt Pomadasys argenteus

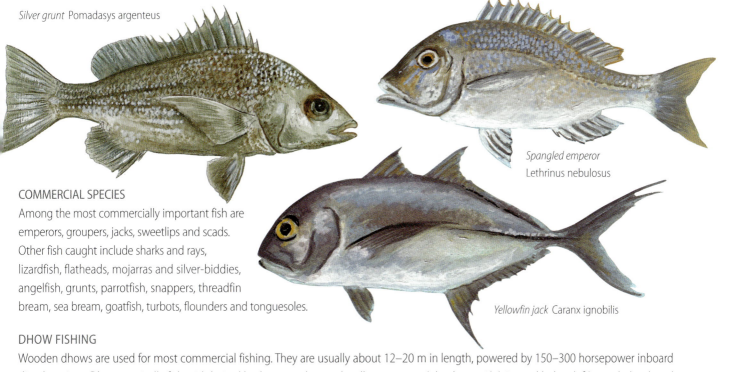

Spangled emperor Lethrinus nebulosus

COMMERCIAL SPECIES

Among the most commercially important fish are emperors, groupers, jacks, sweetlips and scads. Other fish caught include sharks and rays, lizardfish, flatheads, mojarras and silver-biddies, angelfish, grunts, parrotfish, snappers, threadfin bream, sea bream, goatfish, turbots, flounders and tonguesoles.

Yellowfin jack Caranx ignobilis

DHOW FISHING

Wooden dhows are used for most commercial fishing. They are usually about 12–20 m in length, powered by 150–300 horsepower inboard diesel engines. Dhows typically fish with baited basket traps, known locally as *gargoor* (plural *garagir*) (pictured below left), trawls, hook and line (*hadaq*), and trolling lines (*lafah*). Gillnets (*al liekh*), often set on the bottom, are also used. Trap fishing is the most common fishing method. Formerly made from interwoven palm fronds, traps are now manufactured from galvanised steel wire. Species caught include groupers (*hamour*), emperors (*shaeri*) and grunts. Other important species caught in *garagir* include jacks, snappers, sea bream, parrotfish and rabbitfish.

FARMED FISH

Although Arabian waters are rich in marine resources, the demand for the valuable nutrients found in fish as food puts heavy pressure on wild fish stocks. Aquaculture, or fish farming, plays an important part in the sustainable management of fisheries by relieving the pressure on wild fish stocks. The Marine Resources Research Centre (MRRC) of the UAE Ministry of Environment and Water, based in Umm al-Qaiwain, is doing pioneering work in releasing larvae and **fingerlings** of commercially important species into protected marine areas. The species include rabbitfish (*safi*), mullet (*biah*), silver black porgy (*subaiti*) and greasy grouper. *Tilapia nilotica* (*bulti*) have been released into freshwater areas.

Marketable-size rabbitfish Siganus canaliculatus (above) have been reared using aquaculture technology developed at the Marine Resources Research Centre in Umm al-Qaiwain.

HAMOUR

The greasy grouper *Epinephelus tauvina* (pictured below) is one of several *Ephinephelus* species known in local fish souqs as *hamour*. Due to their popularity as food fish, *hamour* populations in Arabian waters have been greatly depleted. In May 2008, the Marine Resources Research Centre, Umm al-Qaiwain, affiliated to the UAE Ministry of Environment and Water, successfully hatched larvae of *hamour* fish. The release of *hamour* larvae and fingerlings into Khors and marine protected areas is part of the Ministry's efforts to replenish the diminished populations of commercial fish species.

FRESHWATER FISHES

Of the world's estimated 10,000 species of freshwater fishes, only 16 occur in the Arabian Peninsula. Freshwater species are under greater threat worldwide than those of other ecosystems due to pollution, climate change and human population increases. In arid regions, such as the Arabian Peninsula, wadis and wadi pools provide essential freshwater habitats for fish, amphibians and invertebrates. Many mountain wadis only contain water for part of the year, but fish manage to survive for extended periods in small, isolated pools. When it rains, the wadis flow again and the fish reproduce and disperse rapidly.

NATIVES

OPPORTUNIST

The Arabian killifish *Aphanius dispar* (above) is noted for its ability to tolerate both fresh water and salt water, as well as water temperatures as high as 46℃. For this reason it is found in coastal lagoons and in mountain wadis and pools. Its opportunistic feeding habits help the killifish to survive in harsh conditions. It can subsist on algae, but it takes live food when available, as well as debris on the beds of wadis.

It also shows a preference for mosquito larvae. For this reason the killifish has been introduced for mosquito control into various man-made bodies of water, including cisterns, agricultural runoff channels, bulldozed ponds and water tanks. It is able to reproduce successfully in all of these environments. The Arabian killifish is found throughout the Arabian Peninsula.

DISCOVERY & DISAPPEARANCE

A small population of the freshwater goby *Awaous aeneofuscus* was discovered in 1997 in a tributary of Wadi Hatta near the border between the UAE and Oman. Most of the fish were observed in some deeper pools a few kilometres downstream from the Hatta Pools. Although rare in Arabia, this species is relatively common in South Africa, where it exists in estuaries and rivers, in running water as well as in slower or stagnant pools.

Annual monitoring of four sites in the area from 1997 showed a decline in the number of these gobies, until only five individuals were sighted in May 2004. After further investigation the following year, scientists concluded that the goby was locally extinct. Prolonged drought during those years may explain its disappearance, along with use of the pools for fishing and specimen collection by private individuals and institutions.

TENACIOUS CLIMBER

Garra barreimiae is one of several *Garra* species that are found in the Arabian Peninsula. *G. barreimiae* is **endemic** to the UAE and northern Oman. These small (4.5–7 cm) fish feed on algae and debris. They have a tendency to swim upstream and have been observed climbing the wet surface of waterfall splash zones, using a specialised mouth plate as a suction device

INTRODUCTIONS

Among the fishes introduced into freshwater habitats in the Arabian Peninsula are mollies *Poecilia* spp. (pictured above). It is thought that these introduced fish originate from private aquaria. *Tilapia* species have been deliberately introduced in recent years as a form of algae, weed and mosquito control. There are now concerns that the presence of *Tilapia* may have an adverse effect on native fish populations.

>> LEARN MORE : USEFUL WEBSITES

GENERAL INFORMATION ON FISH

http://www.fishbase.org/search.php – large, worldwide database of species information on fish – over 30,000 species

http://www.uaeinteract.com/nature/marine/fsh06.asp – list of fish in Arabian waters with links to information on individual fish families

http://www.enhg.org – the Emirates Natural History Group has numerous articles about fish in its searchable online bulletins – use the search facility on the home page

FISH ANATOMY

http://www.earthlife.net/fish/anatomy.html – part of the large Earthlife website, with links to information on specific aspects of anatomy (e.g. swim bladder) – well-illustrated

http://www.seaworld.org/infobooks/BonyFish/anatomy.html – fish anatomy in straightforward point form with diagrams

SHARKS

http://www.arabianwildlife.com/archive/vol1.1/shark.htm – information and photographs of sharks found in Arabian waters

http://www.elasmodiver.com/Shark_Facts.htm – a list of useful facts about sharks from a shark dive site

http://www.whalesharkproject.org/ – information on the whale shark

SEA HORSES

http://seahorse.fisheries.ubc.ca/why.html – website dedicated to conservation of seahorses

CORAL REEF FISHES

http://www.coralrealm.com/homepage.html – attractive educational website about coral reefs, including fish associated with them

http://www.nature.org/joinanddonate/rescuereef/explore/photos.html – a section of the Nature Conservancy's website devoted to coral reefs

http://www.arabianwildlife.com/archive/vol3.1/redbutr.htm – article on the butterflyfishes of the Red Sea

DANGEROUS FISHES

http://www.uae.gov.ae/uaeagricent/fisheries/dangersmarine_e.stm – list and descriptions of dangerous marine animals from the UAE Ministry of Agriculture

http://www.arabianwildlife.com/archive/vol2.1/stone.htm – Arabian Wildlife article on the stonefish

GAME FISH

http://www.arabianwildlife.com/current/sailfish.html – excellent article about the sailfish and the process of tagging

FRESHWATER FISHES

http://www.enhg.org/trib/trib07.htm and http://www.enhg.org/trib/V16N2/TribulusV16N2P34.pdf – details of the discovery and eventual demise of the freshwater goby

FOR YOUNGER CHILDREN

http://www.enchantedlearning.com/subjects/fish/printouts/ – information and printouts on bony and cartilaginous fish

FISH GLOSSARY

ampullae of Lorenzini: special sensory organs in the heads of **cartilaginous** fish that pick up electrical signals in the surroundings

cartilaginous: consisting of soft cartilage rather than bone

caudal fin: tail fin

denticles: tooth-like structures found instead of scales on the bodies of some fish (e.g. sharks)

dorsal fin: a stabilising fin located on the back of many fish and marine mammals

endemic: native to a particular region

fingerling: young fish in its first or second year

gill rakers: bony parts of the gill that prevent food particles from entering the gill chambers

gill filaments: feather-like projections of the gills across which oxygen and carbon dioxide are exchanged as part of the breathing process

gill lamellae: small membranes that make up the **gill filaments**

hermaphrodite: having both male and female reproductive organs in the same body

lunate (tail): crescent-moon shaped

monogamous: mating system in which a single male and single female form an exclusive breeding relationship

nare: nostril

operculum: a hard, bony flap that protects the gills of a fish

osmosis: process by which water moves from an area where the concentration is higher to one where it is lower, in an effort to equalise the concentration

oviparous: fertilised eggs develop and hatch outside the body

oviviviparous: young develop within eggs that remain inside the mother's body until they hatch or are about to hatch

pectoral fins: first set of fins behind the head

pelvic fins: pair of fins on the abdomen of a fish below or behind **pectoral fins**

pharyngeal jaws: second set of jaws inside the mouth of an animal, distinct from the main jaws

photo-receptors: specialised cells in the eye that are able to detect and react to light

prehensile: an appendage specially adapted for grasping and grabbing

retina: the inside back surface of the eyeball that converts images to electrical signals, which are sent to the brain along the optic nerve

salinity: the amount of salt in water

spiracle: small opening on each side of a shark's head, used in respiration (breathing)

symbiotic: a relationship in which two species live in close association for mutual benefit

tapetum lucidum: an adaptation in nocturnal species in which a reflective layer behind the retina of the eye intensifies the image

truncate (tail): tail with cut-off appearance (see illustration on page 156)

urea: waste product formed by the breakdown of protein

viviparous: giving birth to live young instead of laying eggs

vertebrates/birds

BIRDS

The Arabian Peninsula is rich in birdlife, due in great part to its position on major bird migration routes. Widespread coastal wetlands, including mangroves, mud-flats and intertidal areas provide important habitats for large numbers of migratory birds, whilst man-made freshwater habitats, such as water reservoirs, sewage treatment ponds and artificial lakes and lagoons, provide stop-over points further inland. Situated at the crossroads of three main zoogeographical regions (Palaearctic, Afrotropical and Oriental), Arabian resident species include examples from each region, depending on which part of the Arabian Peninsula is under consideration. The extreme south-west corner is home to a number of African species, whilst many birds in the UAE and Oman originate from India. Residents in the remaining regions are mostly Palaearctic species.

LONG DISTANCE TRAVELLER

The great knot *Calidris tenuirostris* is known to breed only in the extreme east of Siberia, with most of the population spending the winter in north-western Australia. A small number, however, appears in the Arabian Gulf each autumn and over-winters in western Abu Dhabi, whilst another population arrives in central Oman. This migration is unmatched by any other species visiting the Arabian Peninsula.

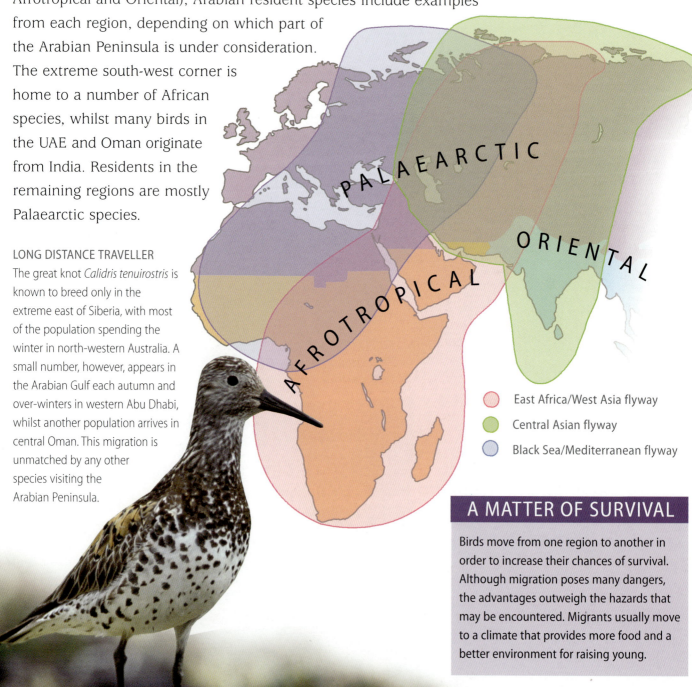

East Africa/West Asia flyway

Central Asian flyway

Black Sea/Mediterranean flyway

A MATTER OF SURVIVAL

Birds move from one region to another in order to increase their chances of survival. Although migration poses many dangers, the advantages outweigh the hazards that may be encountered. Migrants usually move to a climate that provides more food and a better environment for raising young.

THOSE MAGNIFICENT FLYING MACHINES

Most birds are perfectly adapted for life in the air. They have a number of unique adaptations for flight, evolved since the first birds appeared around 150 million years ago.

FACTS ABOUT FEATHERS

Feathers are actually modified scales. In addition to being essential for flight, feathers are also used for other purposes. Soft down feathers lie against the skin and provide insulation to keep the bird warm. Contour feathers protect the bird from the elements and aid flight by giving a smooth, aerodynamic shape to the body. Strong, stiff flight feathers in the wings and tail are essential for flying, assisting the bird to change direction and speed. The colour and arrangement of feathers may act as camouflage or be used to attract a mate.

WINGS

Birds' wings are really modified front legs, adapted for lifting the bird off the ground and enabling it to move efficiently through the air. Short, rounded wings assist rapid takeoff and turning, whilst long, wide wings are useful in gliding and soaring. By altering the angle of the wings a bird can propel itself forward or change direction. To slow down, a bird tilts its wings back and fans out its tail feathers, creating more resistance.

LIGHTWEIGHT SKELETONS

Bird skeletons are both lightweight and strong, making them ideally suited for flying. Many of the bones are hollow, but reinforced with internal struts. The keel-shaped breastbone is relatively large, since it must support the powerful muscles needed for flight. Heavy jaws and teeth have been replaced by beaks of various shapes and sizes, depending on the type of food eaten.

BIRD'S EYE VIEW

Birds require exceptionally good eyesight when flying, in order to avoid obstacles and predators and to locate food. Some birds have more light receptors in their eyes than humans do, allowing them to see much greater distances.

HEART AND LUNGS

Like mammals, birds breathe in oxygen and breathe out carbon dioxide, but in addition to lungs, birds have a number of special air sacs (usually nine) that extend into the bones. These help to push air through the respiratory system. Birds breathe more efficiently than mammals, transferring more oxygen with each breath. To assist oxygen circulation, birds have a strong heart that beats much faster than the human heart.

TOWN, PARK, GARDEN

Prior to modern development, even the common house sparrow was absent from most of the region. Birds associated with human habitation now prosper in towns, forestry plantations, shelter belts and agricultural settings. Other native species have expanded their ranges from the better-watered mountain districts and moved into parks, gardens and other green areas sustained through artificial irrigation.

GREY FRANCOLIN *Francolinus pondicerianus*

The grey francolin is one of a number of naturalised species, exotics probably released by humans, which have become successfully established in the wild. Grey francolins roost in trees and are usually found not far from water. They have a loud, raucous call that can be heard at dawn and dusk.

OLIVACEOUS WARBLER *Hippolais pallida*

This migrant visitor is now a resident breeder on Abu Dhabi Island. Its favourite habitat is leafy gardens, where it feeds in the canopy and outer branches of trees. The olivaceous warbler can easily be confused with other warblers. The crown feathers are raised (see image) when the bird is alarmed.

EXOTIC ESCAPEES

The ring-necked parakeet *Psittacula krameri* (above) is one of a wide variety of exotic species released over the past 20 years that have become 'naturalised'. They are considered to be a pest in fruit orchards. As a result, further imports have been officially banned.

<< COLOURFUL RESIDENTS

The Indian roller *Coriacas benghalensis* (far left) and green bee-eater *Merops orientalis* (left) are examples of species that continue to steadily expand their ranges. This may be due to the increases in woodland and parkland areas and the creation of entirely new habitats.

TIRED TRAVELLERS >>

The importance of green urban landscapes for migrant birds is probably considerable, given the scale of planting over the past 30 years. Tired and hungry migrants overflying the empty quarter in spring, or after crossing the Gulf in autumn, now find somewhere to rest and refuel before continuing their journeys. Among those most commonly found are the Scops owl, nightingale (pictured), thrush nightingale, tree pipit, marsh warbler, spotted flycatcher, semi-collared flycatcher, red-backed shrike, golden oriole and European nightjar.

WHITE-CHEEKED USURPER

Although no native species has been seriously affected by the increase in introduced species of birds, there is now good evidence that the white-eared bulbul *Pycnonotus leucogenys* has displaced the native white-spectacled bulbul *P. xanthopygos* in some locations.

PURPLE SUNBIRD >>

The purple sunbird *Nectarinia asiatica* has taken advantage of urban plantations and gardens and is now found in most suitable areas, where it is continuing to spread and increase in number.

RUFOUS BUSH ROBIN *Cercotrichas galactotes*

The rufous bush robin is a European migrant species that breeds widely in desert date groves inland and close to the mountains. It is now also found nesting in an ever-increasing number of parks, gardens and plantations along the Gulf coast. Often seen hopping in shaded areas on the ground.

CHIFFCHAFF *Phylloscopus collybita*

This small olive-brown warbler is a common **passage migrant** and winter visitor. It is very similar to the willow warbler, but can be distinguished by its black legs. The chiffchaff prefers areas with a good degree of tree cover. It feeds on small insects, constantly flicking its tail as it does so.

MOUNTAINS AND WADIS

The mountains and wadis of the Arabian Peninsula support a rich variety of birdlife. Some valleys have permanent pools and streams, while others depend on rainfall to bring water to the dried-up river beds. Birds are most plentiful in the better-watered wadis, but some are equally at home at higher elevations and in more arid regions.

VULTURES

Vultures have a bare neck and head, which enables them to reach inside the carcasses they feed on. Many have a highly developed sense of smell, which helps them locate dead animals.

EGYPTIAN VULTURE

Smallest of the Old World vultures, the Egyptian vulture *Neophron percnopterus* is a resident Arabian species as well as a migrant and winter visitor. Although widespread, the numbers of Egyptian vultures are declining. Mainly found in mountainous areas, these birds construct untidy nests, which are used over a number of years. They are usually composed of vegetable matter, along with material scavenged from village refuse dumps.

ARABIAN RESIDENT

Until recently, the lappet-faced vulture *Torgos tracheliotos* was not considered widespread in Arabia. Thanks to the ABBA (Atlas of Breeding Birds of Arabia) Project, this species is now believed to be a resident breeder in the UAE, Yemen, Oman and Saudi Arabia. Flocks of these **raptors** may sometimes be seen at feeding sites or soaring overhead.

BONELLI'S EAGLE *Hieraaetus fasciatus*

Bonelli's eagle is a rare, but widely-distributed resident of mountainous terrain in the UAE, northern Oman, Yemen and in parts of Saudi Arabia. There are a few records of this small eagle as a migrant and winter visitor in northern Arabia, as well as along the coastline of the Arabian Gulf.

SHORT-TOED EAGLE *Circaetus gallicus*

Few breeding records exist in Arabia for this large, long-winged eagle, but due to the isolated, rocky regions that it frequents, records are difficult to compile. **Passage migrants** and winter visitors are believed to move from the head of the Arabian Gulf in a diagonal line across the Arabian Peninsula.

LONG-LEGGED BUZZARD *Buteo rufinus*

A small number of this widespread, but rare, Arabian resident are believed to breed in the UAE, Oman, Yemen and Saudi Arabia, with an estimated total of around 800 pairs. Long-legged buzzards also occur widely as winter vistors and as migrants, mainly during November.

SCRUB WARBLER *Scotocerca inquieta*

A typical resident of rocky hillsides, semi-desert and sandy scrubland, this shy little bird bears a resemblance to the graceful prinia, but has more contrast, along with a dark eye-stripe on the head and streaks of colour on the breast. Often observed hopping on the ground near bushes.

HOODED WHEATEAR *Oenanthe monacha*

A resident of rocky mountain gorges, hillsides and desert, which builds its nest in rock crevices. Seems to favour areas with limestone outcrops. Males are black with distinctive white crown. Tail is white except for central tail-feathers, which are black. Females are brownish, with cream-coloured underside.

TRUMPETER FINCH *Bucanetes githagineus*

A small, ground-dwelling finch found on rocky hillsides, in wadis, stony desert and semi-desert. Feeds on seeds and insects. A sociable bird, often seen in pairs or small groups, but may form large flocks in winter. Has a preference for drinking at midday during hot weather.

INDIAN SILVERBILL *Euodice malabarica*

A small, finch-like bird, the Indian silverbill has a thick, silver-grey or horn-coloured bill. This gregarious seed-eater feeds in small groups on the ground or in low shrubs. It builds a domed, straggly nest in a bush up to about 3 m off the ground. Favours scrubland, palm groves and cultivated areas.

LONG-BILLED PIPIT *Anthus similis*

The long-billed pipit favours mountain habitats up to an elevation of 3000 m, with broken, rocky ground and some vegetation. Nests on the ground in a deep, cup-shaped nest, but often perches in trees. Resident in UAE, Oman, Yemen, Jordan and south-western corner of Saudi Arabia.

VISITORS TO THE MOUNTAINS

During the winter months, resident species are joined by a limited variety of winter visitors, which include red-tailed wheatear *Oenanthe xanthoprymna* (pictured below right), black redstart *Phoenicurus ochruros* (below left), desert lesser whitethroat *Sylvia curruca minula*, chiffchaff, plain leaf warbler *Phylloscopus neglectus* and occasionally a blue rock thrush *Monticola solitarius* (below centre). More species occur on migration, but the diversity remains relatively low. Autumn migration through the mountains is less pronounced than in spring, and mostly involves the same species.

DESERTS AND DUNES

Sand deserts cover most of the Arabian Peninsula, presenting birds with a hostile environment in which to survive. In order to cope with the scarcity of water, extremes of temperature and limited shelter, desert birds have developed various physical and behavioural adaptations. Many desert birds have a light, sandy-coloured plumage that reflects the heat, as well as Various other adaptations aid in protecting eggs and hatchlings from the extreme climatic conditions of the desert.

Pharoah eagle owl
Bubo ascalaphus

TAKING A DIVE

The hoopoe lark *Alaemon alaudipes* is a widespread **breeding resident** of coastal dunes, as well as inland desert and *sabkha* scrublands. This species is noted for its spectacular display flight (pictured above) in which it whistles melodiously, whilst it makes a steep climb, before dropping dramatically out of the sky in a vertical dive.

GHAF GROVES

Groves of *ghaf* trees *Prosopis cineraria* grow in the deserts of the UAE, Oman and south-east Saudi Arabia, providing valuable food, shelter and nesting places for birds in an otherwise harsh and barren environment. Among the species associated with *ghaf* groves are the brown-necked raven *Corvus ruficollis* (pictured left), yellow-throated sparrow, and nesting migrant turtle doves. On the ground, under the tangled roots of the *ghaf* tree, the desert eagle owl (pictured above) may make its nest.

BIRDS OF SAXAUL WOODLAND

Stands of the shrubby tree *Haloxylon persicum* (*ghada*) in the UAE, as well as in the Eastern Province, central and northern parts of Saudi Arabia, form 'dew forests'. The trees are able to take droplets of water from the atmosphere, which then fall to the ground beneath the plants. Dew forests provide a habitat for such species as long-legged buzzard, little owl (below) and hoopoe lark in summer. In winter, eagles, kestrels, stone curlew, desert wheatear and flocks of short-toed larks occur regularly.

BAR-TAILED LARK *Ammomanes cincturus*

This lark is distinguished from other species of lark by a black bar at the end of its tail, most easily seen during the moments of take-off and landing. A resident of the Arabian deserts, it may be seen in flocks of around 20 birds. Lays two to five eggs in a nest on the ground, beside a rock or clump of grass.

BLACK-CROWNED SPARROW-LARK *Eremopterix nigriceps*

Unlike other larks, this species has a thick bill that resembles that of a finch. Male is quite distinctive with a black crown, white cheeks and forehead. Gathers in small flocks, except during the breeding season when it forms pairs. Prefers areas of desert scrub for nesting. Lays two or three eggs.

DESERT WHEATEAR *Oenanthe deserti*

A common winter visitor to coastal dunes, sand desert and *sabkha* scrubland. Prefers to perch on low bushes, from which it can watch for spiders and insects. When in flight this species is easily distinguished from other wheatears by a black tail without any white patches at the sides.

DISAPPEARING ACT

The cream-coloured courser *Cursorius cursor* nests where the intense heat shimmer permits it to slip away from its nest unnoticed.

COAST AND ISLANDS

The coastline of the Arabian Peninsula is of major international importance for visiting waterfowl, in particular for long-distance migrant shore birds. For example, an estimated 250,000 shore birds can be present on the UAE's Arabian Gulf coast at any one time in peak migration periods. Taking into account the likely turnover of birds on this, the west Asian-African flyway, several million individuals must pass through the area over the course of a year. In addition, offshore islands offer essential nesting sites for a wide variety of sea birds, whilst mangrove lagoons provide safe feeding, nesting and roosting places for many bird species.

OFFSHORE BREEDING

Offshore islands are important habitats for colonies of nesting sea birds, Many species occur in internationally-important numbers, including a number of tern species. The sooty gull *Larus hemprichii* (pictured above) and the red-billed tropicbird *Phaethon aethereus* (juvenile pictured left) also breed on islands off the UAE coast.

The Socotra cormorant *Phalacrocorax nigrogularis* (see page 187), a species **endemic** to the Arabian Gulf, breeds in significant numbers in colonies off the coasts of the UAE, Saudi Arabia, Bahrain and Oman.

Birds of prey are also represented among the breeding birds on the offshore islands. The sooty falcon *Falco concolor* delays breeding until mid-summer, when it is able to feed chicks on south-bound migrant birds, easily caught over the sea.

The osprey *Pandion haliaetus* also breeds offshore, the majority of birds occuring in the Red Sea, with a smaller number in the Arabian Gulf.

In Arabia, these fish-eating **raptors** are only found in marine habitats.

A GOOD NEWS STORY

Surveys by the Environment Agency – Abu Dhabi (EAD) during the 2007 breeding season revealed a record increase in the number of red-billed tropicbird on Qarnein, one of Abu Dhabi's islands. Of the 217 nests recorded, 155 nests were active, with chicks, eggs or adult birds present at the time of observation – nearly a 150 per cent increase from previous estimates.

ARCTIC NESTERS

Many Arctic-nesting shore birds visit the Arabian Peninsula in the autumn, most of them refuelling for their onward journey to eastern or southern Africa. The extensive mud-flats along the coastline yield large quantities of shellfish and other nutritious invertebrates for the migrants. Species include turnstone *Arenaria interpres*, ringed plover *Charadrius hiaticula*, curlew sandpiper *Calidris ferruginea* (pictured right), little stint *C. minuta* and sanderling *C. alba*.

BLACK-WINGED STILT *Himantopus himantopus*

This graceful black and white bird is easily identified by its very long, pink legs and needle-like black bill. White body and black wings are a distinctive feature in flight. Common **passage migrant**, winter visitor and casual summer breeder. Usually lays four eggs in an untidy nest close to shallow water.

GREATER SAND PLOVER *Charadrius leschenaultii*

This medium-sized plover is a summer visitor to breeding areas on inland mud-flats as far south as Jordan and Syria. Winter visitor and passage migrant on intertidal mud-flats, beginning in late June and reaching a peak in September and October. Khor Kalba and Khor al Beidah in the UAE are favourite sites.

BROAD-BILLED SANDPIPER *Limicola falcinellus*

A rather inconspicuous bird with short legs and a heavy bill. Its plumage resembles that of a snipe. Mixes with groups of dunlin. A **passage migrant** from Scandinavia and Arctic Russia. Some Russian birds winter on coastal mud-flats around the Arabian Gulf, whilst others travel to India and Ceylon.

DUNLIN *Calidris alpina*

Common and widespread wader, large numbers of which spend winters on Arabian coasts. Chicks feed themselves on insects as soon as they hatch. Females abandon their young after about six days, to begin migration south. Males remain with chicks, but follow females before young birds are fledged.

FASCINATING FACTS ABOUT CRAB PLOVERS

• The distinctive black and white crab plover *Dromas ardeola* is a rare wader that appears to have no close living relatives. Genetic studies suggest that the species diverged from the pratincoles and coursers some 35 million years ago!

• Unlike other waders, crab plovers breed underground, digging out burrows that are over 2 m long in raised sand banks close to the seashore.

• Crab plovers lay a relatively large, single white egg, whereas other waders generally lay two or more coloured eggs camouflaged with spots or other markings.

• Although other waders include crabs in their diet, the crab plover is unique in its reliance on this food source all year round.

• Crab plover chicks develop rapidly, enabling them to join their parents at feeding grounds, thereby reducing the energy required by adults to fly to and fro between the nest and feeding area.

• Only about ten breeding colonies of crab plover are known worldwide, two of which are located on UAE offshore islands. The most westerly colony is situated on the Saudi Arabian Farasan Islands in the Red Sea.

GULLS AND TERNS

Gulls and terns, are represented on every continent, including Antarctica. Most nest on the ground in colonies, usually laying between one and four eggs. Both parents help with incubation of the eggs and feeding the young birds. Gulls are heavy-bodied, sociable birds with a variable diet, eating virtually whatever is available. Terns have lighter, more streamlined bodies, allowing them to swoop rapidly over water in their search for food, plunging head first into the sea to catch fish. They usually occur in flocks, some of which may be very large.

Sooty gull in adult plumage

CHANGING COLOURS

All gulls change their plumage from juvenile to adult. This occurs through a series of moults, during which the bird loses its old feathers and replaces them with new ones. Moulting happens twice a year, in spring and autumn. During the spring moult it is only the body feathers that are replaced, but in autumn the tail and wing feathers are also replaced. Juvenile plumage is the first set of feathers to grow in after a baby bird loses its down feathers. For some of the larger gulls, it may take up to four years to fully change to adult plumage. Juvenile gulls are usually brownish with darker patterning and bars.

Sooty gull in juvenile plumage

Sooty gulls lay one to three eggs and the chicks are covered with down (see photo above). Nests are just a scrape on the ground, but may be located near a rock or vegetation.

<< AGGRESSIVE FORAGERS

Gulls hunt for food in a wide range of habitats, including refuse dumps, landfills, and other places associated with human activity, such as piers and harbours, fishing boats and agricultural land. They are particularly characteristic of the intertidal zones, but they also feed in other marine and freshwater areas, using various methods, including walking on the ground, swimming and diving into the water, and swooping from the air.

The Siberian gull Larus heuglini (pictured left) is one of a number of migrant species commonly seen on the Arabian Peninsula. This large gull breeds in the tundra regions of Russia. This individual has pink legs, but the legs are more commonly yellow.*

taxonomic status under review – BirdLife International (2009) For details see RESOURCES on page 192

WHITE-CHEEKED TERN *Sterna repressa*

Significant numbers of white-cheeked tern nest in dense colonies on offshore islands in the Arabian Gulf and the Red Sea, as well as off the Oman coast. After laying eggs in May and June, the colonies disperse in July and birds may be found at inshore locations. Rarely seen after mid-November.

SANDWICH TERN *Sterna sandvicensis*

This medium-sized tern may be seen in large numbers along the coasts during most of the year. Usually nesting in colonies on islands and sandy coasts, it lays from one to three eggs in a shallow scrape. The wings and back are very pale grey. Adult birds have a long slender, black bill with a yellow tip.

SWIFT TERN *Sterna bergii*

Although rarely seen, this tern is resident in the Arabian Gulf, nesting in colonies on sandy or rocky shores, usually on offshore islands. Also known as the greater crested tern, this large species has a black crested cap broken by a white forehead. The thick, greenish-yellow bill curves downwards.

The long, slim yellowish-orange bill of the lesser-crested tern Sterna bengalensis helps to distinguish it from the somewhat similar swift tern.

FEEDING HABITS

Terns feed over water, usually diving for fish (see photos above). They may plunge from overhead, or dip into the water from a hovering position. Sometimes terns follow shoals of large fish or groups of marine mammals, both of which force smaller fish to the surface. Foraging usually takes place early in the day and later in the afternoon, and may be influenced by the tidal cycle. Terns are more specialised feeders than gulls, with a diet consisting mainly of fish, although some terns will also take insects.

▶▶ FOCUS ON **FLAMINGOS**

FLAMINGO FACTS

- The greater flamingo, *Phoenicopterus ruber*, bred in Arabia in the summer of 1993 for the first time in 70 years, on a salt lake at Al Wathba, about 40 km inland from the UAE capital, Abu Dhabi. It was the first ever recorded breeding on the mainland of the Arabian Peninsula, and the first in the Gulf since 1922.

- In 2009, biologists from the Environment Agency – Abu Dhabi (EAD) discovered a new breeding colony of flamingos while conducting a survey of the coastal areas west of Abu Dhabi. Altogether, the biologists counted 1,954 nests at two sites in the colony, including 224 currently active nests. They recorded more than 1,800 flamingos, along with 800 chicks, in the inter-tidal areas between Musaffah and Bu Al Siaief Musaffah, making it the biggest successful nesting in the UAE and possibly in the entire Arabian Peninsula.

- Both male and female flamingos participate in constructing a nest mound, made from a combination of mud, feathers, grass, twigs and small stones. A shallow depression is made at the top of the mound, in which a single egg is laid.

- Flamingos may stamp on the mud when feeding, in order to bring the micro-organisms they feed on to the surface.

- Flamingos are filter feeders. The inside of the bill is lined with a very efficient filtration system, somewhat similar to that of whales. The bill is placed in the water upside down and the tongue is pulled back, allowing water to enter the partly-opened bill. As the tongue moves forward again, the water is forced out, leaving behind the food particles on which the flamingo feeds.

THE TRAVELS OF SINDIBAD

MARCH 2006. The Environment Agency – Abu Dhabi (EAD) reported that the first of the greater flamingos fitted with satellite trackers had successfully migrated to the skies of Iran. Sindibad, as the bird was named by the Agency, began his journey from Abu Dhabi's coast, stopping briefly along the coastline of Ra's al-Khaimah, before heading to Khor Al Beidah in Umm al-Qaiwain. Two days later, the flamingo moved north across the Arabian Gulf, into Iran.

JUNE 2006. EAD reported that Sindibad had continued his travels, moving from Iran into Turkmenistan, stopping at important wetland sites along the way. Satellite tracking showed that the feathered traveller had flown a total of approximately 2,100 km, making use of 11 sites on his route for feeding and resting.

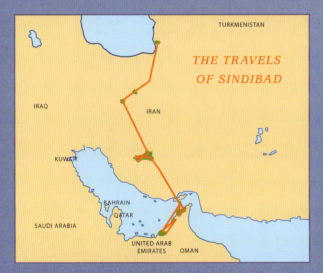

THE TRAVELS OF SINDIBAD

APRIL 2007. Sindibad was once again on his travels, beginning his second spring migration from Khor Al Beidah, Umm al-Qaiwain on March 9, 2007. He flew 132 km across the Gulf to the Iranian coast. Since he has been tagged, Sindibad has traveled more than 5,000 km (point to point distances) and spent 95 days wintering in the UAE.

In January 2006, five greater flamingos at Abu Dhabi's Al Wathba Wetland Reserve were captured and fitted with plastic rings and satellite transmitters by the Environment Agency – Abu Dhabi (EAD). This was done in order to learn more about the movements of these birds. The following month a similar exercise was undertaken by Dubai Municipality, in partnership with EAD and Dubai's Wildlife Protection Office at Dubai's Ra's Al Khor Wildlife Sanctuary.

The birds tracked in 2007 showed similar patterns of movement to the birds tracked in 2006. In both years the birds used the coastal and inland wetlands to rest and feed, underlining the importance of conserving such wetlands.

OTHER WATER BIRDS

Among the many other species that rely on saltwater or freshwater wetland habitats are herons, egrets, spoonbills, cormorants, bitterns, rails, ducks and kingfishers. Some of these are residents of the Arabian Peninsula, whilst others make use of the region's wetlands as a stopover on long migratory journeys. Still others spend a portion of each year as visitors, returning to their cooler places of origin as the summer heat approaches.

BIRDS IN MANGROVES

Mangroves are a vital habitat in which birds may feed, nest, find shade or seek shelter from predators. Among the few species of bird that nest in mangroves of the Arabian Gulf are western reef heron and striated heron. Smaller nesting species include the reed warbler, graceful prinia and palm dove. Many birds, including chiffchaffs, whitethroats and marsh warblers, use the mangroves for brief migratory stopovers.

Of special interest is the crab-eating *Halcyon chloris kalbaensis* (pictured below), an endemic subspecies of the collared kingfisher found only in the mangroves of Khor Kalba in the UAE and Khor Liwa in Oman. It is one of the rarest birds in the world.

Spoonbills use their sensitive, spoon-shaped bills to sweep through the water in search of food.

HERONS AND THEIR RELATIVES

In addition to herons, this group of wading birds includes egrets, bitterns, storks, ibises and spoonbills. They share physical characteristics that make them well-adapted for walking and feeding in shallow water: long legs, powerful bills and flexible necks. Keen eyesight helps in locating their aquatic prey, which includes fish, frogs, crabs and snails.

MAN-MADE WETLANDS

Man-made wetlands, such as golf course lakes, fish ponds, sewage lagoons and dammed reservoirs, are a magnet for water birds.

Among the **breeding species** that frequent these areas are little grebes, moorhens, black-winged stilts, red-wattled plovers, little ringed plovers and reed warblers.

Migrants include the little bittern, purple heron (see bottom of facing page), glossy ibis, spotted crake, collared pratincole and citrine wagtail.

Various ducks, such as the pochard, shoveler, garganey (right) and pintail, are among the **winter visitors**, along with the common snipe, marsh sandpiper, water rail, and others. In recent years, species such as the coot, white-tailed plover, black-necked grebe and avocet have been added to the list of birds breeding in these man-made habitats.

FASCINATING FACTS ABOUT SOCOTRA CORMORANTS

- The Socotra cormorant *Phalacrocorax nigrogularis* is **endemic** to the Arabian Peninsula. According to the IUCN, only nine breeding colonies remain of 28 formerly occupied sites: all except one or two of the presently known breeding colonies are situated in the Arabian Gulf – in the UAE, Saudi Arabia, Bahrain and Qatar.

- Not all Socotra cormorants breed at the same time, and colonies may contain eggs and hatchlings at various stages of development. As a result, the colonies are able to accommodate larger numbers of birds.

- Two to four pale blue eggs are laid in a circular depression with raised sides. Nests are placed close together, resulting in frequent squabbles between neighbouring birds.

- Chicks are pink and naked when newly hatched, but the body quickly becomes covered with down. The face and underside of the neck remain bare.

- Herring gulls gather at the edge of the colonies, and prey on both small and large chicks. As chicks mature, they are sometimes left in crèches protected by a few adult birds.

- Socotra cormorants are a coastal species, seldom seen inland.

- In spite of the large number of birds that congregate in Socotra cormorant colonies, this species is listed as vulnerable, due to its small range and the dwindling number of colonies.

- Habitat loss and degradation due to the expansion of human settlement, along with pollution, are listed as the main causes for the decline of this Arabian species.

▶▶ FOCUS ON **HOUBARA BUSTARD**

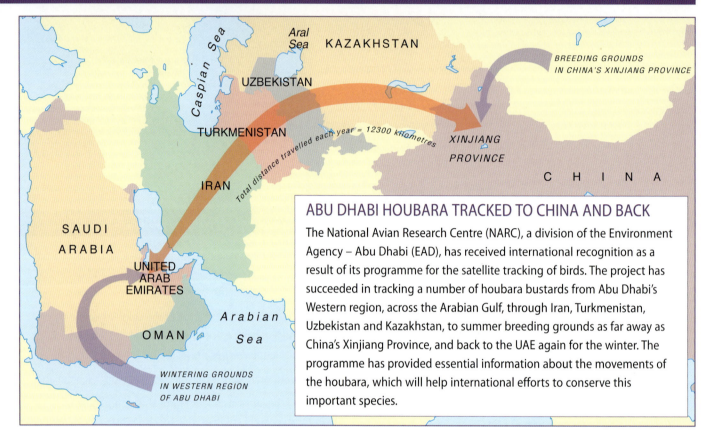

BREEDING GROUNDS
IN CHINA'S XINJIANG PROVINCE

Total distance travelled each year = 12300 kilometres

KAZAKHSTAN

Aral Sea

Caspian Sea

UZBEKISTAN

TURKMENISTAN

XINJIANG PROVINCE

IRAN

C H I N A

SAUDI ARABIA

UNITED ARAB EMIRATES

Arabian Sea

OMAN

WINTERING GROUNDS
IN WESTERN REGION
OF ABU DHABI

ABU DHABI HOUBARA TRACKED TO CHINA AND BACK

The National Avian Research Centre (NARC), a division of the Environment Agency – Abu Dhabi (EAD), has received international recognition as a result of its programme for the satellite tracking of birds. The project has succeeded in tracking a number of houbara bustards from Abu Dhabi's Western region, across the Arabian Gulf, through Iran, Turkmenistan, Uzbekistan and Kazakhstan, to summer breeding grounds as far away as China's Xinjiang Province, and back to the UAE again for the winter. The programme has provided essential information about the movements of the houbara, which will help international efforts to conserve this important species.

INTERNATIONAL COOPERATION

In April 2007, EAD announced the release of 18 houbara bustards in the mountains of Baluchistan, a province of Pakistan. The captive-bred birds were released into the wild with the cooperation of the Houbara Foundation International Pakistan (HFIP). Bred from birds of Pakistani origin, these houbara have been tagged in order to track their movements and to determine whether birds can be successfully reintroduced. NARC will also assist HFIP in conserving the habitat of these birds.

Since releases began in the UAE in 2004, a total of around 800 captive-bred birds have been released in NARC's strategy to restock depleted wild populations of houbara and to re-establish those that have become extinct.

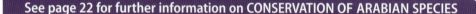

See page 22 for further information on CONSERVATION OF ARABIAN SPECIES

SHOWING OFF >>
The male houbara attracts females during the mating season by strutting around with his head thrown back and chest thrust forward. At the same time he spreads out a white crest of feathers on his head and an impressive fan of white feathers on his chest.

CAPTIVE-BRED HOUBARA NEST IN UAE DESERT

Since the spring of 2004, NARC in Sweihan, Al Ain, have released into the wild several groups of captive-bred houbara.

A conservation programme to preserve the endangered bird from extinction was launched in 1989 by the late HH Sheikh Zayed bin Sultan Al Nahyan. In May 2007, EAD (of which NARC is a part) confirmed that three chicks, hatched by one of the captive-bred females, had been found in the desert.

The discovery of the chicks affirmed Sheikh Zayed's belief that the UAE could provide a suitable habitat in which the birds would breed successfully. In 2008, 25 chicks were born to 12 females that nested in the wild.

In January 2010, 70 captive-bred houbara were released in the Western Region of Abu Dhabi Emirate. Some of these birds were equipped with either radio or satellite transmitters for monitoring purposes. Satellite tracking has shown that some of the released captive-bred houbara moved as much as 200 km away from the release site. A wild-born chick from one of the released females even travelled 600 km to Oman.

FASCINATING FACTS ABOUT HOUBARA

- Although the houbara is an excellent flyer, it spends long periods on the ground, and is able to run at speeds of up to 40 km/h.
- According to satellite tracking information, the houbara can fly as much as 1200 km between stop-over points, and can manage 700 km within a 24-hour period.
- Houbara may walk several kilometres each day while feeding.
- In order to avoid being caught by falcons, the houbara excretes a slimy, green liquid in the direction of the falcon, resulting in temporary blindness and sticky feathers, which prevent the predator from flying.
- The houbara has no oil gland with which to preen its feathers, so it keeps its feathers clean by dust-bathing.
- Like most desert species, the houbara can survive long periods without drinking. It obtains liquid from the plants and insects that it eats.

FALCONS

Falcons have played an important role in Arabia for many centuries. These birds of prey were originally used by the Bedu to hunt houbara and other birds, such as the stone curlew, which provided an essential source of protein in the diet of the desert nomads. Although peregrine and saker falcons are the birds most commonly used in falconry, a number of other species also occur in the Arabian Peninsula. As wild stocks have decreased due to habitat loss and hunting, captive breeding programmes have been introduced to relieve pressure on both falcons and their prey.

See page 13 for more information about falconry

WIDESPREAD RESIDENT

The most common of all the falcons in Arabia is the kestrel *Falco tinnunculus*. It may be seen hovering, not only in desert regions, but also over cities across the Arabian Peninsula. In addition to the large resident population, there is also a substantial number of winter migrants.

Kestrels hunt during the day, taking a wide variety of small mammals, birds and reptiles, as well as insects. They usually hunt from about 15–20 m above the ground, diving rapidly onto their prey from above. This species is an important predator of agricultural pests such as mice.

VULNERABLE SUMMER VISITOR

The sooty falcon *Falco concolor* mainly occurs as a summer visitor to the Arabian Peninsula, migrating from wintering grounds in Madagascar and, less often, the east coast of Africa, to a number of islands off Abu Dhabi Emirate and a number of other Arabian Gulf sites.

A recent survey by the Environment Agency – Abu Dhabi (EAD) indicated a sharp drop in the breeding population, which now consists of only a few pairs.

In efforts to save the sooty falcon from extinction, EAD has been instrumental in forming a new agreement the 'African-Eurasian Memorandum of Understanding on Birds of Prey' that will aid conservation efforts across international borders. On a regional level, studies by EAD and BirdLife International show that immediate action is required to conserve the remaining nesting sites on the Abu Dhabi islands and elsewhere in the Arabian Gulf.

FASCINATING FACTS

- Like most birds of prey, female falcons are larger than males.

- Male and female plumage is usually similar, but males may be slightlybrighter and have more pronounced markings.

- Since it is important for their feathers to be in top condition for flight, falcons spend considerable time in preening and bathing in dust or water.

- Falcons have superb eyesight, which is essential for catching fast-moving prey.

- Falcons do not build nests from gathered material such as grass or leaves. Instead they make a 'scrape' – a shallow depression in the ground.

- Breeding takes place once a year, when food is at its most plentiful. Females lay from one to six eggs, which are incubated for between 28 and 35 days. For the first seven to ten days, the female feeds the chicks with food caught by the male, who provides food for both the female and the chicks during the first half of the **fledgling** period.

- Some falcons, such as the peregrine, have adapted well to urban living, nesting on tall buildings and hunting pigeons and other city wildlife.

Although it is one of the two species most frequently used in falconry, the saker falcon Falco cherrug *(pictured above) is rarely seen in the wild in Arabia. Sakers are zealous and persistent hunters, a characteristic that makes them highly sought after by falconers. In 2004, the IUCN classified the saker as endangered in the wild, having undergone rapid population decline, particularly in its Central Asian breeding grounds.*

FASTEST ON THE PLANET

With the exception of rainforests and Arctic regions, the peregrine falcon *Falco peregrinus* (right) has a worldwide range. Peregrines are generally regarded to be the fastest creatures on the planet, able to reach speeds up to, or exceeding, 290 km/h in a steep dive. Their speed and superb hunting ability has made them a favourite choice for falconers.

Peregrine falcons feed almost exclusively on other birds. Occasionally, small mammals and reptiles may be eaten. After catching prey using its talons, a peregrine kills its victim by severing the neck vertebrae with its sharp, curved beak. The prey is usually plucked and eaten at a favoured eating perch.

As a species at the top of the food chain, peregrines suffered serious population declines in some parts of the world, due to the use of organochlorine pesticides such as DDT. They are no longer considered to be endangered, thanks to pesticide controls and various programmes of captive breeding and reintroduction into the wild.

>> LEARN MORE : USEFUL WEBSITES

GENERAL INFORMATION ON BIRDS

http://www.arkive.org/threatened-species/birds/ – information and superb photographs and videos of threatened bird species worldwide (listed alphabetically); includes Arabian species

http://www.bbc.co.uk/nature/class/Bird – part of the BBC Nature website; excellent photographs

http://www.pbs.org/lifeofbirds/ – companion website to David Attenborough's television series 'The Life of Birds'

http://www.birdlife.org/index.html – Birdlife is an international organisation with partners in many regions, working to conserve birds, their habitats and global biodiversity.

http://www.birdlife.org/datazone/species/downloads/BirdLife_Checkli st_Version_2.zip [.xls zipped 1 MB] BirdLife International (2009) The BirdLife checklist of the birds of the world, with conservation status and taxonomic sources

http://www.rspb.org – website of the UK-based Royal Society for the Protection of Birds; features international conservation issues, wildlife webcams and topics such as wildlife gardening and bird-watching

ARABIAN BIRDS

http://www.arabianwildlife.com/nature/bird/index.html – lots of information about birds of the UAE, much of which is generally applicable to the Arabian Peninsula

http://www.birdsoman.com/ – excellent photographs of birds and other Arabian wildlife, along with regularly updated birding reports

http://www.uaebirding.com – superb website with useful information, checklists and a very extensive collection of photographs of birds found in the Arabian Peninsula; this site also contains the UAE Nature Forum at http://www.uaebirding.com/forum/ – provides useful information and photographs, as well as an opportunity to post questions related to Arabian wildlife

http://www.birdlife.org/action/science/sites/mideast_ibas/index.html – section of the Birdlife International website featuring important bird areas of the Middle East

http://www.arabianwildlife.com/current/waders.html – article on the wading birds of the Arabian Peninsula

http://www.arabianwildlife.com/archive/vol2.3/majfly.htm – information on vultures, eagles and lesser kestrel

BIRD ANATOMY

http://www.all-birds.com/Anatomy.htm – part of a larger, informative website on birds; deals with flight, types of beaks and feet, and other aspects of bird anatomy

http://www.biology4kids.com/files/vert_bird2.html – useful, straightforward page on anatomical features of birds

http://www.paulnoll.com/Oregon/Birds/Avian-flight.html – excellent text and photographs explaining the anatomy of bird flight

FALCONS AND FALCONRY

http://www.i-a-f.org/new/ – website of the International Association for Falconry and Conservation of Birds of Prey

http://www.falconhospital.com/web/default.aspx – website of the Falconry Hospital, Abu Dhabi

BIRD MIGRATION

http://www.npwrc.usgs.gov/resource/birds/migratio/index.htm – section of the large United States Geological Survey website containing extensive information about bird migration (scroll down for contents)

http://wetlands.org/Whatwedo/Flywaysforwaterbirds/tabid/772/Defau lt.aspx – one of a series of pages on the Wetlands International website featuring water bird migration

http://www.followthebird.org/ – linked to the Wetlands International site and includes interactive map to follow purple heron migration

http://www.birdlife.org/flyways/index.html – Birdlife International's Flyways Programme – follow links on this page for more information

http://www.birdlife.org/flyways/africa_eurasia/borntotravel/index.html – video about migratory birds that use the Africa-Eurasian flyway (which includes the Arabian Peninsula)

FOR YOUNGER CHILDREN

http://www.enchantedlearning.com/subjects/birds/ – information and printouts on birds

BIRD COMMUNICATION

http://www.bl.uk/listentonature/specialinterestlang/langofbirdsconten ts.html – information on the language of birds and samples from the British Library collection of 8,000 bird songs

BIRD GLOSSARY

breeding species: bird species that reproduce on the Arabian Peninsula

endemic: native to a specific region

fledgling: a young bird that has developed its flight feathers and has learned to fly

flyway: the flight path followed by birds on their migratory journeys

migrant: refers to birds that make seasonal journeys from one location to another, due to availability of food or changes in weather or habitat conditions

passage migrant: birds that stop off in a given location, such as the Arabian Peninsula, during their annual migratory journey

raptors: birds of prey, including falcons, eagles, hawks and owls

resident: a non-migratory species that completes its lifecycle within a given region

winter visitors: birds that spend the winter months on the Arabian Peninsula, but do not breed there

ertebrates/land mammals

MAMMALS

Mammals are warm-blooded vertebrates that have a number of characteristics in common: body hair at some stage of their development, lungs to breathe air, three middle ear bones and modified sweat glands, called **mammary glands**, which produce milk for offspring.

All the mammals of the Arabian Peninsula are placental mammals, meaning that they bear live young, which, until they are born, obtain oxygen and nourishment via a **placenta** attached to the wall of the mother's **uterus**.

Grazing mammals, such as gazelles (below), usually live in herds. Belonging to a group is an effective defence against predators.

LIVING IN THE DESERT

Mammals that live in the desert have evolved methods of surviving the heat and shortage of water and food. Those that are active during the daytime find a shady place to rest when the sun is at its hottest. Many desert mammals, such as Blanford's fox *Vulpes cana* (left) are active only in the night hours, or at dusk and dawn. During the day they sleep in caves or burrows.

Desert mammals are usually light-coloured. This helps to reflect the sun's heat away from the body. Few desert mammals use sweating or panting as methods to cool themselves because these both result in water loss. Instead they have developed the ability to survive greater increases in body temperature than most mammals.

Most desert mammals have thin coats of fur. Since they are usually **herbivores**, large mammals obtain most of their water needs from the vegetation that they eat.

MAMMALS

| HEDGEHOGS AND SHREWS | BATS | CARNIVORES | EVEN-TOED HOOVED ANIMALS | HYRAXES | HARES | RODENTS | PRIMATES |

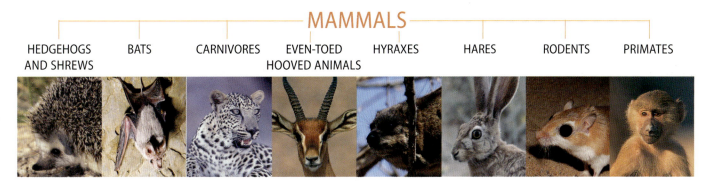

FUR COATS

True hair is unique to mammals. All mammals have hair at some stage in their lives. Marine mammals such as whales have hair as embryos.

Hairs grow from **follicles** (holes in the skin), which extend through the outer layer of skin (**epidermis**) into the lower layer (**dermis**). Each follicle is attached to a tiny muscle. Some animals can control these muscles and make their hair stand on end.

Mammals have several different kinds of hair. Guard hairs protect the inner hairs or fur. In some animals, such as the hedgehog (see photo at left), guard hairs have been modified into protective spines or quills. Underneath the guard hairs is an under-layer, which can consist of as many as three different types of hair: wool (grows continuously), fur (grows to a limited length) and down or fuzz. Whiskers are a special type of hair. They are stiff and very sensitive due to nerves located at the base. Whiskers help an animal to receive information about its surroundings.

Hair has several purposes. It insulates the body against both cold and heat and protects against injury and radiation from ultraviolet rays. The colour of individual hairs combine to form patterns in the fur. These patterns may help the animal to blend in with its surroundings or serve as a warning to others of its own species or to potential predators.

hair shaft

epidermis

follicle

sebaceous gland

dermis

muscle

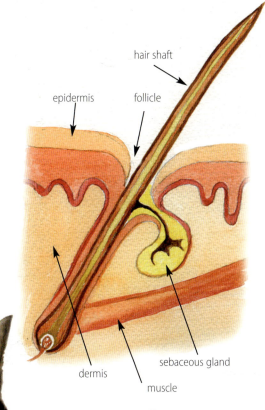

LEARNING TO SURVIVE

Mammal babies are often quite helpless when they are born. They require a prolonged period of care after birth. Since all mammals suckle their young, this helps to build a bond between the mother and her offspring. During infancy, the duration of which varies greatly between species, the young animal has an opportunity to observe and learn various skills that are important for survival.

HEDGEHOGS AND SHREWS

Three species of hedgehog occur in Arabia. They live in a variety of habitats, ranging from gardens and plantations to sandy and gravel plains, desert and mountainsides. Most widespread of the three species is the Ethiopian hedgehog *Paraechinus aethiopicus*, which is found over much of north-east Africa and throughout Arabia. Savi's pygmy shrew, perhaps the smallest mammal in the world, was discovered in the UAE only as recently as 2000, but southern Arabia, Bahrain and Oman are also known to be part of its extensive range.

When they are born, young hedgehogs have very soft, rubbery spines covered by a fluid-filled membrane, which soon dries and shrinks. Within hours the spines start to grow rapidly.

<< BRANDT'S HEDGEHOG

Brandt's hedgehog *Paraechinus hypomelas* (see photographs left and above) ranges from India to Afghanistan and Central Asia, and south to Iran and Arabia, where its population is widely scattered. Larger than the Ethiopian hedgehog, it also has bigger ears, white-based dark spines and a black face and snout. It occurs most frequently in rocky areas, but not at the highest elevations.

Mainly **nocturnal**, Brandt's hedgehog becomes active only after sundown when the temperature drops, although after rainfall it may be active during daylight, taking advantage of the abundance of emerging insects. This species rests curled up into a ball in debris, in the shade of dry bushes or in holes in the ground. Resting places are changed daily but are made semi-permanent by females with young too small to follow their mother.

ARABIA'S SMALLEST MAMMAL

Savi's pygmy shrew (also known as the pygmy white-toothed shrew) *Suncus etruscus* is the smallest mammal in Arabia. Measuring a mere 69 mm from nose to tail tip, it has a long tail, tiny eyes and rounded ears projecting from dense velvety, grey-coloured fur. Characteristic of the family is its long, pointed snout, which juts beyond the bottom lip. The heart of the Savi's pygmy shrew is believed to beat at a remarkable 20 times a second. These shrews are exceptionally nervous creatures and are extremely difficult to keep alive in captivity. Their metabolic rate is so high that they cannot survive for more than a few hours without food. They consume vast amounts of their preferred diet of insects, usually more than their own body-weight every day.

WHAT'S ON THE MENU?

Although hedgehogs have poor eyesight, their acutely developed sense of smell enables them to detect food. Favoured prey includes beetles, termites, centipedes, millipedes, grasshoppers and moths. Essentially carnivorous, besides arthropods, they eat small mice, lizards and the eggs and chicks of ground-nesting birds. Their diet even occasionally features amphibians, plant matter and fruit.

ETHIOPIAN HEDGEHOG >>

The Ethiopian hedgehog *Paraechinus aethiopicus* occurs over much of north-east Africa and throughout Arabia, including desert environments, although not in extensive mobile dunefields. It may also be found in gardens and other cultivated areas, open woodland, sandy and stony plains, and on mountainsides.

BATS

Bats are the only mammals that are truly able to fly. All bats belong to the order Chiroptera (meaning 'hand-wing'), which is divided into two groups: fruit bats, and the smaller, mainly insect-eating species. Most bats are nocturnal, and spend the day roosting in caves, rock crevices, trees and dark corners of buildings. In spite of their sinister reputation in myth and folklore, bats are of great assistance to humans in keeping down insect populations. Fruit bats play a vital role in seed dispersal and pollination.

FASCINATING FACTS

- Contrary to popular myth, bats are not blind. They see quite well, and fruit bats can even see in colour.

- Bats are not flying mice; they are more closely related to primates than rodents.

- Bats are unlikely to become tangled in human hair. Insect-eating bats use echolocation to navigate accurately at great speed in total darkness.

- A bat may eat up to 3,000 insects in a single night.

- Bats are very clean animals and spend a lot of time grooming their silky fur.

- Only three species of bats out of more than 1,000 species worldwide are vampires, and only one of these will attack humans.

- In cold countries bats hibernate through the winter. In Arabia they are active all year round.

- There are more than 1,000 bat species worldwide and they are found on every continent except Antarctica.

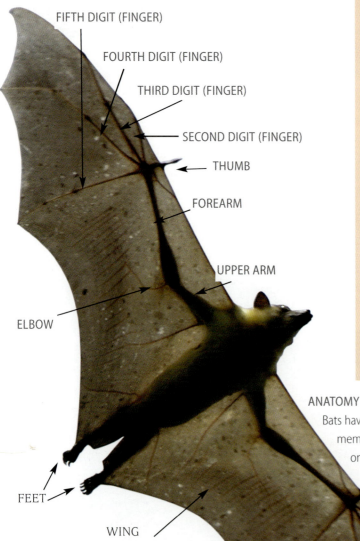

FIFTH DIGIT (FINGER)

FOURTH DIGIT (FINGER)

THIRD DIGIT (FINGER)

SECOND DIGIT (FINGER)

THUMB

FOREARM

UPPER ARM

ELBOW

FEET

WING MEMBRANE

The straw-coloured fruit bat Eidolon helvum *(pictured above) is mainly found on the African continent, but is also known to occur in the south-west of the Arabian Peninsula.*

ANATOMY

Bats have four very long fingers and a short thumb in each wing. The wing membranes are attached to the fingers and to the legs. Bats have a claw on the second finger in addition to the claw on the thumb. These are used in movement and to manipulate fruit and leaves.

Bat wings contain the same bones as a human hand. A thin, strong membrane spreads across these bones, connecting them to the bat's back and legs, like the fabric and ribs of an umbrella. The thumb clings to surfaces when the bat alights. Most bats take off by dropping from a hanging position, and many cannot take off from the ground. Bats land by slowing down until they stall and grab hold of a branch or other surface. Some bats perform a flip and then grab hold!

FRUIT BATS

Fruit bats belong to the order Megachiroptera. Only two species of fruit bat occur in the Arabian Peninsula: the Egyptian fruit bat *Rousettus aegyptiacus* (pictured below) and the straw-coloured fruit bat *Eidolon helvum*. As their name suggests, fruit bats live on fruit and the nectar of flowers. They play an important role in both pollination and seed distribution. Although they have relatively large eyes and are able to see reasonably well, fruit bats rely mainly on their excellent sense of smell to find food. Unlike other bats, most fruit bats do not use echolocation. One exception is the Egyptian fruit bat *Rousettus aegyptiacus*. Fruit bats are nocturnal and usually spend daylight hours roosting in large colonies, mainly in trees or caves. They are often found in date groves.

Insect-eating bats in the Arabian Peninsula are usually recorded close to human habitation, but they also occur in remote areas of both deserts and mountains, where they roost in crevices of rocky outcrops as well as in abandoned buildings.

SLOW REPRODUCTION

Most bat species give birth to a single offspring in each breeding season. The wings of a young bat are not strong enough to be used for flight, so the babies cling to their mother's belly fur for the first six weeks to four months, depending on the species. Like all mammals, young bats feed on their mother's milk. Bats have a relatively long life span, with some species known to survive as long as 40 years.

NAVIGATION AND COMMUNICATION

Most bats communicate and navigate using high-frequency sounds. Using echolocation, they can detect even the smallest obstacles in the total darkness of their surroundings. >> see page 52 for more information on echolocation.

WOLVES AND FOXES

The family Canidae includes coyotes, dogs, foxes, jackals, and wolves. In Arabia, this family is represented by the Arabian wolf *Canis lupus arabs*, the golden jackal *Canis aureus*, and three fox species. All **canids** are **carnivores** or flesh eaters, but some species supplement their meat diet with plant matter and invertebrates such as beetles and their larvae. Adapted for endurance more than speed, canids may pursue their prey over long distances. Prey is usually killed by grasping the back of the neck and violently shaking it, often breaking the neck.

ARABIAN WOLF

The Arabian wolf is similar in size and build to a medium-sized domestic dog – smaller than its North American and European relatives. Its short-haired coat varies in colour from pale brown to grey on the back and flanks, while the neck and belly are creamy-white. During the winter, the coat is noticeably thicker and longer, especially around the neck. Unlike wolves in other regions, the Arabian wolf is not a pack animal and generally lives in pairs or small family groups. It is capable of killing animals up to the size of a goat, but commonly eats carrion and invertebrates. Most hunting takes place at night.

Though once widespread throughout the Arabian Peninsula, wolves are now only found in parts of Jordan, Oman, Saudi Arabia and Yemen. Since hunting was banned in Oman, the wolf population has increased significantly, raising hopes that the species will re-establish itself in other regions where hunting is no longer a threat.

BLANFORD'S FOX

Vulpes cana has a patchy range in Arabia, including southern Oman and Saudi Arabia. Recent research has shown it to be common throughout the Hajar Mountains and Jebel Hafit in the United Arab Emirates. It is restricted to the rocky mountains of the peninsula, avoiding the foothills and plains inhabited by the Arabian red fox. Slightly bigger than *V. rüppelli*, this beautiful fox is readily distinguished by its long, extremely bushy tail and large, prominent ears. The soft, woolly fur, much thicker in winter, has a reddish-brown tint or greyish-buff cast. Sharply defined black tear marks extend from the internal angle of the eye to the upper lip. The feet are smaller than those of the Arabian red fox or Rüppell's fox and, unlike these species, the pads are bare, providing sure footing in rocky terrain. Extremely agile and an exceptional jumper, this nocturnal animal feeds on invertebrates, reptiles, small mammals and fruit.

RÜPPELL'S SAND FOX

Vulpes rüppelli (pictured above) is a shy, secretive desert species that ranges across North Africa, and eastwards from Arabia to Afghanistan and Pakistan. As the range of the red fox has increased with the spread of human habitation, the territory of this species has decreased.

The uniform creamy-white or pale reddish brown colouring of these foxes provides excellent camouflage in their desert surroundings. The pads of their feet are almost entirely covered by hair, presumably as an adaptation to walking in loose sand.

ARABIAN RED FOX >>

Vulpes vulpes arabica is found throughout the Arabian Peninsula in a variety of habitats, from rocky mountains to sandy desert, coastal plains and even small, offshore islands. This highly adaptable species has benefited from the expansion of human habitation, particularly from associated rat and mice populations.

Although it is the largest type of fox in Arabia, the Arabian red fox is smaller than its European equivalent. Primarily reddish-brown, the throat and belly vary from black to off-white. The tail is greyish-buff with a white tip.

HONEY BADGER (RATEL)

The honey badger *Mellivora capensis* occurs in Saudi Arabia, eastern Yemen, Qatar and possibly Oman. In August 2005, three specimens were recorded near Ruwais in western Abu Dhabi. Its world range extends through much of Africa and Asia, as far east as Nepal. With its nomadic habits and secretive behaviour, the honey badger is difficult to track, which may account for the scarcity of sightings. Its conservation status is uncertain, but at present it is not on the IUCN Red List of endangered species.

FEROCIOUS HUNTER
Honey badgers are known for their fearless hunting instinct. They have a diverse diet that includes invertebrates, lizards, rodents and mammals, but they are particularly noted for their ability to kill snakes, including those that are highly venomous. As their common name suggests, they also raid the hives of honeybees.

Large front claws, a strong, stocky body and a keen sense of smell enable the honey badger to hunt much of its rodent and reptile prey by digging into their underground burrows.

MONGOOSES

Two species of mongoose occur in the Arabian Peninsula. The white-tailed mongoose *Ichneumia albicauda* (pictured right) is a native species that ranges from south-east Arabia and north-east Africa south to the Cape. A subspecies of the Indian grey mongoose *Herpestes edwardsii ferruginens* appears to be native to the Gulf Coast of Saudi Arabia, while *H. edwardsii* itself appears to have been introduced into the UAE.

WHITE-TAILED MONGOOSE
The white-tailed mongoose is nocturnal and feeds mainly on insects. However, it may also eat small mammals, reptiles and birds, and supplements its mainly meat diet with berries and fruit. Daylight hours are spent resting in the abandoned burrows of other animals or under vegetation.

HYAENAS

Of the four hyaena species found worldwide, the striped hyaena *Hyaena hyaena* is the only species present in Arabia. The characteristic sloping back is due to its well-developed forequarters, used for digging, and the shorter, less muscular hindquarters. The striped hyaena can increase its apparent size by fluffing out its fur and raising the mane along its back. Together with body posture, ear position and tail movement, this ability is used to communicate with other animals. Despite its awkward-looking gait, the striped hyena is surprisingly agile. Its range extends throughout north Africa, and from west Asia north and east to Central Asia and Nepal.

NATURE'S RECYCLER

The striped hyaena plays an important role in desert habitats, where dry conditions slow down the decomposition of organic matter. With its large head and powerful jaws, the hyaena is able to crush and swallow large bones and body parts that other animals leave behind after a kill. The hyaena has a specialised digestive system, which allows it to extract nutrients out of these remains, and to break down bone and other tough organic matter into a form that allows it to return to the soil.

Hyaenas are ideally suited to desert life, being able to go for long periods without water. Although capable of hunting and bringing down large animals, hyaenas are primarily scavengers. Their diet includes animal carrion, reptiles, rodents, insects and a variety of fruit and vegetable matter. The pictures above show a hyaena foraging at night in a date palm grove.

CATS

Among the carnivores, the members of the cat family Felidae are the most specialised hunters. Though they vary considerably in size, all of the world's cats are remarkably similar in general appearance, with agile, muscular bodies, ideally suited for stalking and bringing down their prey. Of a total 39 species worldwide, four species of cats occur in Arabia: Arabian leopard, caracal, Gordon's wildcat and the sand cat.

GORDON'S WILDCAT >>

The genetic purity of the Gordon's wildcat *Felis silvestris gordoni,* which is restricted to the UAE and northern Oman, is under severe threat as a result of interbreeding with feral domestic cats.

Wildcats occur in semi-desert, on open plains and in more rocky terrain, but not in true desert areas of the peninsula. Almost entirely **nocturnal**, wildcats prey on rodents, small birds, insects, lizards and snakes. Their water needs are met from their food. Although predominantly **carnivorous**, wildcats will also eat some vegetable matter.

Highly adaptable, wildcats are now found with increasing regularity in and around human settlements where, unfortunately, they are considered to be pests and often killed.

<< SAND CAT

The sand cat *Felis margarita harrisoni* is Arabia's smallest **felid**, being slightly smaller than Gordon's wildcat, from which it can be easily distinguished both by its conspicuously large ears and broader head and by its sandy colour. Long, wiry, sandy-coloured hairs grow between the black paw pads, almost covering them, and assist the sand cat in walking over loose sand. The ears are also protected by coarse hairs, which prevent sand from entering.

Predominantly **nocturnal**, the sand cat feeds mainly on small rodents, although insects, reptiles and the occasional small bird are also taken. Adapted perfectly for life in an arid environment, the sand cat rarely drinks, obtaining most, if not all, of the moisture it requires from its food.

Arabia is at the centre of the sand cat's range and the species is clearly at home in sandy deserts, although it may also be found in rocky areas. The range extends north as far as Central Asia, while to the west it crosses the Sahara.

THE EYES HAVE IT

Although cats cannot see in complete darkness, they do have excellent night vision, due to the special structure of their eyes, which can let in a great deal more light than the human eye can.

The pupil of most cats' eyes is a vertical slit, which can open very wide to allow as much light in as possible. The slit can also narrow to prevent too much light entering. In addition, cats can lower their eyelids to allow in even less light.

Like a number of other primarily **nocturnal** animals, cats have a reflective layer behind the **retina**, which functions like a mirror and reflects light back into the eye, allowing better vision at night. This layer, known as the *tapetum lucidum*, is what causes the eyes to glow at night when a light is shone at them.

ARABIAN CARACAL *Caracal caracal schmitzi*

Caracal means 'black ears' in Turkish and it is this characteristic, along with the long tufts of black hair on the tips of the ears and the short muzzle, that makes this species so distinctive.

Like most desert animals, the caracal can survive for long periods without drinking water, obtaining fluids from its prey. Mainly **nocturnal**, it also hunts in the cooler early morning and late afternoon hours to catch birds, rodents, reptiles and even young or small **ungulates**. A remarkable jumper, the caracal is known for its ability to catch birds in flight, aided by its large paws and long claws. The long canine teeth are highly specialised for catching, holding and killing live prey, while the teeth towards the rear of the mouth are used to tear or slice food into smaller pieces.

Although this solitary animal is less vulnerable than many other carnivores in Arabia, experts believe that its numbers are steadily declining.

The caracal occurs throughout Africa and Arabia, across much of west Asia north to Kazakhstan, and east to northern India.

CHEETAH FACTS

• The cheetah, with its small head, long limbs and deep chest cavity, is the fastest land animal in the world, capable of bursts of speed up to 110 km/h.

• Sadly, the cheetah is now extinct in Arabia, and is endangered throughout its range due to hunting and environmental pressures such as loss of habitat and population decline in prey species.

• The cheetah is the only cat species without the ability to retract its claws. This allows more traction when running at speed.

ARABIAN LEOPARD

The Arabian leopard *Panthera pardus nimr* is the largest and most powerfully built of the Arabian cats, but is the smallest of the 15 subspecies of leopard. Predominantly pale golden yellow-brown, its coat fades to a pale yellow or white on the belly and is interspersed with widely spaced rosettes, adaptations that help to camouflage the leopard in rocky terrain. The long tail is used to balance while climbing or when reclining in trees.

Leopards favour the rugged mountains of the Arabian Peninsula and once occurred wherever there was permanent water and sufficient prey. Their distribution extended from the Musandam in the north-east, along an almost continuous band parallel to the coast, through southern Oman into Yemen, and north to Tabuk in Saudi Arabia. Although perhaps never common, persecution by humans, along with rapid development, has seen their range decrease dramatically. Experts estimate that the total population now numbers less than 250 individuals, scattered in small, isolated populations in Oman, Saudi Arabia, the UAE and Yemen.

As numbers of traditional prey species such as the Arabian tahr *Hemitragus jayakari*, Nubian ibex *Capra nubiana*, mountain or Arabian gazelle *Gazella gazella cora* and the birds, chukar *Alectoris chukar* and sand partridge *Amnoperdix heyi*, have decreased, leopards have been forced to prey upon domestic livestock, bringing them into direct conflict with humans.

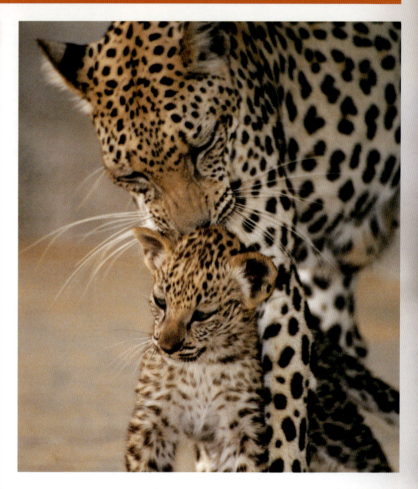

In order to find enough food and water to survive, leopards require large territories. A male's territory may overlap those of several females and is patrolled continuously to prevent other males from occupying the same area. Normally solitary animals, leopards only come together to mate.

After a gestation period of up to 100 days, a litter of one to three cubs is born, hidden in a cave or under an overhang. The cubs are deaf and blind at birth, and although their eyes open after five to six days, it is not until they are two weeks old that they will begin to explore their immediate surroundings in the den. They generally do not emerge from the security of the den until they are at least four weeks old, by which time their coordination has improved dramatically. During these first weeks, the female will move the cubs from one den to another several times to reduce the risk of them being discovered.

The cubs remain with their mother for up to two years while they learn the skills necessary to survive on their own. Females will not breed again until the cubs have left. Such a slow reproductive rate is a major factor in the leopard's decline.

For information on conservation of endangered species, see page 22 ▶

ROCK HYRAX

At first glance, the rock hyrax *Procavia capensis* looks like a rodent, but in fact this native of southern and western Arabia has more in common with elephants than rats! At one stage, hyraxes were placed in the same order as elephants due to similarities in their skulls and feet, but now hyraxes have their own order, Hyracoidea. This contains a single family, Procaviidae, with seven hyrax species. Modern DNA analysis has recently added further evidence of the link between elephants and the hyraxes.

FASCINATING FACTS

• Hyrax teeth are quite different from those of other small animals. The two long, sharp, upper **incisors** (cutting teeth) look like miniature tusks and are used for defence. The bottom **incisors** are used for grooming. Instead of **canine teeth**, hyraxes have has a space next to the incisors, followed by **molars**, which grow continuously, as they are worn down by constant grazing and browsing.

• Hyraxes have blunt-toed feet. Secretions from sweat glands in the feet, along with a network of tiny muscles in the rubbery soles, help the hyrax to gain traction when climbing rocks and trees. The forefeet have four toes each whilst each hindfoot has three. The nails are flat and hoof-like, except for the second toe on each hind foot, which has a long, curved claw used for grooming.

• Hyraxes are sociable animals that live in colonies, often established over centuries. Older males act as lookouts, giving a shrill warning whistle to the others when a predator approaches. Hyraxes always urinate in the same spot, producing heavy crystalline deposits on the rocks due to the high concentraion of minerals in the urine. These deposits were once used in traditional medicine.

CAMEL

The camel or dromedary *Camelus dromedarius* was first domesticated between 4000 and 2000 BC.

Ideally suited to life in the desert, the camel is known as *Ata Allah* (God's gift) and has been an integral part of Arabia's long history, supplying transport, milk, meat, wool, leather and fuel (dried dung) for human use. In the modern world, though humans are no longer dependent on the camel, this 'ship of the desert' is now highly prized as a racing animal, capable of speeds up to 20 km/h.

SURVIVING IN THE DESERT

Camels can survive for long periods without drinking and are able to withstand substantial (up to 30 per cent) dehydration, compared to a tolerance of about 15 per cent in most animals. Their ability to tolerate fluctuations in body temperature of nearly 8°C celsius means that camels do not need to cool themselves by sweating. They are also able to tolerate high levels of salt in their plant food. When they have access to water, camels are able to rehydrate rapidly and can drink up to 130 litres in about ten minutes.

Contrary to popular belief, the camel's hump contains fat, not water. This fatty hump supplies the camel with essential nutrients in times of food scarcity. The size of the hump varies, depending on how much and often a camel eats..

Camel physiology is specially adapted for life in arid desert conditions. Each foot has two toes and broad, leathery pads that spread to prevent the foot from sinking into the sand. As protection from blowing sand, camels can close their nostrils, have a double row of long eyelashes and have ears that are covered with fur both inside and out. Thick, leathery lips allow camels to feed on thorny desert plants.

Females usually give birth to a single calf after a gestation period of 15 months. Calves are able to walk within 24 hours of birth, but remain with their mothers until they reach maturity at around four years of age.
Mothers nurse their offspring for one to two years. Camel's milk is sweet and very nutritious. It has less fat and lactose than cow's milk, but contains more potassium, iron and vitamin C.

Camels are strong, muscular animals, capable of carrying heavy loads over long distances. Their endurance, combined with their other unique qualities, made camels essential and valuable components of the nomadic life for thousands of years.

▶▶ FOCUS ON **ARABIAN ORYX**

FASCINATING FACTS

- Oryx rarely run but can walk long distances at a steady pace, covering up to 50 km in a night.

- Oryx can go without fresh water for more than nine months at a time.

- Oryx meet virtually all their water requirements from the plants that they eat and by feeding around dawn when water from fog and dew on leaves is at its maximum.

- It has been claimed that Arabian oryx follow the smell of rainfall.

- Oryx possess a complex method of ensuring that the temperature of the blood reaching the brain remains substantially below that of the body. Warm arterial blood on its way to the brain is cooled by passing through a sinus of venous blood returning from the nasal passages, which has been cooled down by panting.

DESERT DWELLERS

Arabian oryx are very well-adapted to life in the desert. Unlike most grazing antelope species, they live in small groups rather than large herds. The brightness of their white coats makes them highly visible within their surroundings. This may be important in enabling members of a group to locate one another, as well as in reflecting heat away from the body.

REPRODUCTION

After reaching sexual maturity at 1–1.5 years of age, a female oryx will usually calve every year, as long as there is adequate food and water. During periods of prolonged drought, birth rates decline and females may not have enough milk to feed their calves. Birth usually takes place away from other oryx. For the first few weeks, calves spend most of the day lying in a shady spot, drinking from their mother, who will visit them up to 14 times a day.

For information on conservation of endangered species, see page 22

SAVED FROM THE BRINK

The Arabian oryx *Oryx leucoryx* once roamed the entire Arabian Peninsula, but it became extinct as a wild species in the early 1960s. Having been reintroduced into very large reserves in the UAE, Oman, Jordan and Saudi Arabia, the Arabian oryx is no longer considered critically endangered by the World Conservation Union, IUCN.

GAZELLES

Gazelles are small to medium-sized members of the antelope family, characterised by their long, ringed horns and their ability to run and jump. Four species of gazelle have been identified in Arabia. The Arabian gazelle *Gazella gazella* is further divided into four subspecies. At one time, gazelles were widespread across the Arabian Peninsula, but their numbers have decreased dramatically due to hunting and encroaching human development.

ARABIAN GAZELLE

The mountain gazelle has a pure white belly with a dark to black stripe on its flanks that changes to dark beige or brown on the back, the neck and the head. The facial markings consist of various shades of brown with two white stripes extending from the eyes towards the nostrils.

FASCINATING FACTS

• Male and female sand gazelles *Gazella subgutturosa marica* have differently shaped horns, males often having sharp, hooked tips to their horns, which are broader in diameter than those of the females.

• The male sand gazelle has large scent glands on his face. Scent marking is not a very useful activity for animals with large, constantly changing territories; however, sand gazelles may have small winter territories where the ability to mark with scent glands is an advantage.

• Sand gazelles are mainly browsers, eating grass, herbs and woody plants depending on availability. On islands, the tubers and shoots of the parasitic desert hyacinth *Cistanche tubulosa* are frequently sought by sand gazelles.

Sand gazelles often give birth twice in a year, usually in spring and autumn, and are the only antelopes that regularly give birth to twins. The young are hidden for the first few days until they are strong enough to move with the herd.

SAND GAZELLE

The sand gazelle has an extensive range from Arabia and south-west Asia to the Transcaucasus, Central Asia, Mongolia and western China. It is quite distinct from the Arabian gazelle and only very distantly related. Sand gazelles are light buff-coloured above, with a white under-belly and face, the only contrast being their black nose and mouth and large black eyes. They usually rely on concealment to escape detection, their first response to danger being to freeze. Only on a predator's continued approach do they flee.

The *idhmi* or mountain gazelle *Gazella gazella* inhabits the gravel plains, foothills and mountains along the outer fringes of the Arabian Peninsula. Its range is often associated with *Acacia*. Unlike many **ungulates**, the mountain gazelle is generally seen singly or in small groups.

USEFUL FACTS

- Fawns are usually born singly during January and August and remain hidden in a hollow or under shrubs for the first few days. Females are able to give birth twice a year, as their **gestation period** is just less than six months, although this is uncommon, even amongst captive herds.

- The chest, belly, backs of the limbs and inner thighs are pure white. The dominant colour on the back is a light reddish, sandy brown, with a dark stripe along the flanks. Individual variation is extensive, with the stripes in some individuals substantially darker than in others.

- Gazelles have a characteristic gait of bouncing or 'pronking' along stiff-legged with all four limbs landing together. This is generally seen when they are playing or alarmed.

For information on conservation of endangered species, see page 22

NUBIAN IBEX

The Nubian ibex *Capra nubiana* is a goat-like **herbivore** found in arid, rocky, desert mountain regions in isolated parts of Arabia, as well as in north-eastern Africa. Classified by the IUCN as endangered, the Nubian ibex is under threat from habitat loss and degradation and from poaching. Among the protected areas providing sanctuary for this now rare species are the reserves at Yalooni, Huqf and Wadi Sirab in Oman, At-Tubayq in northern Saudi Arabia and Hawtat Bani Tamim, near Riyadh. The Mujib Reserve in Jordan has established a successful captive breeding programme, from which a number of Nubian ibex have been returned to the wild.

JUST LOOK AT THOSE HORNS!

Among the most distinctive features of the Nubian ibex are the magnificent backward-curving, ridged horns of the bucks (males). The smooth sandy-coloured coat fades to almost white on the undersides, and bucks have a darker stripe along the back and on the front legs. Older males have a beard. During the rutting season in October, the sandy colouring of the males becomes considerably darker.

MOUNTAIN DWELLERS

The Nubian ibex is active during the day, often leaving its **nocturnal** resting place on the cooler upper slopes to negotiate a steep descent to the lower levels in order to graze on grass and other vegetation.

During the winter months, the ibex looks for more sheltered spots at lower elevations in which to rest and to avoid seasonal rains.

Unlike many desert mammals, the Nubian ibex drinks frequently, and is, therefore, vulnerable to drought and polluted water sources.

FAMILY LIFE

The mating season occurs in late summer. The largest mature males use their horns to spar with one another as they fight for breeding rights. After mating takes place, females usually give birth about five months later to a single offspring, although twins, and even triplets, are occasionally born. Young kids stay with their mothers in a small herd of females until they reach maturity at two to three years of age. Nubian ibex live to about 17 years of age.

FASCINATING FACTS

- Although other species of tahr are found in India and the Himalayas, the Arabian tahr *Hemitragus jayakari* is found only in the mountains of the UAE and northern Oman. It has been recorded in wadis on the east coast of the UAE, and there is also a critically small population on Jebel Hafit.

- Births appear to take place almost throughout the year, with November being a possible exception. The gestation period is 140–145 days.

- If tahr are found in groups, these are always small, consisting of a female and kid or a male and female with a kid. Males are usully solitary, and never associate with another male.

- Highly territorial, males scrape the soil with their hooves, marking it with dung and urine. Vegetation in the area is also 'horned'. Male tahr rub their chests against rocks to scent-mark with glandular secretions.

- This species requires access to water to survive, usually visiting favourite waterholes in the late evening or early morning. This dependence has led to a steady decline in the species' population as hunters lie in wait to ambush them.

DESCRIPTION

Weighing approximately 23 kg, the tahr is relatively small, although it is both strong and agile. The stocky males have compact, solid horns, impressive manes that extend right down the back and reddish-tinted leg tassels. With age, their manes grow longer, they develop a beard and their striped faces become blacker.

FEMALES

In contrast to the males, the females have slender horns, much shorter, less obvious manes and lack the leg tassels. The lightweight summer pelt becomes a coarsely shaggy coat in winter to provide insulation. Both males and females have rubbery hooves that provide traction on steep slopes and cliffs.

CALVES

The calves are grey in colour at birth, changing to greyish-brown around the same time as their horns start to grow. No doubt the Arabian leopard was the tahr's natural enemy, but today it is the destruction of their natural habitat by feral goats, as well as poaching, that keep their numbers dangerously low.

For further information on the conservation of Arabian species, see page 22 ▶

HARE

The Cape hare *Lepus capensis* has a wide range across a wide variety of habitats and climatic types. It is found throughout Africa, the Middle East and Central Asia as far as eastern China. Numerous subspecies have been described, eight of which are found in Arabia. The Cape hare was, until recently, thought to be the same species as the European hare *L. europaeus* (also known as the brown hare). Regional and seasonal differences in coat colour within subspecies make identification difficult.

BIG EARS
Like a number of other desert mammals, the hare has unusually large ears compared to its body size. This adaptation assists the hare to locate others of its own species, as well as being a means of cooling the body.

FASCINATING FACTS

• Unlike rabbits, the hare does not live in burrows. Instead, it spends the day motionless with its ears folded back, relying totally on its camouflage, remaining in shallow **scrapes** (forms) under bushes or in the open. If it is flushed from its **form**, a hare will not return to that same spot for several months.

• Desert Cape hares are small, having an average weight of approximately 1 kg, compared to 3.9 kg for a European hare. Within the species *L. capensis*, however, there is huge variation – the mean body mass of Cape hares in China is approximately 2.2 kg in autumn, whilst Cape hares of the Sahara desert, which utilise a different type of habitat altogether, are reportedly much larger.

• Cape hares have a much lower metabolic rate than European hares, which keeps the body temperature down. They can also tolerate drinking water of 6 per cent salinity, (sea water is about 3.5 per cent), compared to 2 per cent salinity for European hares.

• In common with other mammals that have adapted to life in the desert, the desert Cape hare does not need to drink water, but obtains all the moisture it needs from the grasses and shrubs it eats.

• As **nocturnal herbivores**, desert Cape hares emerge from their forms shortly after sunset, usually returning to the same resting-place at or around sunrise.

FOOD AND WATER
Desert Cape hares obtain water from their food and, consequently, prefer succulent plants such as *Tetraena mandevillei*. They also eat fresh shoots of *Acacia* shrubs and most grasses. Another favourite food plant is the small **perennial** *Limeum arabicum*.

Both the expansion of human settlement into desert regions and the impact of camel grazing on the flora have had a significant effect on the hare's habitat. Many plains formerly covered by succulent vegetation are now totally barren, through over-grazing and, in some cases, over-extraction of groundwater.

REPRODUCTION

Although desert Cape hares breed throughout the year, winter is the main breeding season. In good conditions, they can breed rapidly, having one or two offspring at a time. Females can become pregnant immediately following delivery. During the breeding season males are often seen chasing each other as they try to attract females.

Young hares, or **leverets**, are born fully furred with their eyes open and are able to survive without their mother once they are between seven and ten days old. The baby hares are left by the mother in separate locations, where she visits them a couple of times a night to let them suckle. The advantage of this system is, that if one young is found by a fox or another predator, only that individual will be killed and not the whole litter. Should the mother vanish, then the babies are able to fend for themselves from a very early age.

*Hares have large, round eyes, which allow them a 360 degree view of their surroundings, whilst resting in shallow **scrapes** in soft sand. If it feels secure, a hare may 'cat-nap', closing its eyes and falling into a half-sleep. Deep sleep, however, is rare and brief – no more than a few minutes per day. During deep sleep the eyes are closed and the hare lies on its side. If it senses danger, a hare will press itself close to the ground and become rigid and motionless, relying on its sandy-coloured coat for camouflage. When it is too hot for their ears to radiate body heat, desert Cape hares may restrict blood flow to the ears and press them flat against their body in order to provide shade.*

RODENTS

There are about 23 species of rodent found in Arabia, most of which are in the mouse and rat family. Together with bats, rodents are the most diverse mammal group in the region, successfully occupying all terrestrial habitats represented, from the most arid deserts to the highest mountains and offshore islands, even if, in some instances, only in close association with man.

JERBOAS

Jerboas are agile little rodents with large hind legs and strong, elongated hind feet, well-suited to jumping distances in excess of their own size. The front legs are short and used for digging and gathering food. A long tail aids locomotion by acting as a counter-balance when leaping. Jerboas can survive without drinking, obtaining water through the metabolisation of the starch in seeds and plants eaten. Two species of jerboa occur in the Arabian Peninsula.

The lesser jerboa *Jaculus jaculus* (pictured right) has large ears and eyes and a stubby snout. As with most small desert mammals, it is only active at night. Most commonly seen on gravel plains and flat sandsheets, the lesser jerboa has tufts of hair between its three toes to enable traction in soft, loose sand.

Unlike *J. jaculus*, the **five-toed jerboa** *Allactaga euphratica* lacks hair between the toes, and occurs in stony foothills and around the grassy margins of wadi systems, but not in true sand desert. Of its five toes, only three are functional.

RATS AND MICE

The **black rat** *Rattus rattus* and **brown rat** *R. norvegicus,* **soft-furred rat** *Praomys fumatus* and **African grass rat** *Arvicanthis niloticus*, along with the **house mouse** *Mus musculus*, are all invasive species. introduced by humans. There are three native species: the Egyptian spiny mouse, the golden spiny mouse and the short-tailed bandicoot rat.

Spiny mice have a stiff, bristly coat, which can stand on end like porcupine's or hedeghog's spines. Colouring varies from one region to another, depending on the surroundings. Unable to conserve water as efficiently as some desert mammals, spiny mice excrete a very thick, concentrated urine. They are dependent on moisture from their diet of succulent plants, berries, small invertebrates and reptiles.

The **Egyptian spiny mouse** *Acomys cahirinus dimidiatus* (pictured left) is dark to reddish-brown in colour with a pale underside. It occurs at all elevations on mainly hard, rocky soils. Unusually for Arabian rodents, the **golden spiny mouse** is active during the day, and is only found in arid, rocky areas. Both species find shelter under ground.

The **short-tailed bandicoot rat** *Nesokia indica* spends little time on the surface. It prefers locations with moist vegetation and soft soil for burrowing out extensive tunnel systems. Its diet consists of leaves and grass roots, but it is known to devour food crops, giving rise to the alternative common name, pest rat.

GERBILS AND JIRDS

Gerbils are small to medium-sized rodents with very acute senses. They are found throughout Africa and the Middle East, and across central Asia, including much of India, to eastern Mongolia. Most species live in dry, open habitats with sparse vegetation, including deserts, sandy plains and mountain slopes.

Gerbils generally have well-furred, long tails and long, narrow, clawed hind feet. Like jerboas, most gerbil species are efficient jumpers. Those living in rocky habitats are often good climbers. There are five species of gerbil that are common in Arabia, as well as a number of other less common species. Of the five common species, three belong to the genus *Gerbillus*, while the remaining two are from the sub-family of Asiatic gerbils known as jirds.

The **Baluchistan gerbil** *Gerbillus nanus* (pictured above) is a tiny species, which lives in sand and salt flats, often using the burrows of other rodents. Its range extends from North Africa to Baluchistan.

The **Wagner's gerbil** *G. dasyrus* is restricted to Arabia and Egypt and has a distinct preference for rocky terrain. It lacks hair on its feet.

The **Cheesman's gerbil** *G. cheesmani* (top right) is widespread in sand and gravel desert areas. Usually nocturnal, it may emerge from its burrow before sunset. The soles of its feet, in common with the lesser jerboa and certain other desert species, are thickly haired. This species ranges throughout Arabia and into the extreme south of Iran.

Unlike the smaller, solitary gerbils, jirds live in large colonies and accumulate large communal stores of food. This may be an ancient adaptation to life in a much colder climate than the present one. The **Libyan jird** *Meriones libycus* and **Sundevall's jird** *M. crassus* (pictured below) are both heavily built, greyish-brown in colour and have a black tuft at the tip of the tail. The head is quite broad, with features similar to those of a hamster. The only visible difference between the two animals are the claws. The Libyan jird's claws are dark to black, whilst those of Sundevall's jird are ivory in colour. Both species favour desert with shrubs and small bushes, and appear to be absent from the mountains.

<< LOCALLY COMMON

The **king jird** *M. rex* is an endemic species, confined to south-western Arabia, in particular, the mountains of Yemen, where it has been found at elevations of 1,350–2,200 m. Its rough fur has a much harsher texture than that of other jirds. The soles of the feet are without hair, reflecting its preference for trees and rocky surroundings. It appears to be active only during the evening and early morning.

BABOONS

The sacred, or hamadryas, baboon *Papio hamadras* is found in the semi-arid and savannah regions of Africa, as well as in Saudi Arabia and Yemen in the south-western Arabian Peninsula. Although long native to Arabia, it is thought that the species must originally have crossed from the other side of the Red Sea.

COMPLEX SOCIAL STRUCTURE

Hamadryas baboon society is organised on a clan basis, with one or two dominant males, each of which heads a group consisting of breeding females, other females, juveniles, infants and elderly baboons. The dominant males ensure that no other males mate with the females in their group. A female rises in the social hierarchy when she ovulates and when she gives birth. Baby baboons are a source of great interest and attention within the group, particularly while they still retain their black infant fur.

A male attempting to establish his own group often befriends a young female, grooming her and caring for her in much the same way as a parent. When she is sexually mature, he will mate with her.

WATCH OUT!

A male baboon shows aggression with a tension yawn, which displays the impressive canine teeth. Staring and moving the head up and down are also forms of threatening behaviour.

FASCINATING FACTS

- Female hamadryas baboons are much smaller than males – approximately 10 kg compared to about 21.5 kg.

- Grooming is a very important part of baboon society. This activity not only helps to control parasites, but also to maintain social relationships within the group, due to its calming effect.

- Hamadryas baboons are **omnivores**. They forage for seeds, roots and leaves, but also eats birds and invertebrates such as termites.

- Male hamadryas baboons are silver-grey in colour, with a long mane and whiskers; females are olive-brown and have no mane. Adults of both sexes have a pink face and rump.

- Baboons are ground dwellers and walk on four legs.

- Hamadryas baboons were considered sacred by the ancient Egyptians, who mummified them and placed them in tombs. They were depicted on temple walls as representations of Thoth, the god of writing and knowledge.

>> LEARN MORE : USEFUL WEBSITES

GENERAL INFORMATION ON MAMMALS

http://animals.nationalgeographic.com/animals/mammals.html – information and photographs on a wide range of mammal species

http://www.iwrc-online.org/kids/Facts/Mammals/mammal_families.htm – useful information about mammals – easy navigation

http://www.worldwildlife.org/species/ – superb website of the WWF with extensive information and a strong empasis on conservation of endangered species

http://www.kidsplanet.org/ – a lively website full of information about mammals and other wildlife; interactive, with excellent navigation

http://www.thewebsiteofeverything.com/ – fact-filled website with a large number of links to further online information about mammals

http://www.arkive.org/threatened-species/mammals/ – easy, searchable alphabetical list of endangered species with superb images, videos and fact files

ARABIAN MAMMALS

http://www.arabianwildlife.com/nature/mammal/index.html – information on Arabian mammals, from jerboas to the Arabian leopard

http://www.arabianwildlife.com/archive/vol2.1/hedge.htm – informative article on Arabian hedgehogs

http://www.arabianwildlife.com/archive/vol2.3/mice.htm – article providing information on some of Arabia's rodents

http://www.enhg.org/bulletin/mammals.htm – a useful interactive list of articles about Arabian mammals that can be found on the Emirates Natural History Group website

www.echoesecology.co.uk/documents/BatsoftheUAE_000.pdf – excellent information on Arabian bats in downloadable PDF format

http://www.breedingcentresharjah.com/Small%20Mammals.html – information and photographs of small Arabian mammals

ENDANGERED ARABIAN MAMMALS

http://www.arkive.org/arabian-oryx/oryx-leucoryx/ – images, video footage and fact file about the Arabian oryx

http://www.arkive.org/arabian-leopard/panthera-pardus-nimr/video-ni00.html – video clip of Arabian leopard with cub in the wild, as well as several images and a fact file

http://www.arkive.org/arabian-tahr/hemitragus-jayakari/video-00.html – video clips showing the Arabian tahr in its natural habitat, along with a fact file and a number of images

http://www.arkive.org/sand-cat/felis-margarita/video-02.html – two superb video clips of the sand cat and its habitat

EXTINCT ARABIAN MAMMALS

http://www.arabianwildlife.com/archive/vol1.2/onager.htm – article on the demise of the onager or wild ass in Arabia

FUN PAGES

http://www.worldwildlife.org/how/fun/index.html – part of the WWF website; games, photographs, e-cards

http://wwf.worldwildlife.org/site/PageServer?pagename=trib_home – this part of the WWF website allows children to create a mini-website to help the WWF's conservation work

FOR YOUNGER CHILDREN

http://www.enchantedlearning.com/subjects/mammals/ – well-presented information on a wide variety of mammals, including classification, evolution, anatomy and behaviour

MAMMALS GLOSSARY

canid: a member of the biological family Canidae, which includes, dogs, wolves, foxes, jackals and coyotes

canine (teeth): sharp, pointed teeth found in mammals, used for puncturing flesh

carnivore: an animal whose diet consists mainly of meat

dermis: the layer of skin under the **epidermis**, containing blood vessels, hair **follicles**, nerve endings and sweat glands

epidermis: outer skin layer covering the body surface of vertebrates

felid: referring to members of the cat family, Felidae, such as leopard and cheetah

follicle: tiny shaft in the skin of mammals through which a hair grows

gestation period: the time period between fertilisation and birth in **placental** mammals

herbivore: an animal that eats only plants

incisor: front teeth of a mammal, used for biting and cutting

leveret: young hare under a year old

mammary glands: milk-producing glands in female mammals

molars: back teeth of a mammal, used for grinding and chewing

nocturnal: active at night

omnivore: an animal that eats both plant and animal matter

placenta: organ that provides nutrients and oxygen to unborn offspring while they are in the mother's womb during pregnancy

retina: membrane on the back of the inside of the eyeball that converts images into electrical impulses, which are then sent to the brain

scrape: a shallow depression in the ground used as a resting place by hares

tapetum lucidum: a reflective layer on the back of the eyeball of some **nocturnal** vertebrates, which aids night vision

ungulates (even-toed): hoofed grazing mammals with an even number of toes on each foot, such as gazelles, camels, oryx and goats

ungulates (odd-toed): hoofed grazing mammals with an odd number of toes on each foot, such as horses

uterus: female reproductive organ in which offspring develop prior to birth

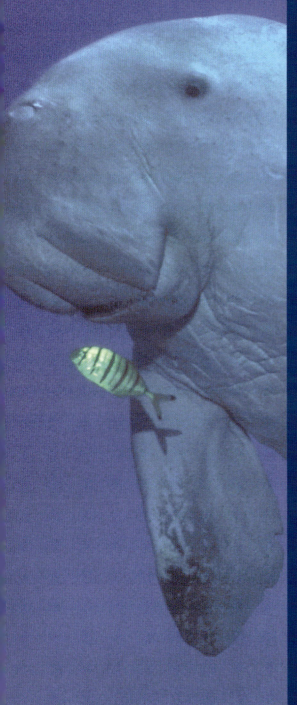

ertebrates/marine mammals

arabian wildlife encyclopedia

WHALES AND DOLPHINS

Whales belong to a group of mammals called **cetaceans**. Like land mammals, have a four-chambered heart, are warm-blooded and have mammary glands with which they feed their young. Unlike fish, which breathe through gills, they breathe air through **blowholes** (nostrils) on the top of the head. Whales are divided into two groups: toothed whales and **baleen** whales. Toothed whales, which include dolphins, use their teeth to catch fish, squid, and other marine life, which they swallow whole. They have a single blowhole (nostril) and use **echolocation** to hunt. Baleen whales are larger than the toothed whales and have two blowholes. They sieve small fish, **plankton** and **krill** from the water by means of **baleen plates**, which are comb-like structures that act as filters. Five species of baleen whale and 16 species of toothed whales and dolphins are known to occur in Arabian waters.

BLUE WHALE

Balaenoptera musculus
(pictured right, at top)
Named after the silvery blue sheen of their mottled skin, blue whales are the largest mammals on the planet. They have been reported in Arabian waters but sightings are rare. On surfacing, the powerful blow shoots straight and high into the air, allowing experienced observers to identify the species immediately.

LOUDEST ANIMAL ON EARTH

Blue whales have very deep voices that transmit at a very low frequency – often below the range of human hearing. Their vocalisations can measure more than 180 decibels (db). Human conversation is measured at about 60–70 db, jet engines at around 140 db, and the louder rock concerts at 150 db. Whale sounds travel over long distances underwater, and are used to communicate with other whales. Tiny crustaceans called **krill** form the basis of the blue whale's diet.

HUMPBACK WHALES

The humpback whale *Megaptera novaeangliae* may reach up to 18 m in length. Male humpbacks are noted for their complex, haunting 'songs', which are thought to be a part of their mating behaviour. While there are occasional humpback sightings in the Arabian Gulf, they are more commonly seen in the Arabian Sea, where scientists have been studying a small group that appear to be the only non-migratory humpback whales in the world. Most humpbacks undertake long seasonal migrations from the warmer waters of their breeding grounds to cooler waters where there is an abundance of food.

BRYDE'S WHALE *Balaenoptera edeni* (above)
The Bryde's whale's preference for warm waters has earned it the alternative common name of 'tropical whale'. Bryde's whales are distinguished from other rorquals by three prominent parallel ridges on the head. The central ridge is the most pronounced, and is the only one present in blue, fin, sei and minke whales. Bryde's whales are found throughout Arabian waters.

In April 2009, a combined team of Environment Agency – Abu Dhabi (EAD) and Critical National Infrastructure Authority personnel recovered the partially decomposed body of a 9-m-long Bryde's whale from the waters off Abu Dhabi. Lacerations to its **fluke** (tail), probably from a large boat propeller, may have been the cause of death.

ECHOLOCATION

Toothed whales use **echolocation** to obtain information about their environment and to locate prey at night or in murky water. The whale sends out high-pitched sounds (usually clicks) that bounce off an object in the vicinity. Some of these echoes return to the whale, which can then determine the object's shape, direction, distance, and texture.

COMMON BOTTLENOSE DOLPHIN *Tursiops truncatus*

The common bottlenose (above) is a large, robust dolphin. In the Gulf of Oman this species frequently exceeds 3 m in length. The beak, from which its common name derives, is relatively short and stubby, with a clear crease separating it from the bulbous forehead. The Indo-Pacific bottlenose dolphin *T. aduncus* is considerably smaller and more slender than the common bottlenose dolphin, and has a relatively longer beak.

KILLER WHALE *Orcinus orca* (below)

This is the biggest and most powerful of the dolphins. With its striking black and white colouration, a killer whale is unmistakable. In an adult male, the huge, triangular **dorsal** fin is sometimes 1.5 m or more high. Killer whales tend to travel in close-knit family **pods** of as many as 30 individuals. Around Arabia they live in the open ocean, but have been known to enter shallower water, including the Arabian Gulf. Prey in Arabian waters may include other **cetaceans** as well as turtles, sea birds and cold-blooded creatures such as fish and squid.

RISSO'S DOLPHIN *Grampus griseus*

A large dolphin, up to 4 m in length, Risso's dolphin lacks a clear beak, and has a stocky, blunt head. The body is robust but tapers off from the dorsal fin to tail, giving the dolphin an almost tadpole-like appearance. Risso's dolphin is a deep-water species, diving for squid and fish over underwater canyons and at the edge of the continental shelf to depths probably exceeding 1,000 m.

FASCINATING FACTS

• A blue whale calf drinks nearly 500 litres of milk per day, and grows in weight while nursing by 85–90 kg daily.

• A 160 tonne blue whale is equal in weight to 2,000 adult humans weighing 80 kg each.

• A large blue whale has a heart that is the size of a small car and has 6.4 tonnes of blood circulating in its body.

• Many **cetaceans**, especially **baleen** whales, migrate over very long distances each year. Grey whales travel the greatest distance, covering 20,000 km each year.

• The sperm whale dives to as much as 3,000 m below the sea's surface to hunt for giant squid.

DUGONG

Besides the **cetaceans**, the only other marine mammal that lives in Arabian waters is the dugong *Dugong dugon*. Dugongs belong to the order Sirenia, which they share with the manatees, or sea cows, of the Americas. Archaeological studies in the UAE indicate that dugongs have been exploited by man for more than 7,000 years. Today, dugongs mostly inhabit the shallow waters around the islands west of Abu Dhabi and between Qatar and Bahrain. There are also records extending up the coast from Abu Dhabi, as far as Umm al-Qaiwain and even Ra's al-Khaimah, as well as north-east towards Qatar and beyond.

*Dugongs and manatees are the world's only **herbivorous** marine mammals. The dugong feeds almost exclusively on seagrasses. The rich and extensive seagrass beds in UAE waters form the most important habitat for dugong in the Arabian Gulf, which hosts the world's second largest population of this species, thought to number at least 5,000.*

SEA COWS OR MERMAIDS?

Dugongs in Arabian waters may reach up to 3 m in length and weigh almost 500 kg. A thick layer of fat gives them a bulky appearance. The ochre brown skin appears smooth but is, in fact, rough and covered in short, thick hairs. Dugongs have small paddle-like flippers positioned far forward on the body and a broad, flattened, powerful tail resembling that of a small whale. Males, considerably larger than females, have ivory tusks believed to be used in fighting other males and for uprooting seagrasses. The small eyes positioned on either side of the head often go unnoticed. Locally, dugongs are known as *arous al-bahr* ('brides of the sea') or *baghr al-bahr* ('sea cows'). They are believed to have given rise to the myth of the mermaid.

THREATS

Although dugongs are protected by law, dugong deaths continue to occur as a by-catch of commercial fishing. Other threats include propeller strikes, pollution from oil, heavy metals and **polychlorinated biphenyls** (PCBs), noise pollution from shipping and other offshore sound sources, and coastal and offshore development.
Measures being used to protect this unique species include detailed scientific study, the use of protected areas, enforcement of fisheries regulations, adequate response to pollution and cooperation with international marine conservation bodies.

>> LEARN MORE : USEFUL WEBSITES

GENERAL INFORMATION ON MARINE MAMMALS

http://www.wdcs.org/index2.php – international website of the Whale and Dolphin Conservation Society (WDCS) – a good site for up-to-date news on cetacean conservation

http://www.nmfs.noaa.gov/pr/species/mammals/cetaceans/ – extensive section of the NOAA website featuring cetaceans, including species information, conservation status, photographs and videos

http://42explore.com/whale.htm – good directory site with links to whale and dolphin websites, including a list of links for teachers

http://www.42explore.com/whale2.htm – this is a companion page to the one above and includes another long list of links, this time for information on specific species of cetacean

http://www.blue-whale.info/ – useful information on the blue whale

http://animals.nationalgeographic.com/animals/mammals/dugong.html – information and video on dugongs

http://www.sirenian.org/dugong.html – informative website devoted to conservation of dugongs and manatees worldwide

http://www.tesag.jcu.edu.au/dugong/ – comprehensive report on international status and conservation action plans for dugongs, available as downloadable PDF

ARABIAN MARINE MAMMALS

http://www.whalecoastoman.com/ – website of the Oman Whale and Dolphin Research Group

http://www.arabianwildlife.com/archive/vol1.1/dolphi.htm – article on whales and dolphins in Arabian waters

http://www.sirenian.org/2008Kwong_AbuDhabi.html – newspaper article about the Abu Dhabi dugong population

http://www.adnoc.ae/AdnocNews_Details.aspx?NewsID=68741029-3586-4ddd-9038-2e493ccfc26b&newid=162&mid=162? – article about fossil whale remains found in Abu Dhabi waters

WHALE AND DOLPHIN SOUNDS ONLINE

http://oceanexplorer.noaa.gov/explorations/sound01/background/seasounds/media/nepblue.html – listen to the sound of a blue whale

http://oceanexplorer.noaa.gov/gallery/sound/sound.html – other sounds from the sea, including humpback, minke and fin whales

http://www.seaworld.org/animal-info/sound-library/index.htm – clear recordings of dolphin sounds, including clicks

FOR YOUNGER CHILDREN

http://www.enchantedlearning.com/subjects/whales/ – lots of facts, fun and activities aimed at younger children; excellent resource for primary level teachers

http://www.ecokids.ca/pub/eco_info/topics/whales/ – a Canadian website with lots of information on whales and their conservation, including activities

http://kids.nationalgeographic.com/Animals/CreatureFeature/Orca – a section of the National Geographic website with facts, images, map, ecards and video on killer whales

USEFUL IMAGES

http://animals.nationalgeographic.com/animals/photos/whales.html – gallery of National Geographic whale images

http://www.photolib.noaa.gov/animals/whales1.html – excellent whale photos from the NOAA photo library

http://www.arkive.org/ – searchable website with many wildlife photos and videos, including superb material on the blue whale, Bryde's whale, killer whale, Risso's dolphin and dugongs – also features useful information on each species

http://animals.nationalgeographic.com/animals/mammals/dugong.html – dugong information and video

http://www.tesag.jcu.edu.au/dugong/ – international status and conservation action plans for dugongs available as downloadable PDF

MARINE MAMMALS GLOSSARY

baleen: material made of **keratin** that is found in **baleen plates;** sometimes called 'whalebone'

baleen plates: long, flat, sheets that hang like curtains in the mouth of toothless whales, used to filter small food organisms from the water

blowhole: a nostril located on top of the head of **cetaceans** with which they breathe – baleen whales have two, toothed whales have one

cetacean: from 'cetus' - Latin for large sea animal; scientific order of marine mammals that includes whales, dolphins and porpoises

dorsal: referring to the back or upper surface of an animal

echolocation: a system of navigation and food location in which **cetaceans** emit clicks and other sounds, then pick up the reflected sound waves that bounce off organisms and other objects in their surroundings

fluke: the flattened tail of whales, dolphins and porpoises

herbivorous: feeding only on plant material

krill: tiny, shrimp-like crustaceans that feed on **plankton** and form an important food source for filter-feeding marine mammals

keratin: a fibrous protein from which hair, nails and baleen are formed

plankton: minute plant (**phytoplankton**) and animal (**zooplankton**) organisms that drift in vast numbers near the surface of the open sea, forming an essential part of the food chain

pod: a group of marine mammals

polychlorinated biphenyls (PCBs): highly toxic synthetic chemicals containing chlorine, used in a wide variety of industrial and commercial applications; notorious for lack of biodegradability and tendency to accumulate in animal tissue

rorqual: species of baleen whale (blue, fin, sei, Bryde's, minke etc) with conspicuous longitudinal grooves or pleats on the throat that allow the mouth to expand when feeding

ventral: referring to the underside of an animal – the opposite of dorsal

INDEX

SCIENTIFIC INDEX

GENERAL INDEX

PHOTOGRAPHIC AND ILLUSTRATION CREDITS

A.N.T. Photo Library/NHPA 160
Pete Atkinson/NHPA 106
BP Archive 14, 15, 209
Rob Baldwin 148, 149
Mark Beech/ADIAS 102
Gary Brown 18, 34, 35, 36, 38, 40, 179
Tina Carvalho, Biological Electron Microscope Facility, Pacific Biosciences Research Center, Honolulu 52, 61, 71, 90
Phil Coates 15
Ronald Codrai 13
Stephen Dalton/NHPA 128-129, 153
Nigel J. Dennis/NHPA 123
Reinhard Dirscherl/FLPA 107, 157
Lorraine Egan (Sharjah Wildlife Centre) 23, 129, 195, 206
Xavier Eichaker 155, 163
Birgit Eichseneher 14, 229, 232
Hanne and Jens Eriksen 16, 17, 23, 28, 32, 35, 40, 41, 46, 48-49, 50, 51, 52, 60, 61, 64, 65, 66, 67, 68, 69, 73, 74, 75, 76, 77, 81, 82, 84, 85, 102, 103, 118, 119, 122, 124, 125, 126, 127, 131, 132-133, 141, 143, 172, 173, 174, 175, 176, 177, 178, 179, 180, 181, 182, 183, 186, 187, 189, 190, 191, 195, 196, 197, 201, 211, 212, 218, 219, 223, 224, 225, 226
Hanne and Jens Eriksen/Trident Press 1 ,2, 3, 5, 8, 13,14, 15, 16, 17, 18-19, 20, 22, 23, 25, 30, 32, 35, 39, 41, 42-43, 48-49, 50, 51, 52, 53, 56, 58-59, 63, 68, 70, 73, 91, 116-117, 118, 127, 167, 171, 173, 174, 175, 180, 181, 182, 183, 184-185, 187, 188, 189, 190, 191, 193, 194, 195, 197, 200, 201, 203, 204, 205, 206-207, 208, 210, 213, 214, 215, 216-217, 218, 220, 221, 227
Gary Feulner 114, 115, 153
David Fleetham/Oxford Scientific 107
Drew Gardner 39, 50, 52, 80, 81, 85, 118, 119, 121, 122, 123, 126, 127, 130, 131, 133, 134, 135, 136, 137, 138, 139, 140, 141, 142, 143, 144, 145, 146, 147, 151, 152, 153, 178, 195, 199
David George 21, 45, 50, 61, 89, 91, 92, 93, 94, 95, 96, 97, 98, 99, 100, 101, 102, 103, 104, 105, 106, 108, 109, 110, 111, 232
Graham Giles 64, 65
Great Images in NASA (GRIN) 26
Michael Gillett 48-49, 67, 69, 70, 74, 76, 77, 79
Christian Gross 142, 196, 201, 205
Martin Harvey/NHPA 125
Daniel Heuclin/NHPA 67, 141, 197, 224
Richard Hornby 32, 37, 40, 46
David Hosking/FLPA 202
David John 44, 45
Marijcke Jongbloed 32, 35, 37, 40, 46
Jumeirah Image Library 210-211
T Kitchin and V. Hurst/NHPA 128, 153
Jürgen Kuchinke 166
Yves Lanceau/NHPA 77
Linda Lewis/FLPA 162
Lucy Monro 13
NASA 26, 28
NASA Earth Observatory 28
NASA Visible Earth 24,
Natural History Museum, London 123
Mark Newman/FLPA 56
Philip Perry/FLPA 202
Linda Pitkin/NHPA 168
Dan Potts 12,
Judy Roberts 13,
Steve Roberts 43, 79
Jany Sauvanet/NHPA 125, 153
Kevin Schafer/NHPA 123
Hagen Schmid 22, 23, 50, 51, 52, 60, 61, 103, 105, 107, 119, 123, 124, 125, 165, 166, 195, 222, 223
Malcolm Schuyl/FLPA 198
Hans Sjoeholm 21
Alex Smailes/Trident 48-49, 161, 168
Dieter Stark 32, 153
Jane Stark/Trident Press 27, 28, 33, 34, 37, 53, 60, 64, 72, 78, 94, 98, 101, 108, 110, 113, 114, 115, 118, 141, 147, 152, 156, 157, 158, 159, 160, 161, 162, 163, 164, 165, 167, 169, 172, 185, 188, 195, 230, 231
Chris and Tilde Stuart 195, 225
Barbara Tigar/Patrick Osborne 80, 83
M. Turkay 103
Peter Vine 25, 168
Tony Waltham 19, 199
Mark Webster/Oxford Scientific 95, 164
Tony Wharton/FLPA 75
Trident Press 10, 11, 12, 15, 20, 33, 42, 43, 119, 203, 209
Peter Whybrow & The Natural History Museum 54, 55
D P Wilson/FLPA 157
Winfried Wisniewski/FLPA 205
Adam Woolfitt/Trident Press 12, 14